HISTORY COMICS

THE GREAT CHICAGO FIRE
RISING FROM THE ASHES

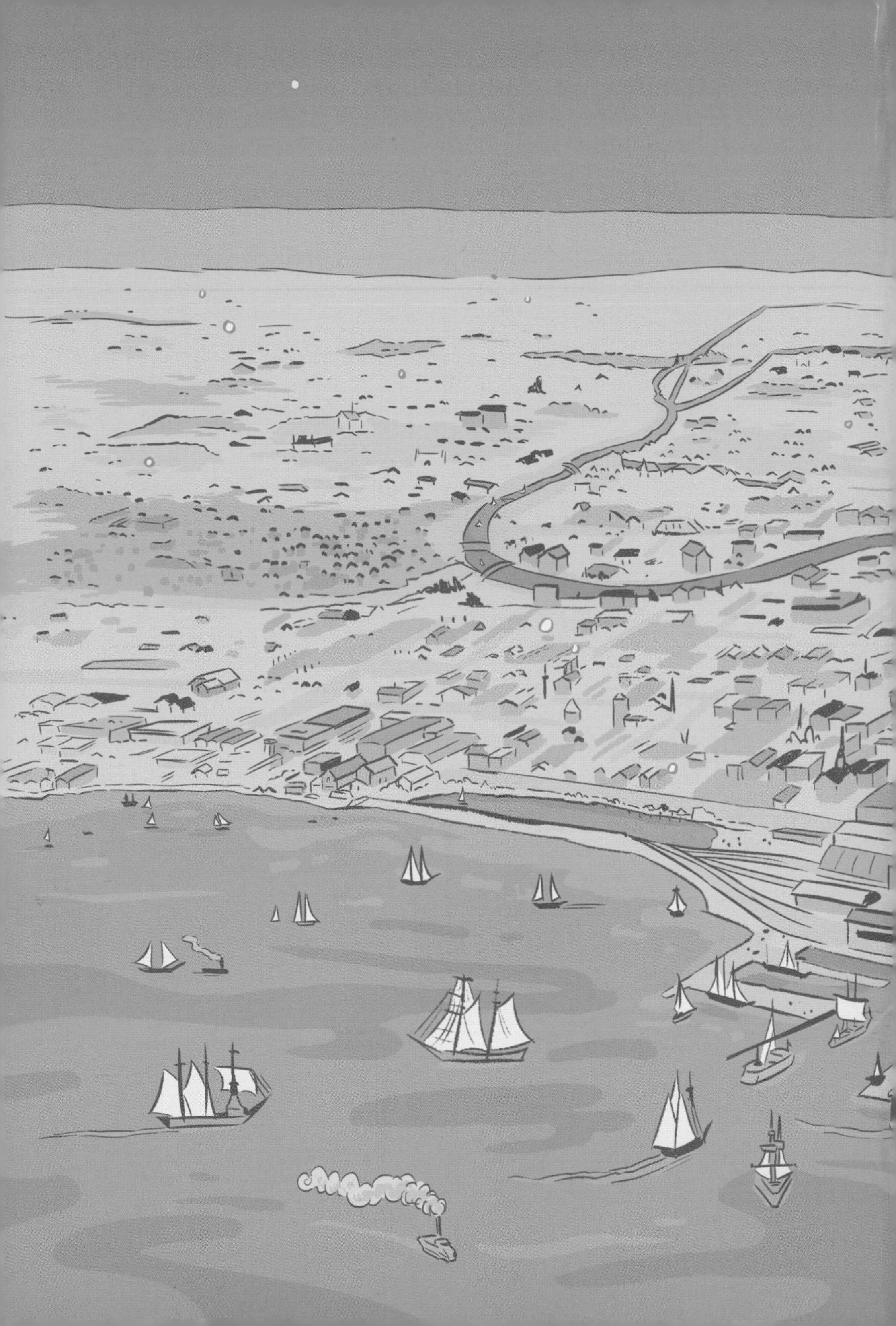

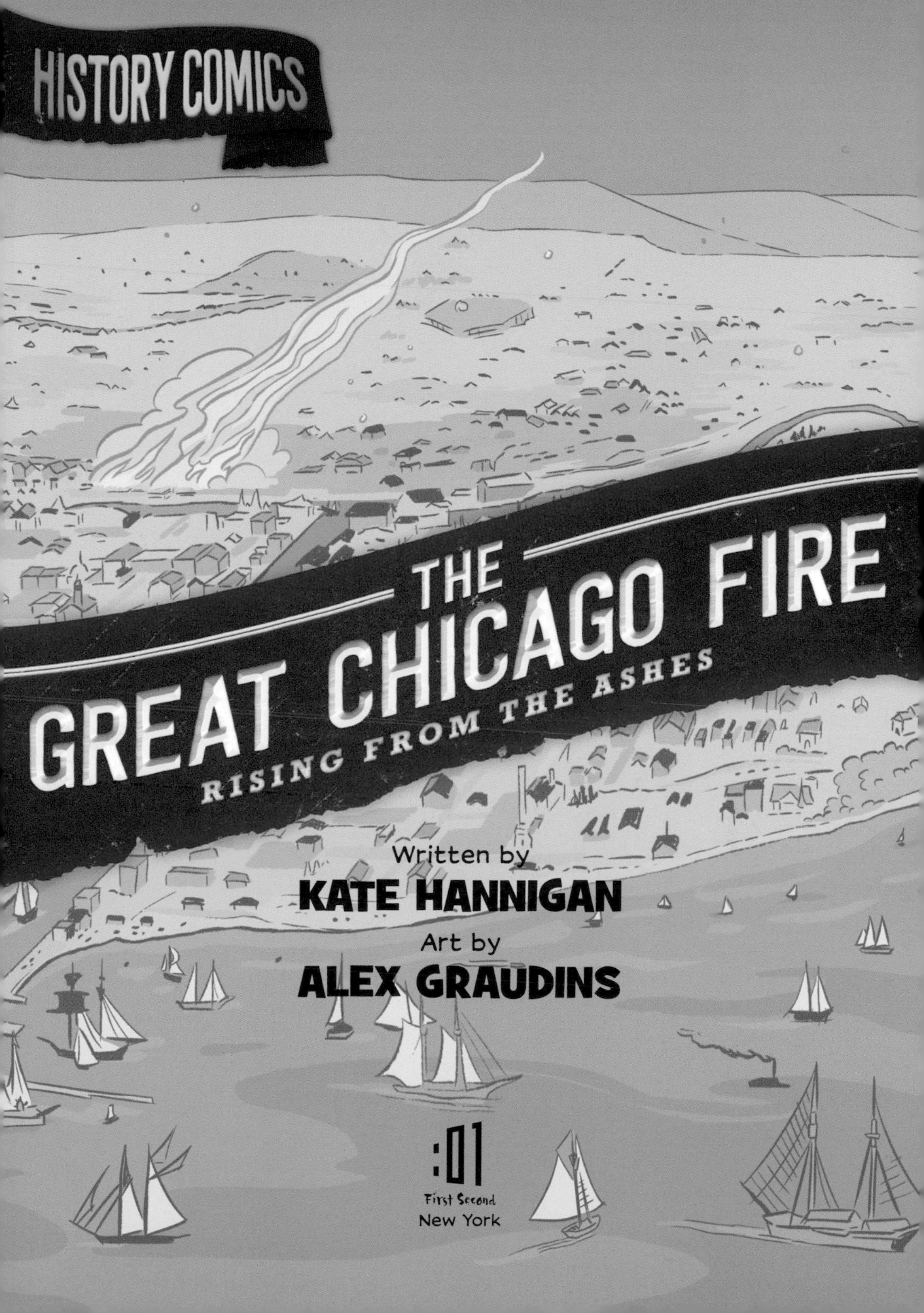

HISTORY COMICS

THE GREAT CHICAGO FIRE

RISING FROM THE ASHES

Written by
KATE HANNIGAN
Art by
ALEX GRAUDINS

:01
First Second
New York

First Second

Published by First Second
First Second is an imprint of Roaring Brook Press, a division of Holtzbrinck Publishing Holdings Limited Partnership
120 Broadway, New York, NY 10271

Don't miss your next favorite book from First Second! For the latest updates go to firstsecondnewsletter.com and sign up for our enewsletter.

Library of Congress Control Number: 2019938065

Paperback ISBN: 978-1-250-17426-0
Hardback ISBN: 978-1-250-17425-3

Our books may be purchased in bulk for promotional, educational, or business use. Please contact your local bookseller or the Macmillan Corporate and Premium Sales Department at (800) 221-7945 ext. 5442 or by email at MacmillanSpecialMarkets@macmillan.com.

FIRST EDITION

First edition, 2020
Edited by Dave Roman
Historical consultant: Ginger Frere
Cover design by Kirk Benshoff
Interior book design by Angela Boyle

Penciled, inked, and colored digitally in Adobe Photoshop CS5 with Kyle Webster's Ratty Inker brush. Lettered with font from Comicraft.

Printed in China by Toppan Leefung Printing Ltd., Dongguan City, Guangdong Province
Paperback: 10 9 8 7 6 5
Hardcover: 10 9 8 7 6 5 4 3 2

BY ART WE LIVE

Do you dream? Have you ever read a story about a real person who might be considered famous or a hero? Do you ever put yourself into the life of the subject you are reading? If the answer to this question is yes, then you understand how you learn from the example of others. It doesn't matter if they are your same age or older than you are. At times, it may seem impossible for you to have an effect on anything or anyone around you. But any small positive effort made by you has a good effect on others whether it is a member of your family, a friend, or even a complete stranger. Because you care and you want to help someone else, you will have an impact on their lives.

When my brother, Dan, and I were in college, he was a member of the Chicago Civil Defense, an organization made up of volunteers who respond to a variety of emergency calls throughout the city to offer additional manpower to support first responders. My brother suggested that during one of my semester breaks from school I go with him to an "extra alarm fire." Fire departments in all cities have preplanned responses for different types of emergencies that require different levels of equipment and manpower. In Chicago there are "Still and Box Alarms" and then "Extra Alarm" responses designated 2-11, 3-11, 4-11, and 5-11. It was a "2-11 or greater" that the Civil Defense responded to on that night. That meant four engines, two trucks, one tower ladder, two battalion chiefs, one district chief, a deputy commissioner on hand, with one air mask truck, plus additional equipment.

At first, I thought I was crazy to follow my brother's suggestion, but we are close in age and interests . . . so I was willing to give it a shot. So on that memorable December evening, naturally after midnight, the phone rang in our home and my brother answered the call. He wrote down the address, and with no experience, I got ready the best I could and went with my brother to my first fire. Despite some cold feet (it was winter in the "Windy City" after all), I was hooked and became interested in the work of the firefighters at the scene of the fire. It took several hours to put out the blaze and wash down, making sure no flames remained hidden behind a wall or in the ceiling. One of the people living in this house didn't make it out alive. You might wonder what my reaction was after getting so close to danger. Well, fast-forward the clock several years and I am now serving as the Catholic chaplain for the Chicago Fire Department. I could never have imagined myself in that position if it hadn't been for the encouragement of my brother.

My brother and I no longer go to fires together due to a job relocation (he lives in Florida with his wife and family). But I do have a companion who comes with me to the fires and other calls I respond to. I never ask her if she wants to come with me. She is always willing to follow me and doesn't complain about the traffic or how long the drive is or what time we return home. Her name is Major and she is a German shepherd. She is trained as a live search and

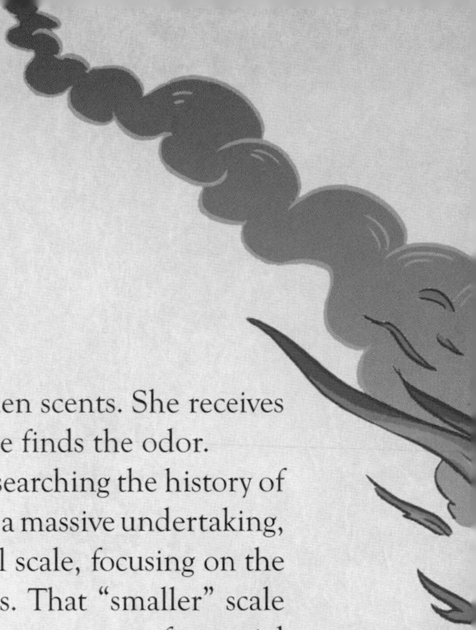

rescue dog able to track specific hidden scents. She receives a praise and/or treat reward when she finds the odor.

I have always had a passion for researching the history of the United States, but that being such a massive undertaking, I reduced the work to a smaller, local scale, focusing on the history of the city of Chicago, Illinois. That "smaller" scale didn't last too long because of the vast amount of material written about our "windy city." I combined a hobby of photography with the gathering of historical material. I would read about an event and travel to the site to take pictures of the area. Eventually I started adding 35 mm slides to my material and offering classes on Chicago history in the parish school. And of course the Great Chicago Fire is something that always sparks a lot of interest.

There are few buildings that survived the 1871 fire. The vast majority of those structures have been torn down to allow for new construction as the city expanded in size. There are some plaques scattered throughout the city to remind people of the Great Chicago Fire, as well as the Columbian Exposition, which was held twenty-two years later and symbolized the city's rebirth. Looking at photos or reading books is going to be your best resource to get a sense of this celebrated event unless you come to Chicago and visit the Museum of Science and Industry. This building was originally the Fine Arts building during the Exposition.

Reading *History Comics: The Great Chicago Fire*, I enjoyed the fictionalized story along with the author's clever way of presenting fun facts about real people and places affected by the Great Fire, all of which is informative and accurate. The graphic novel format allows the reader to put themselves into the events without feeling like they are getting a textbook lesson. You as the reader have the opportunity to see drawings of period clothes, conditions of where people lived, and the struggle to survive during a major disaster. Only a little more than twenty years separated the two events of this story, yet the time periods are very different, and this is an interesting lesson in itself.

I hope reading about the 1871 Chicago Fire and the Columbian Exposition of 1893 may help you realize how far we have come and how much further we might go in the future. And that even one small act of bravery or kindness can have a big impact on society.

—**Rev. John McNalis**, Chicago Fire Dept. chaplain and co-author of *History of Chicago Fire Houses of the 20th Century, 1901–1925*

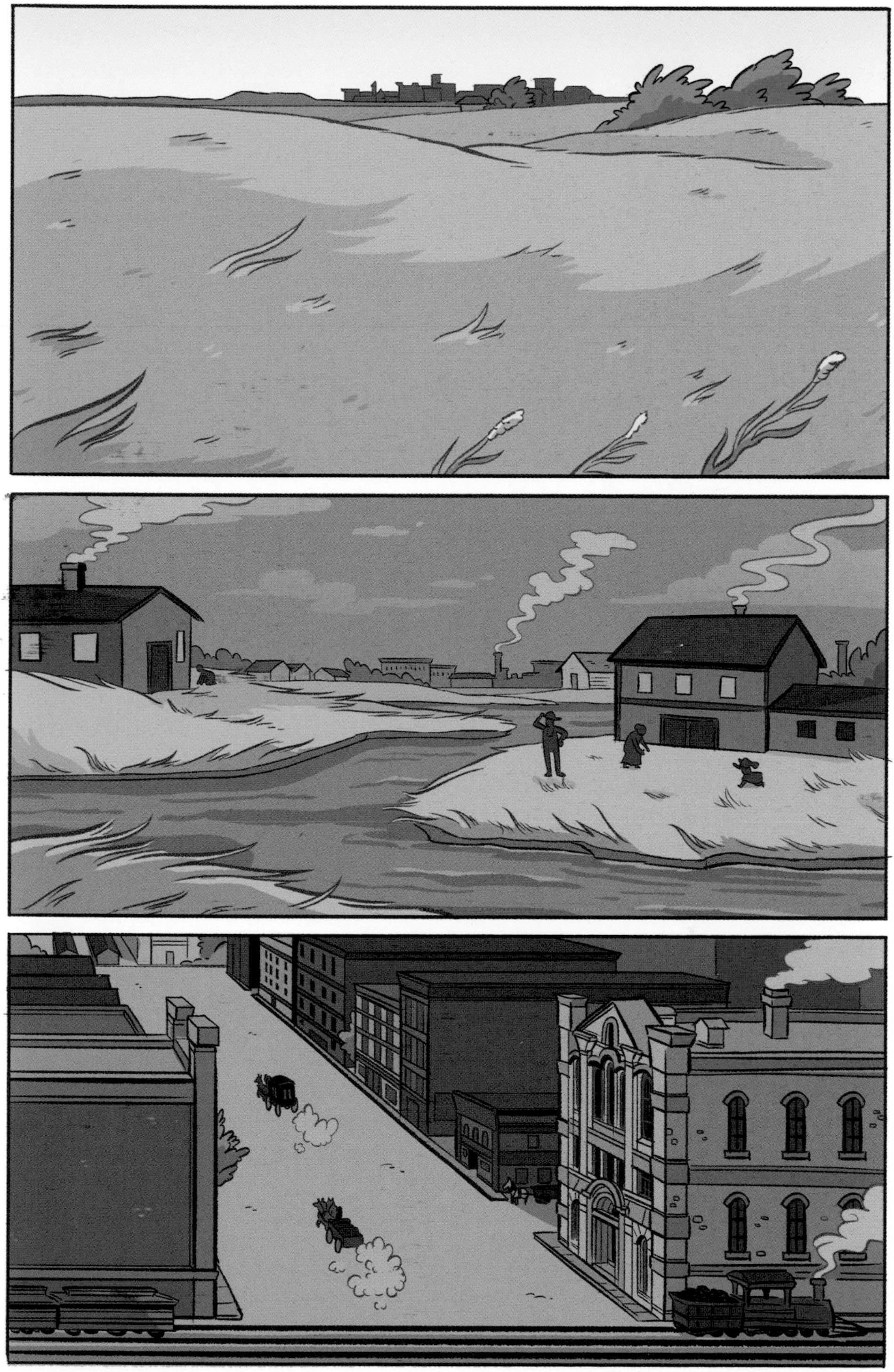

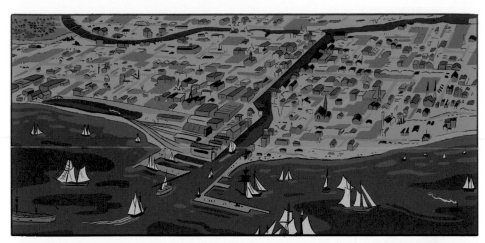

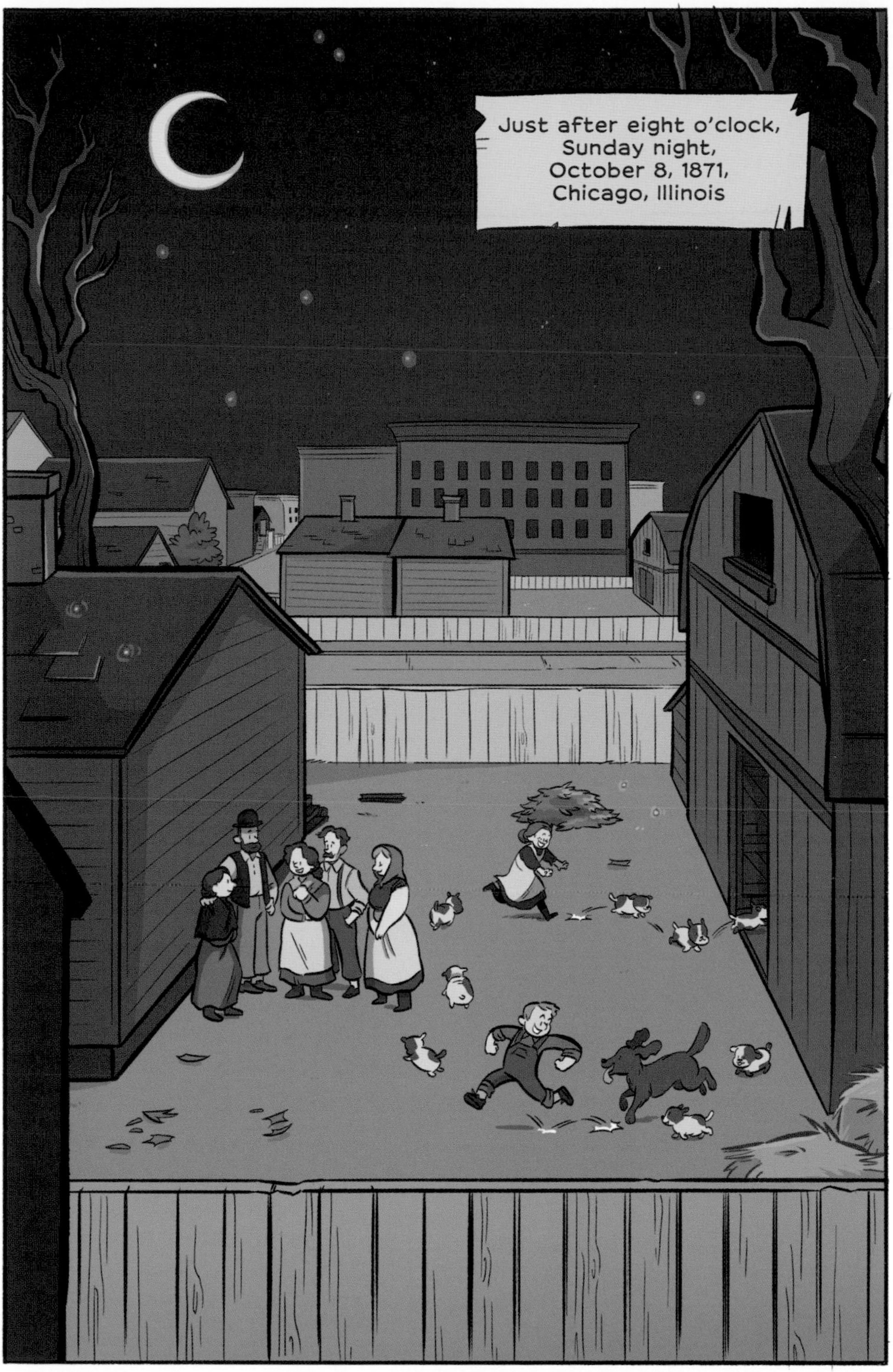
Just after eight o'clock, Sunday night, October 8, 1871, Chicago, Illinois

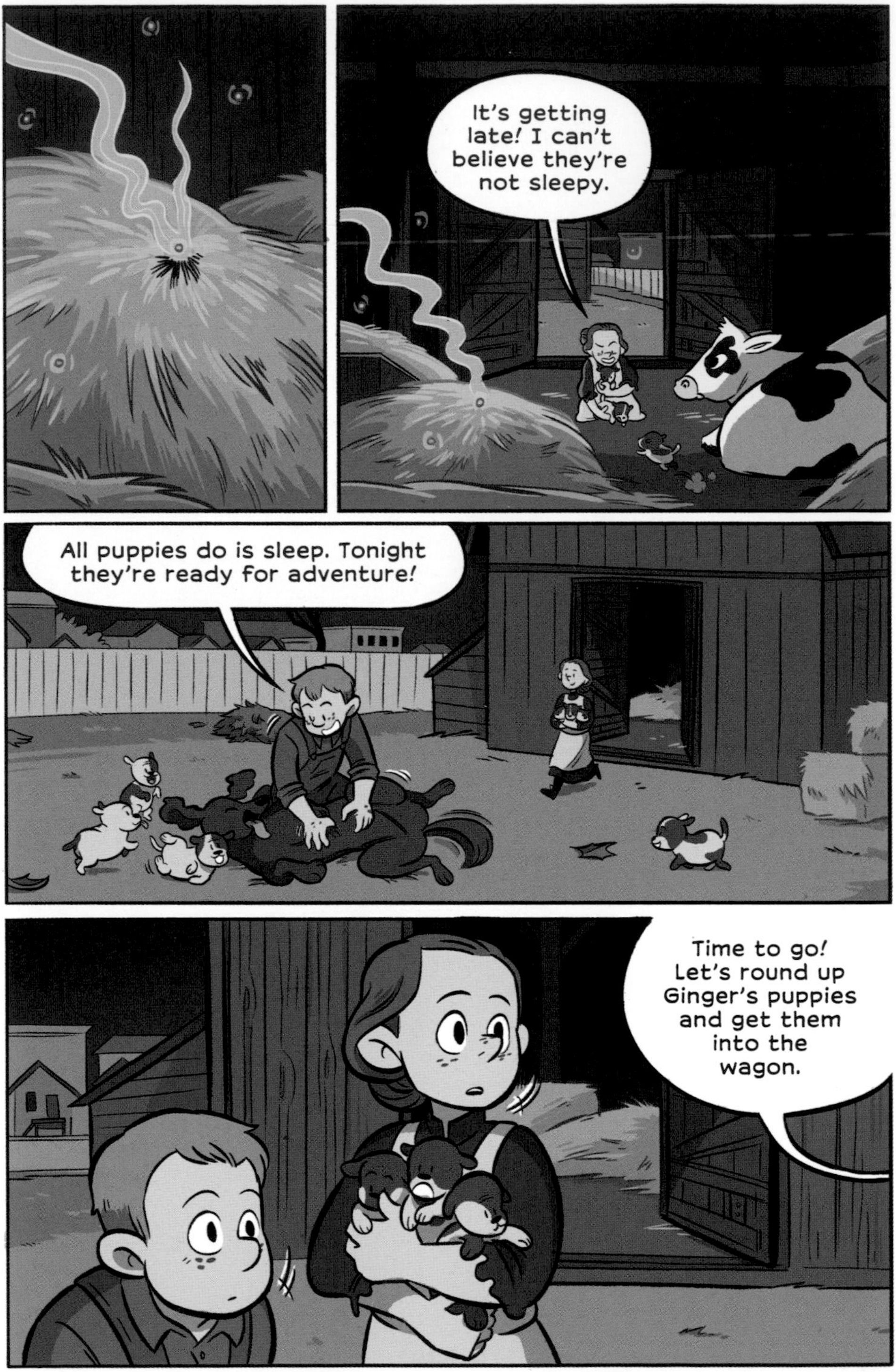
It's getting late! I can't believe they're not sleepy.
All puppies do is sleep. Tonight they're ready for adventure!
Time to go! Let's round up Ginger's puppies and get them into the wagon.

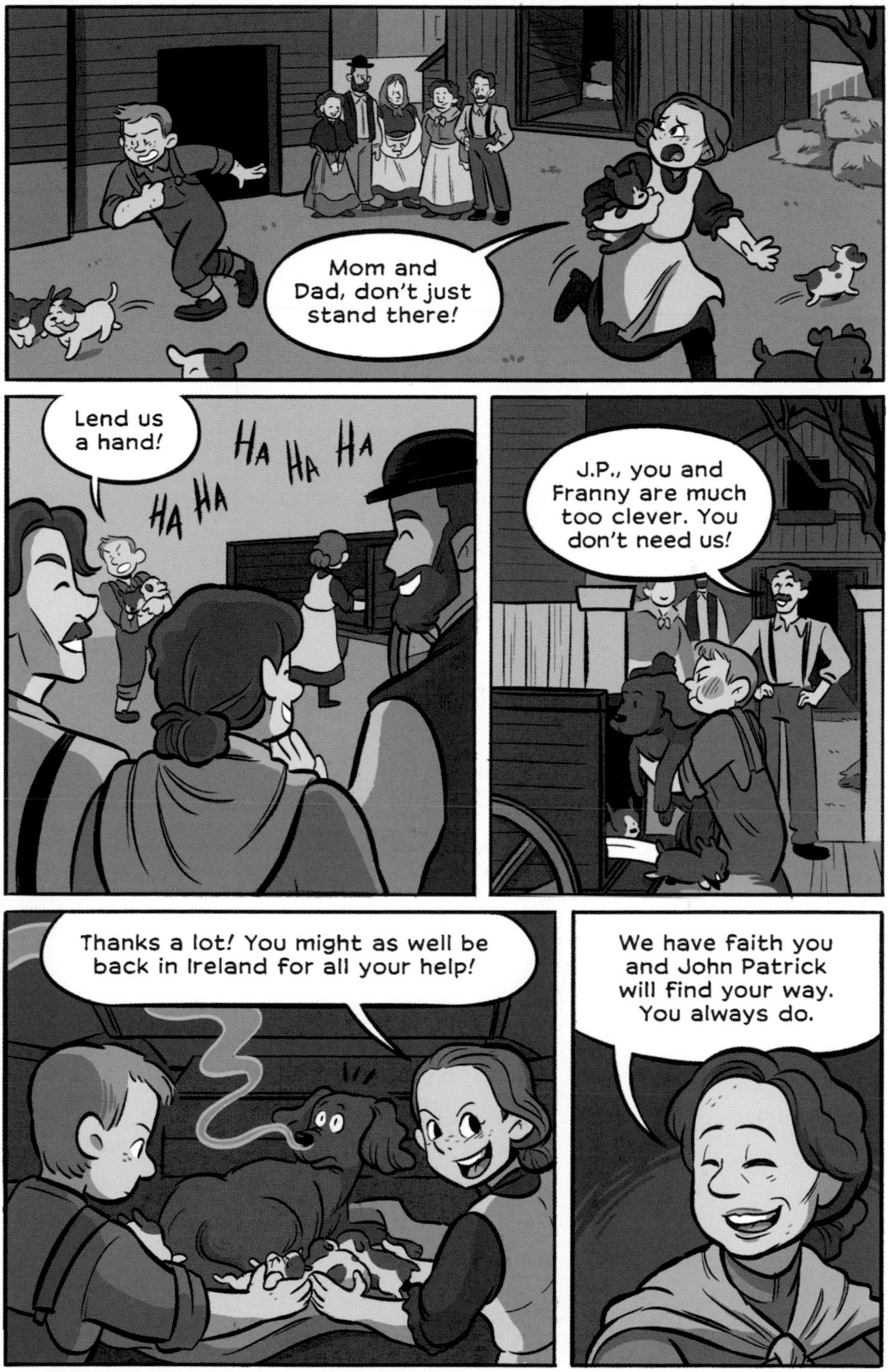
Mom and Dad, don't just stand there!
Lend us a hand!
HA HA HA
HA HA
J.P., you and Franny are much too clever. You don't need us!
Thanks a lot! You might as well be back in Ireland for all your help!
We have faith you and John Patrick will find your way. You always do.

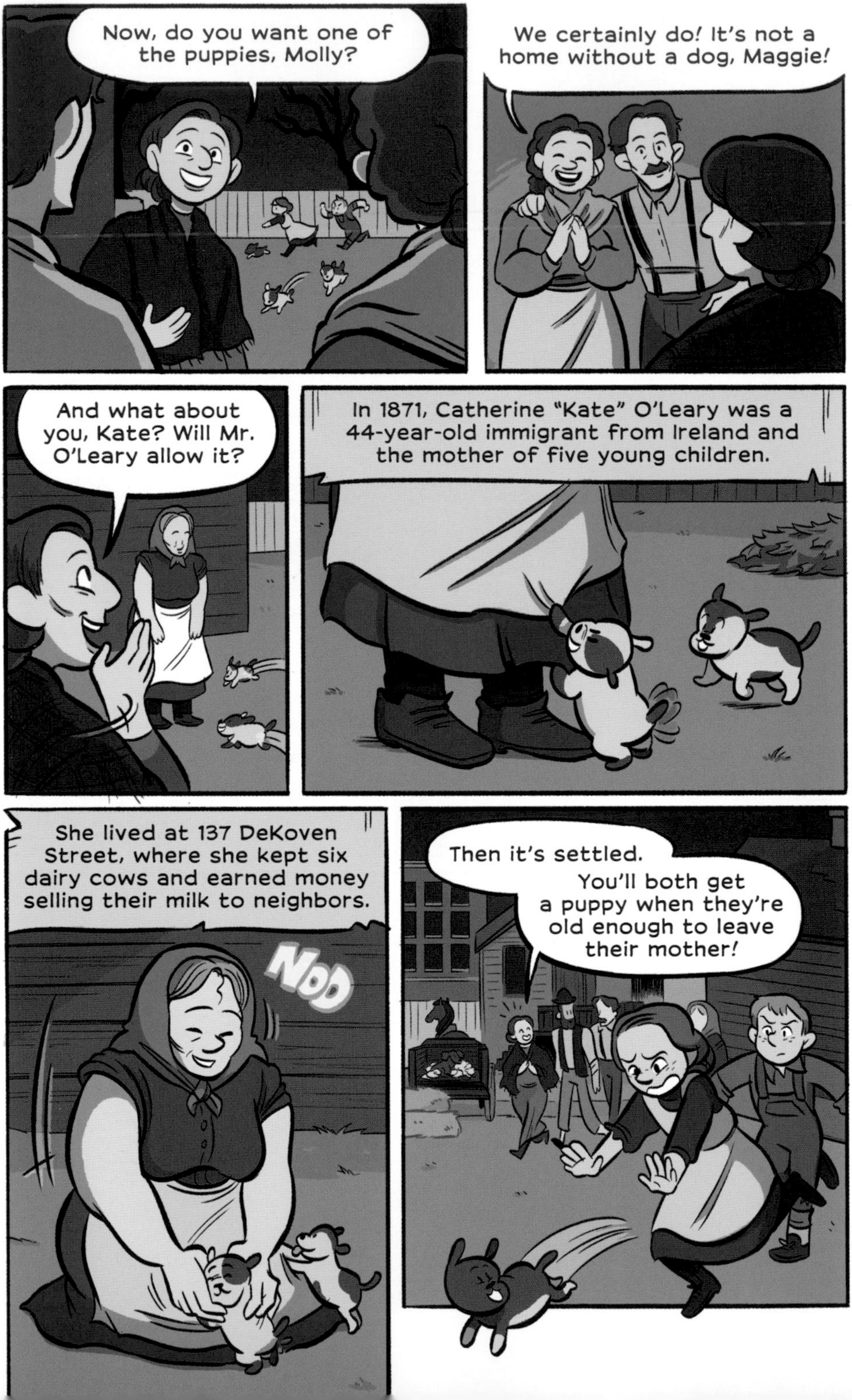

Now, do you want one of the puppies, Molly?
We certainly do! It's not a home without a dog, Maggie!
And what about you, Kate? Will Mr. O'Leary allow it?
In 1871, Catherine "Kate" O'Leary was a 44-year-old immigrant from Ireland and the mother of five young children.
She lived at 137 DeKoven Street, where she kept six dairy cows and earned money selling their milk to neighbors.
NOD
Then it's settled.
You'll both get a puppy when they're old enough to leave their mother!

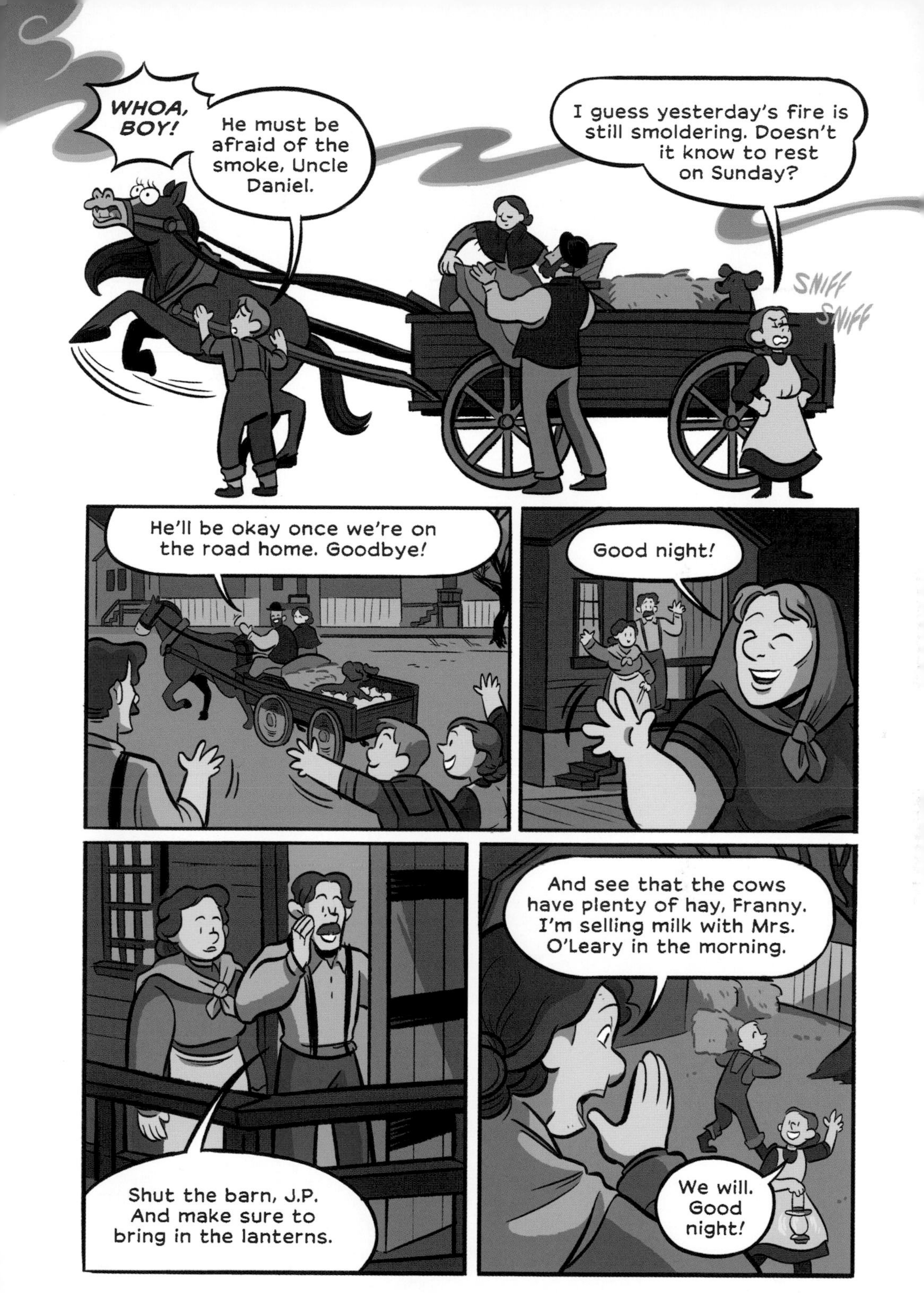
WHOA, BOY!
He must be afraid of the smoke, Uncle Daniel.
I guess yesterday's fire is still smoldering. Doesn't it know to rest on Sunday?
SNIFF SNIFF
He'll be okay once we're on the road home. Goodbye!
Good night!
Shut the barn, J.P. And make sure to bring in the lanterns.
And see that the cows have plenty of hay, Franny. I'm selling milk with Mrs. O'Leary in the morning.
We will. Good night!

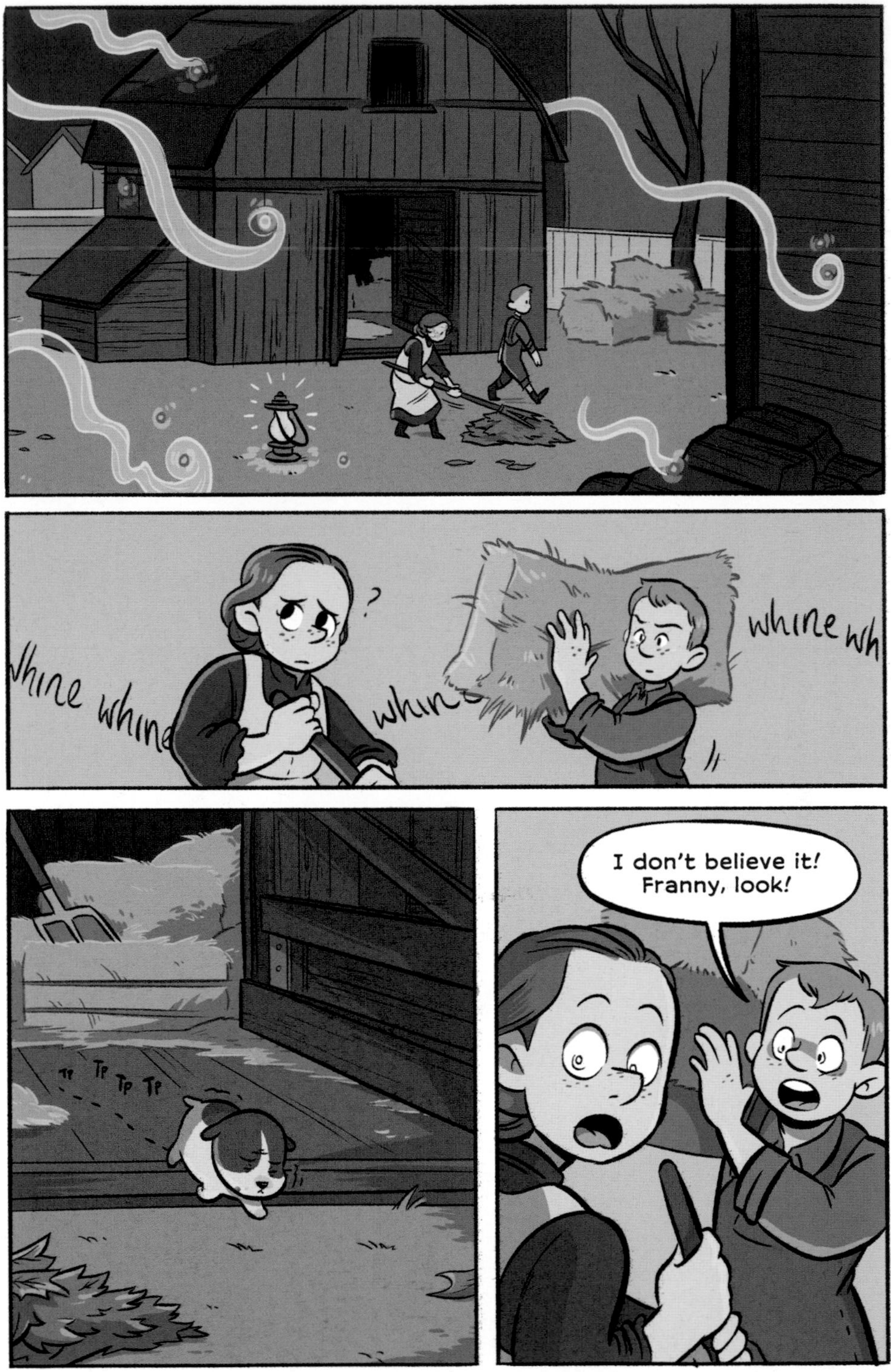
whine whine
whine
whine wh
Tp Tp Tp Tp
I don't believe it! Franny, look!

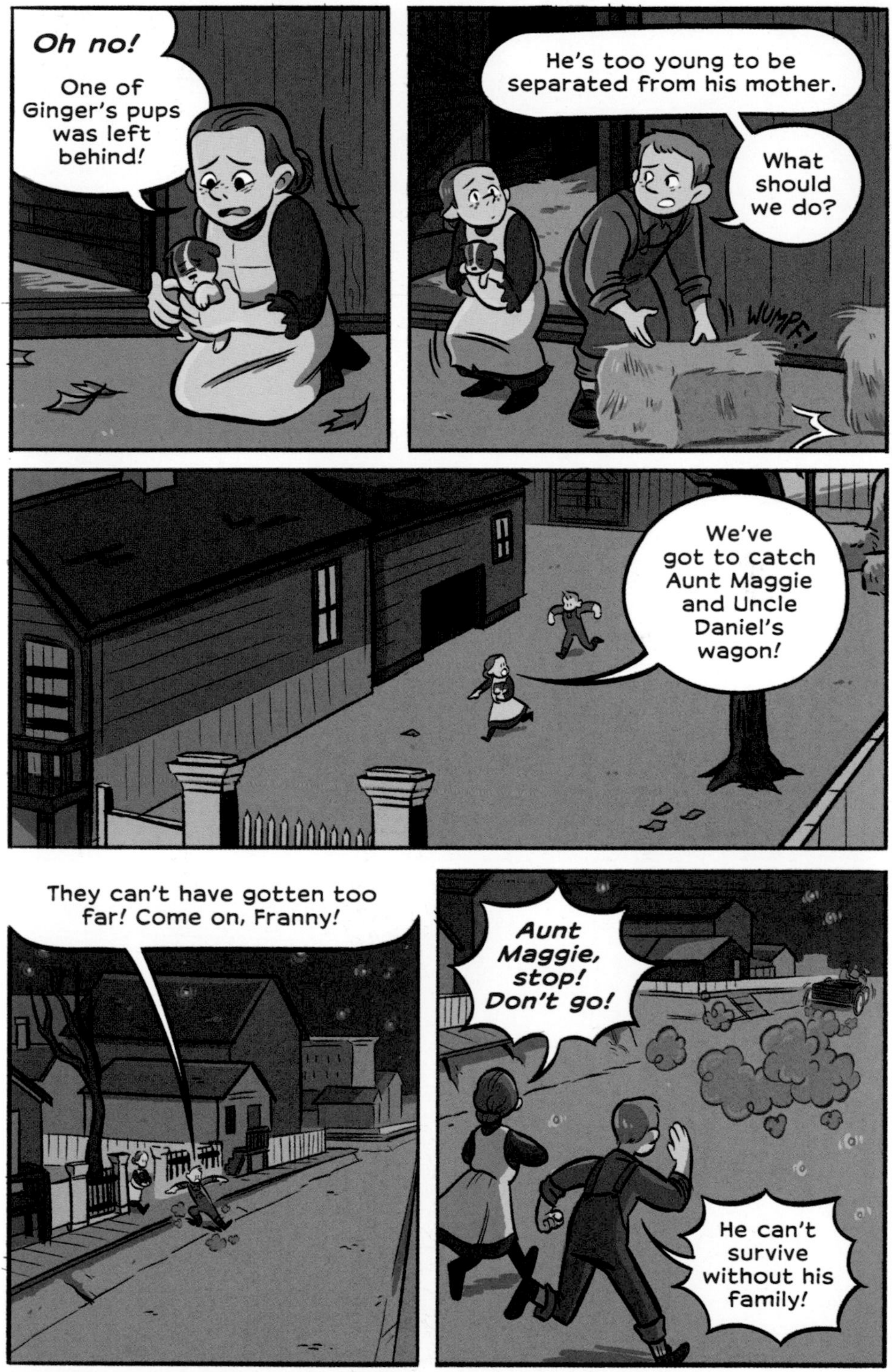
Oh no!
One of Ginger's pups was left behind!
He's too young to be separated from his mother.
What should we do?
WUMPF!
We've got to catch Aunt Maggie and Uncle Daniel's wagon!
They can't have gotten too far! Come on, Franny!
Aunt Maggie, stop! Don't go!
He can't survive without his family!

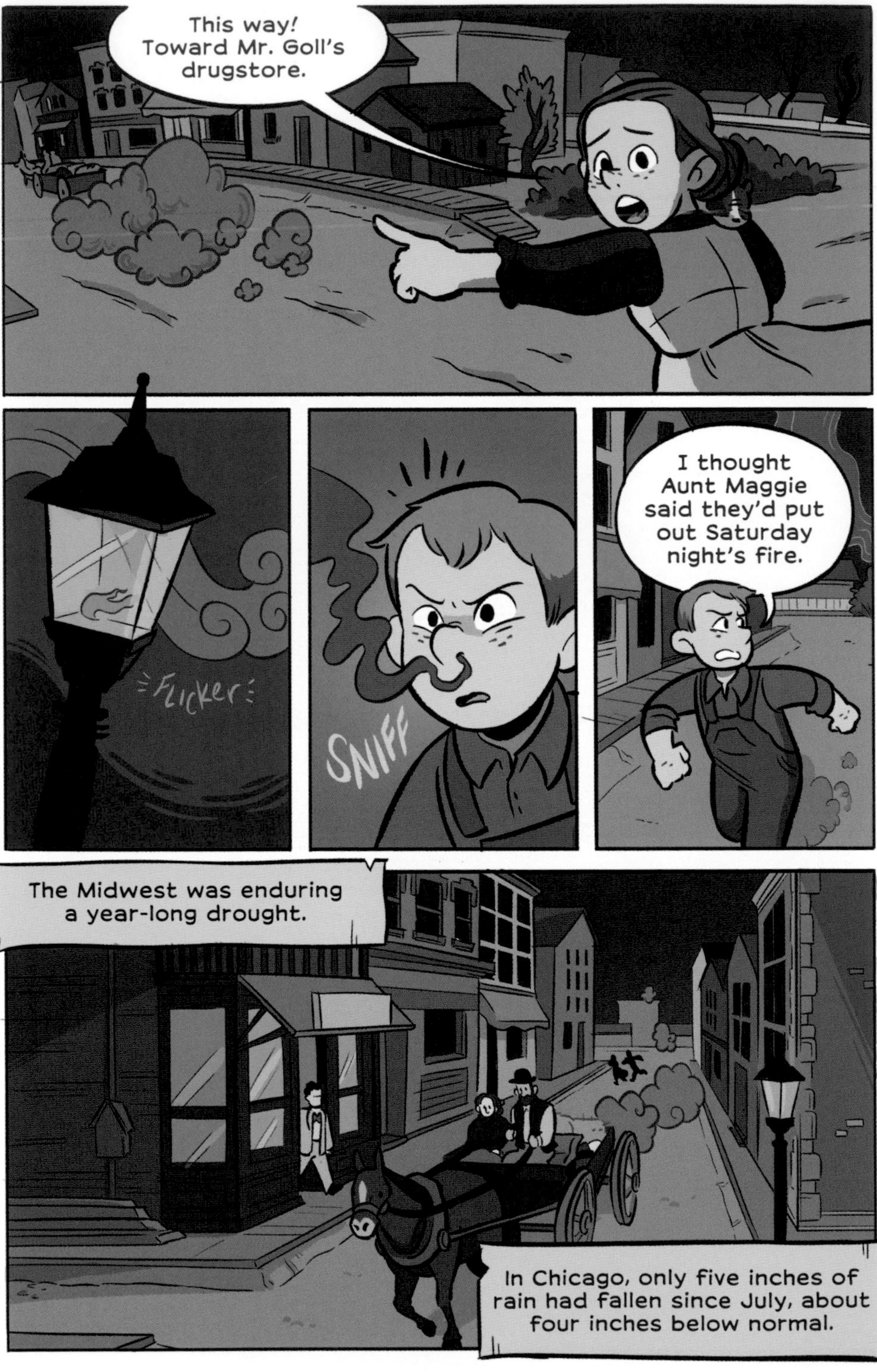
This way! Toward Mr. Goll's drugstore.
FLICKER
SNIFF
I thought Aunt Maggie said they'd put out Saturday night's fire.
The Midwest was enduring a year-long drought.
In Chicago, only five inches of rain had fallen since July, about four inches below normal.

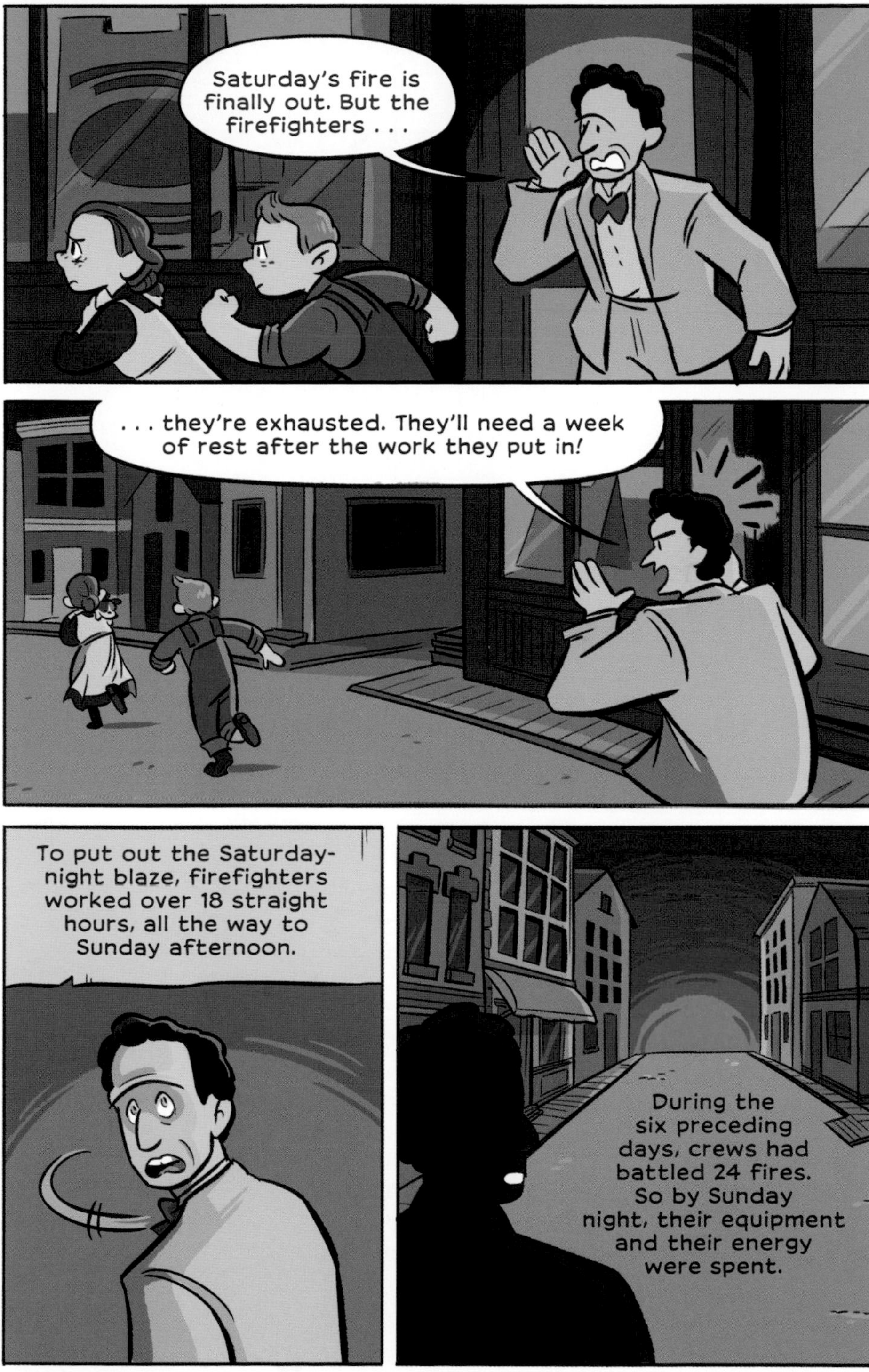
Saturday's fire is finally out. But the firefighters . . .
. . . they're exhausted. They'll need a week of rest after the work they put in!
To put out the Saturday-night blaze, firefighters worked over 18 straight hours, all the way to Sunday afternoon.
During the six preceding days, crews had battled 24 fires. So by Sunday night, their equipment and their energy were spent.

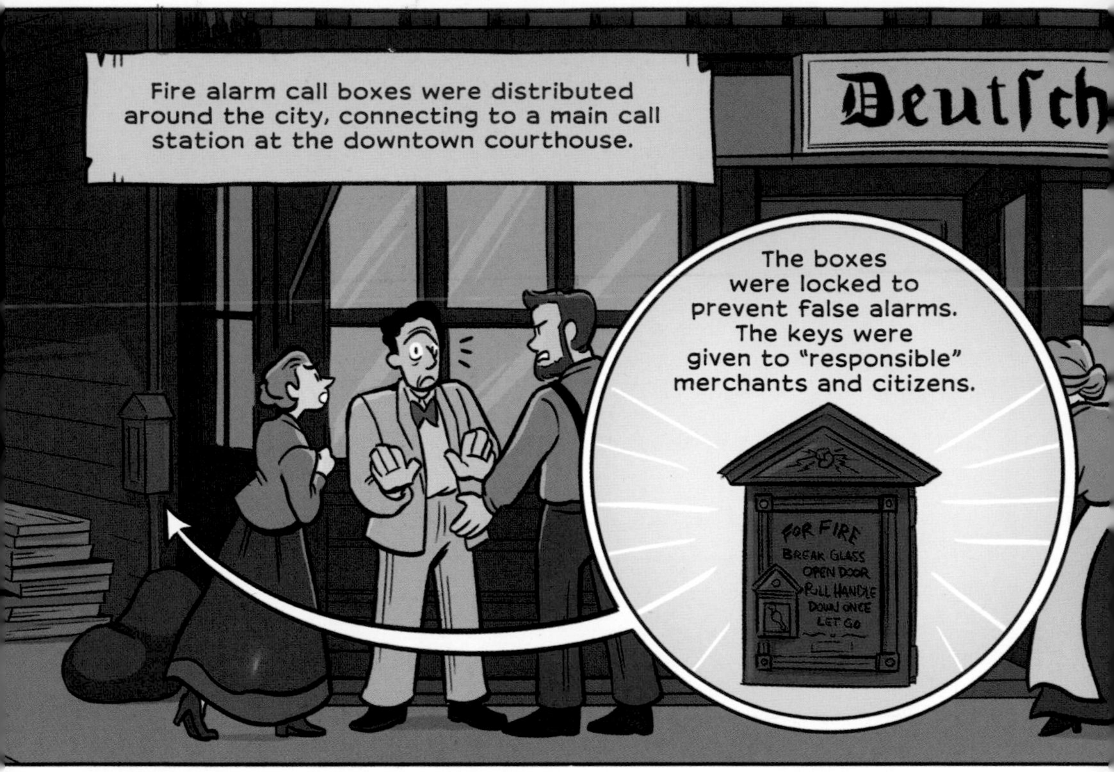
Fire alarm call boxes were distributed around the city, connecting to a main call station at the downtown courthouse.
Deutsch
The boxes were locked to prevent false alarms. The keys were given to "responsible" merchants and citizens.
FOR FIRE
BREAK GLASS
OPEN DOOR
PULL HANDLE
DOWN ONCE
LET GO

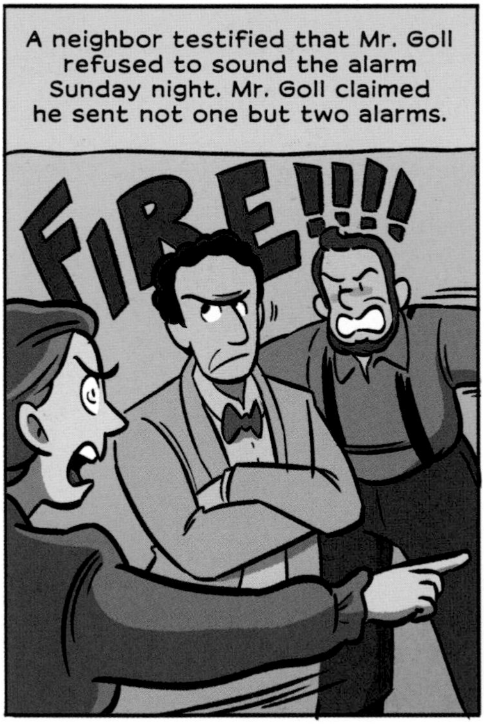
A neighbor testified that Mr. Goll refused to sound the alarm Sunday night. Mr. Goll claimed he sent not one but two alarms.
FIRE!!!!

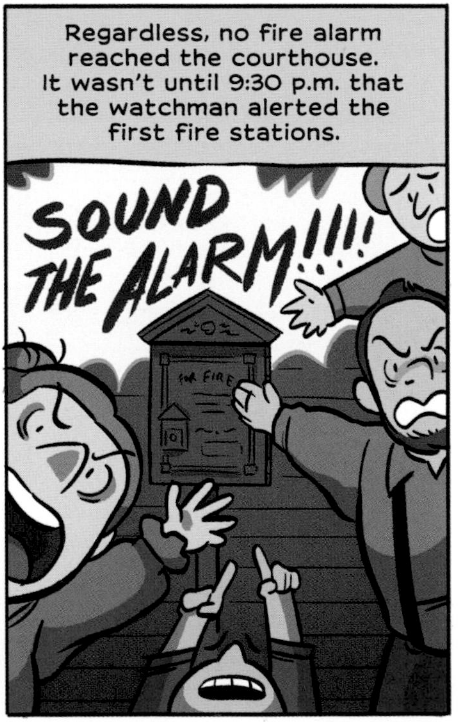
Regardless, no fire alarm reached the courthouse. It wasn't until 9:30 p.m. that the watchman alerted the first fire stations.
SOUND THE ALARM!!!!
FOR FIRE

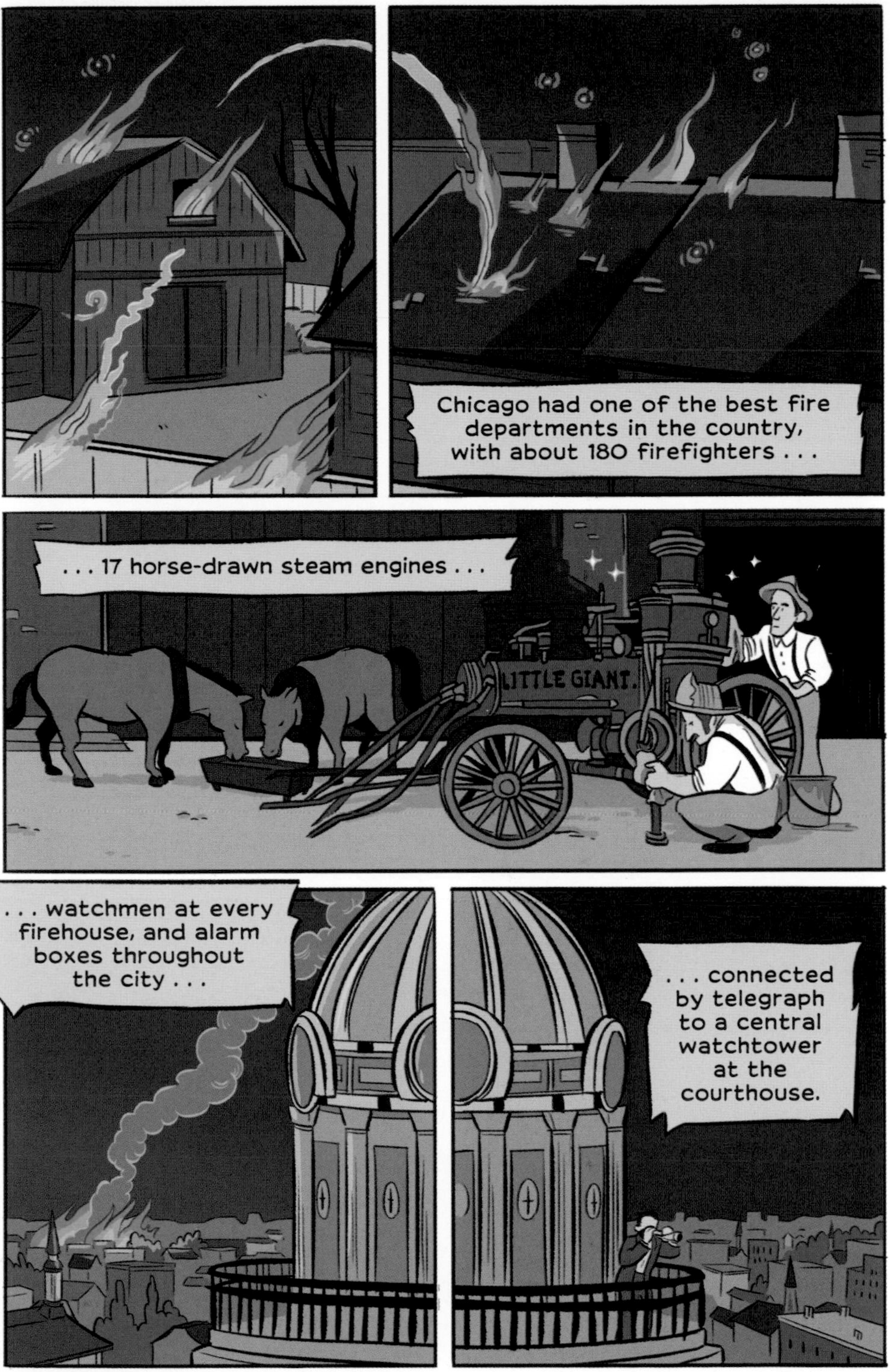
Chicago had one of the best fire departments in the country, with about 180 firefighters . . .
. . . 17 horse-drawn steam engines . . .
LITTLE GIANT.
. . . watchmen at every firehouse, and alarm boxes throughout the city . . .
. . . connected by telegraph to a central watchtower at the courthouse.

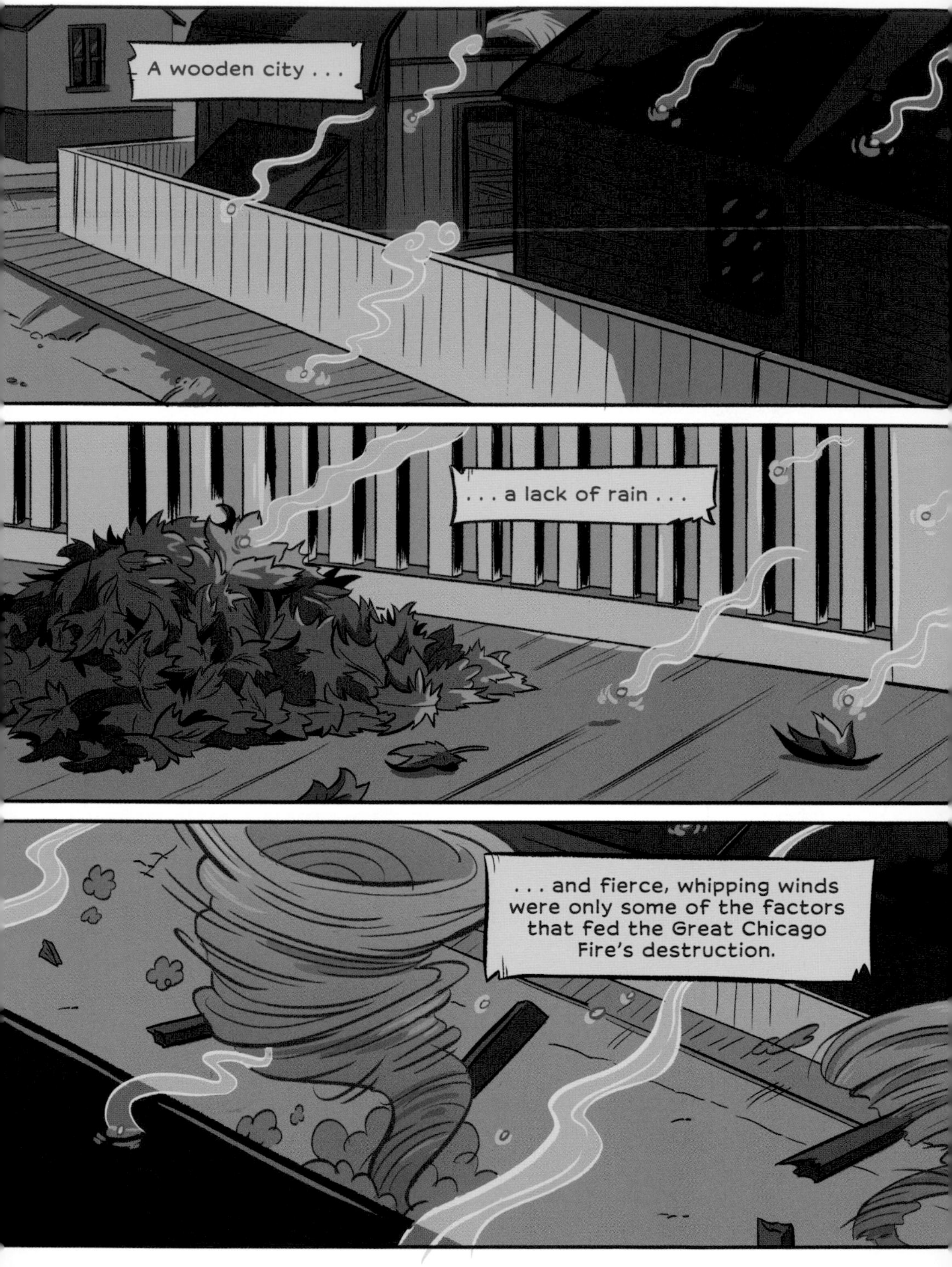
A wooden city . . .
. . . a lack of rain . . .
. . . and fierce, whipping winds were only some of the factors that fed the Great Chicago Fire's destruction.

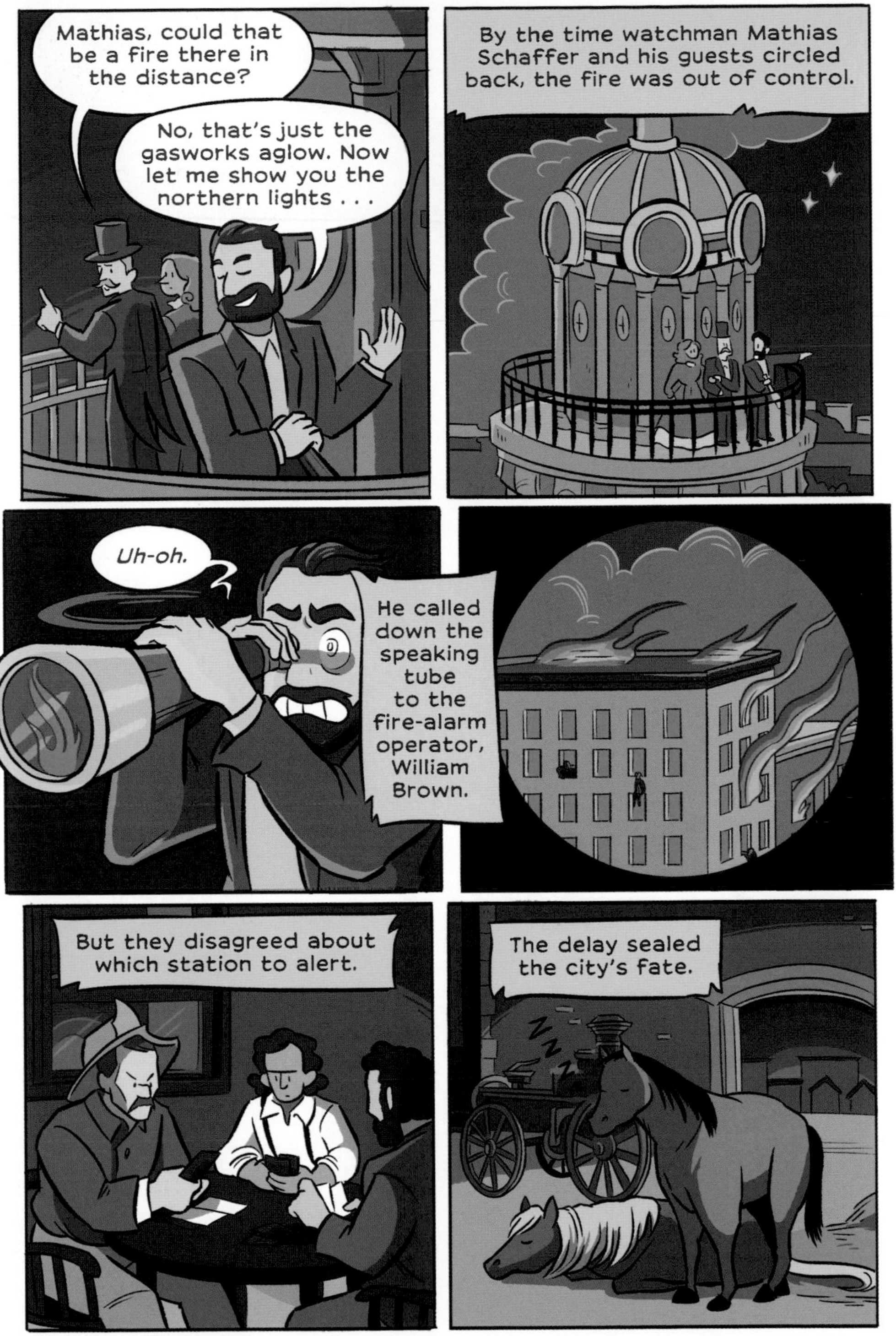
Mathias, could that be a fire there in the distance?
No, that's just the gasworks aglow. Now let me show you the northern lights . . .
By the time watchman Mathias Schaffer and his guests circled back, the fire was out of control.
Uh-oh.
He called down the speaking tube to the fire-alarm operator, William Brown.
But they disagreed about which station to alert.
The delay sealed the city's fate.

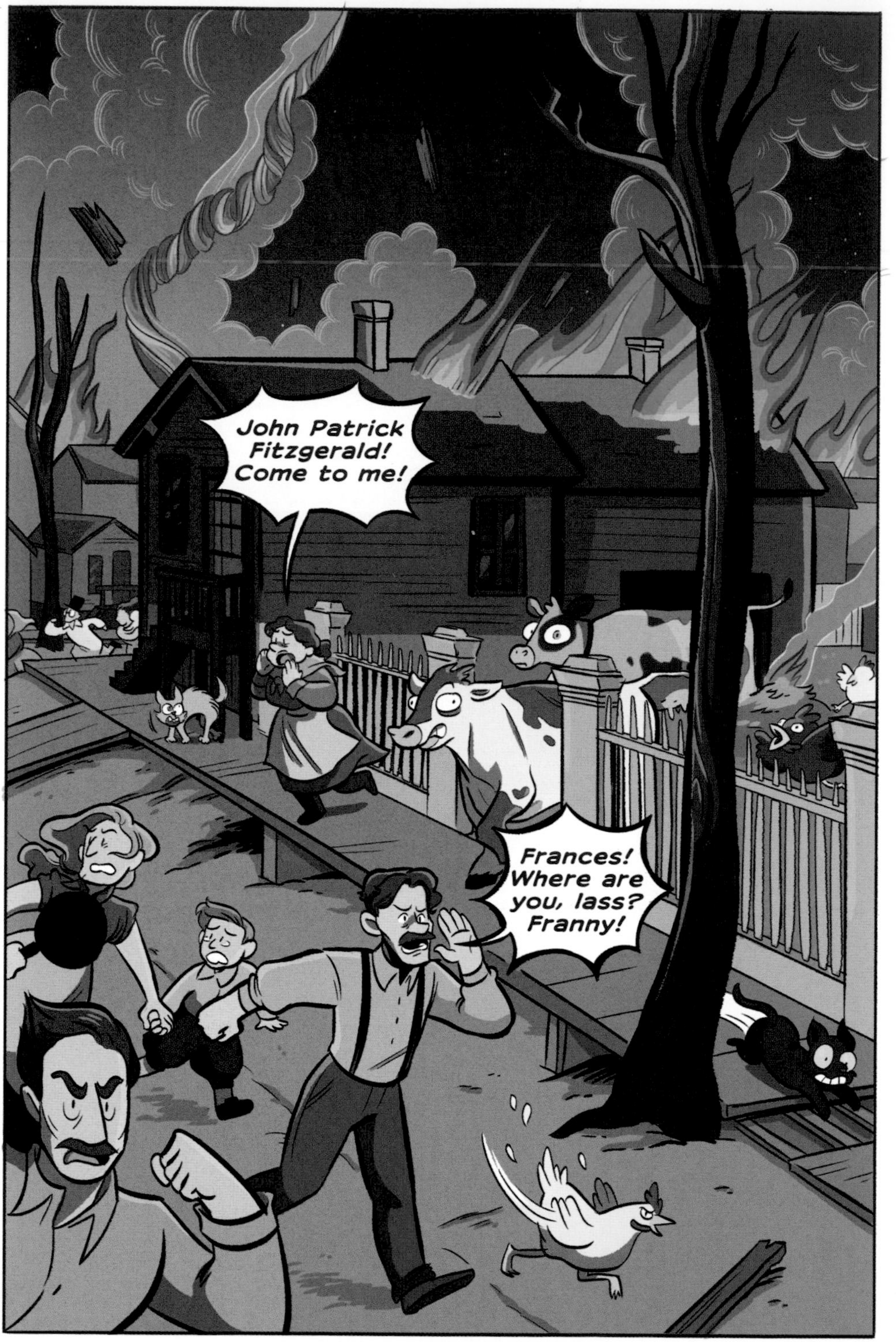
John Patrick Fitzgerald! Come to me!
Frances! Where are you, lass? Franny!

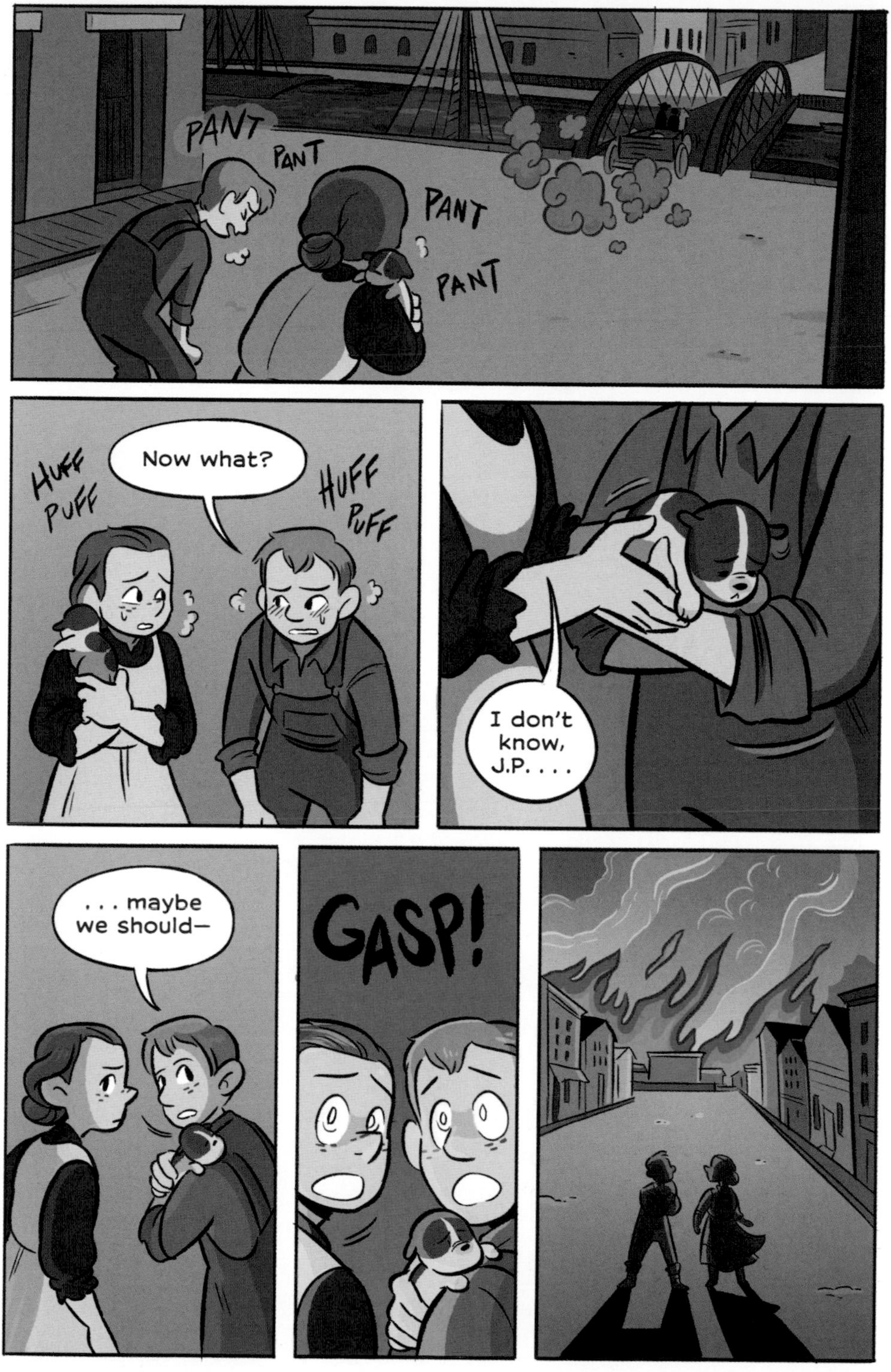
PANT
PANT
PANT
PANT
HUFF PUFF
Now what?
HUFF PUFF
I don't know, J.P. . . .
. . . maybe we should—
GASP!

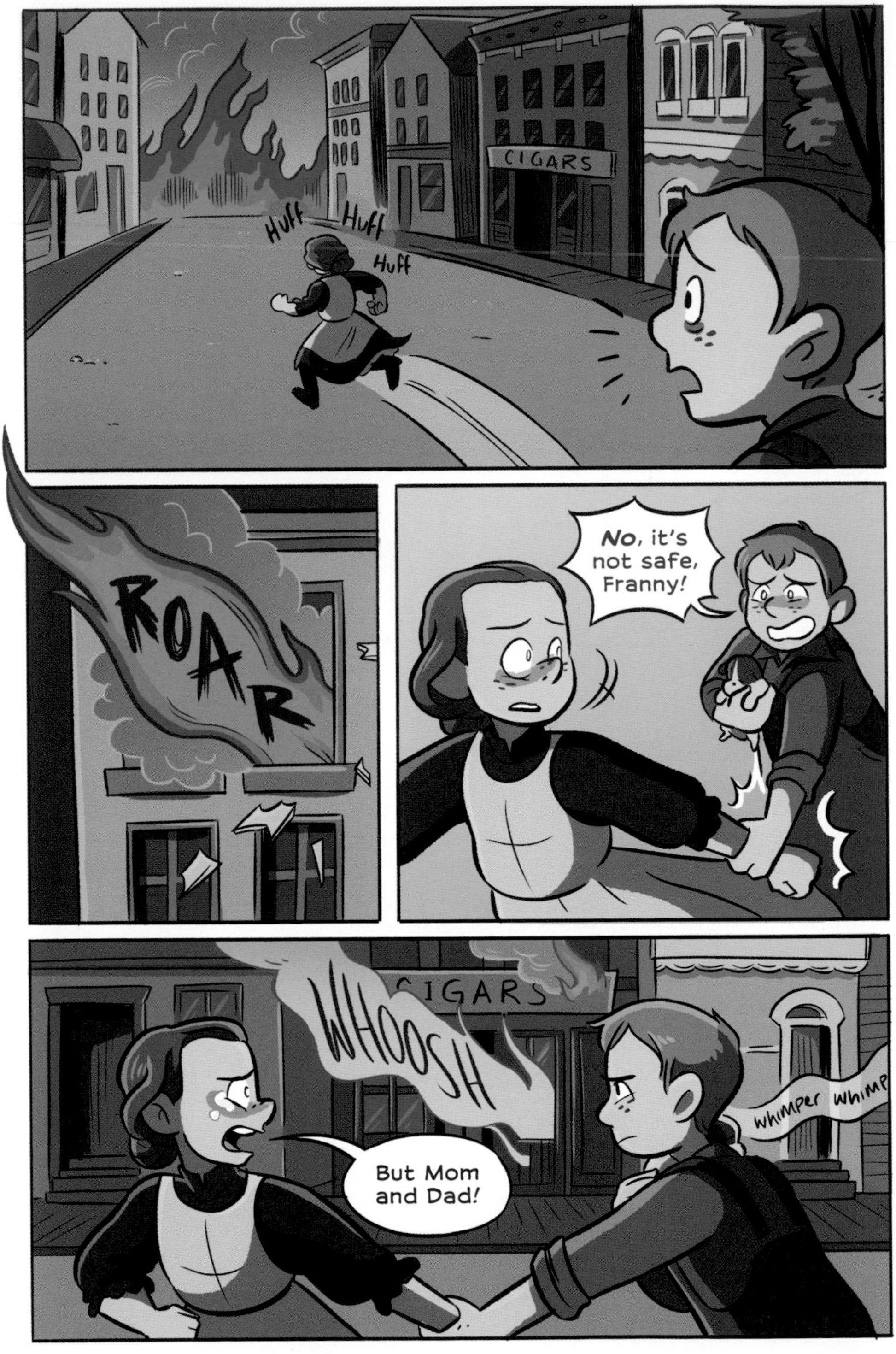
CIGARS
Huff Huff Huff
ROAR
No, it's not safe, Franny!
WHOOSH
CIGARS
whimper whimp
But Mom and Dad!

We'll find them, Franny! But we can't go through the flames!

You're right, J.P. This heat is terrible!

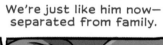

We're just like him now— separated from family.

CRASH!

We're lucky to be alive.

That's what we'll call him— Lucky.

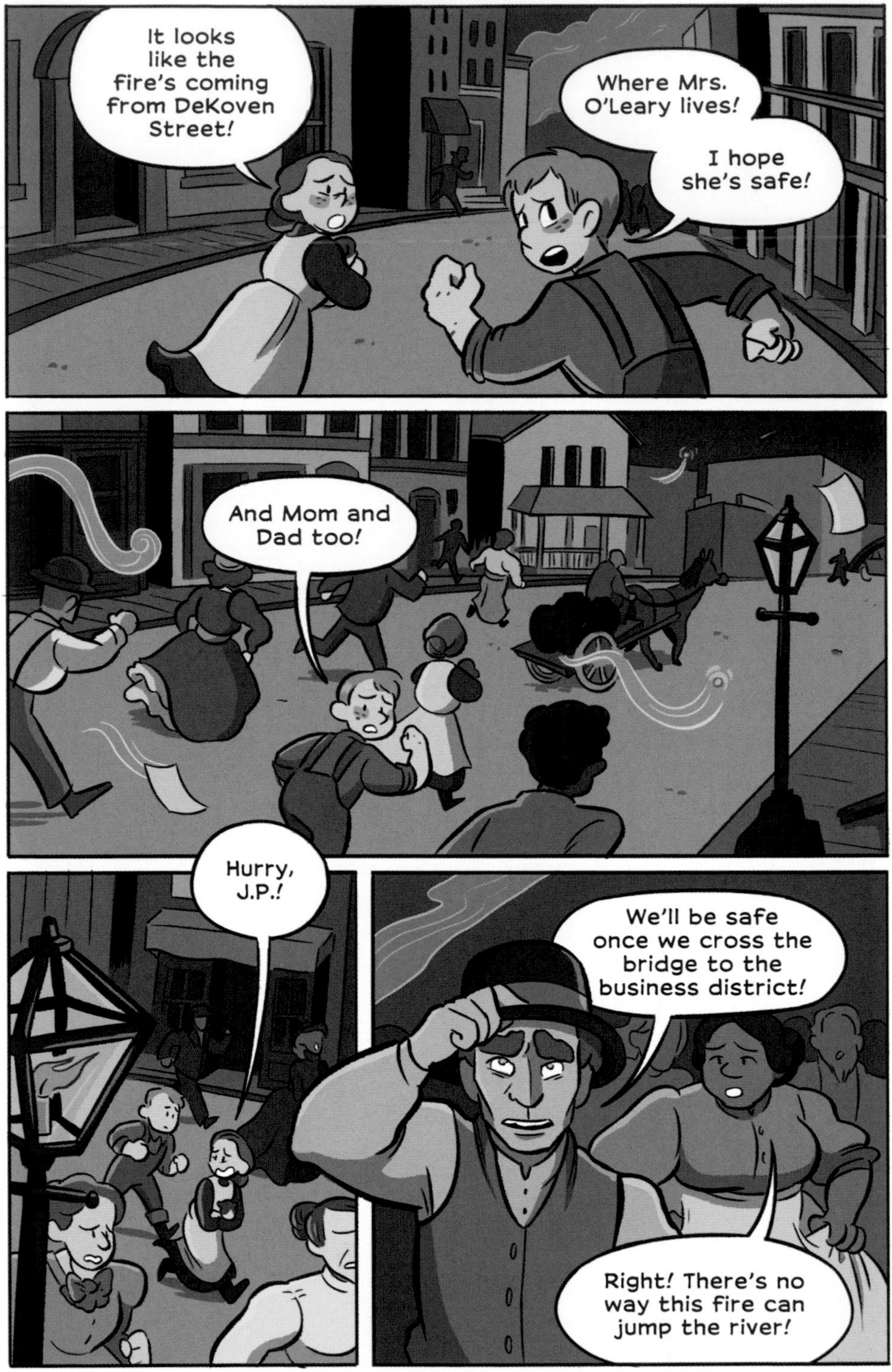
It looks like the fire's coming from DeKoven Street!
Where Mrs. O'Leary lives!
I hope she's safe!
And Mom and Dad too!
Hurry, J.P.!
We'll be safe once we cross the bridge to the business district!
Right! There's no way this fire can jump the river!

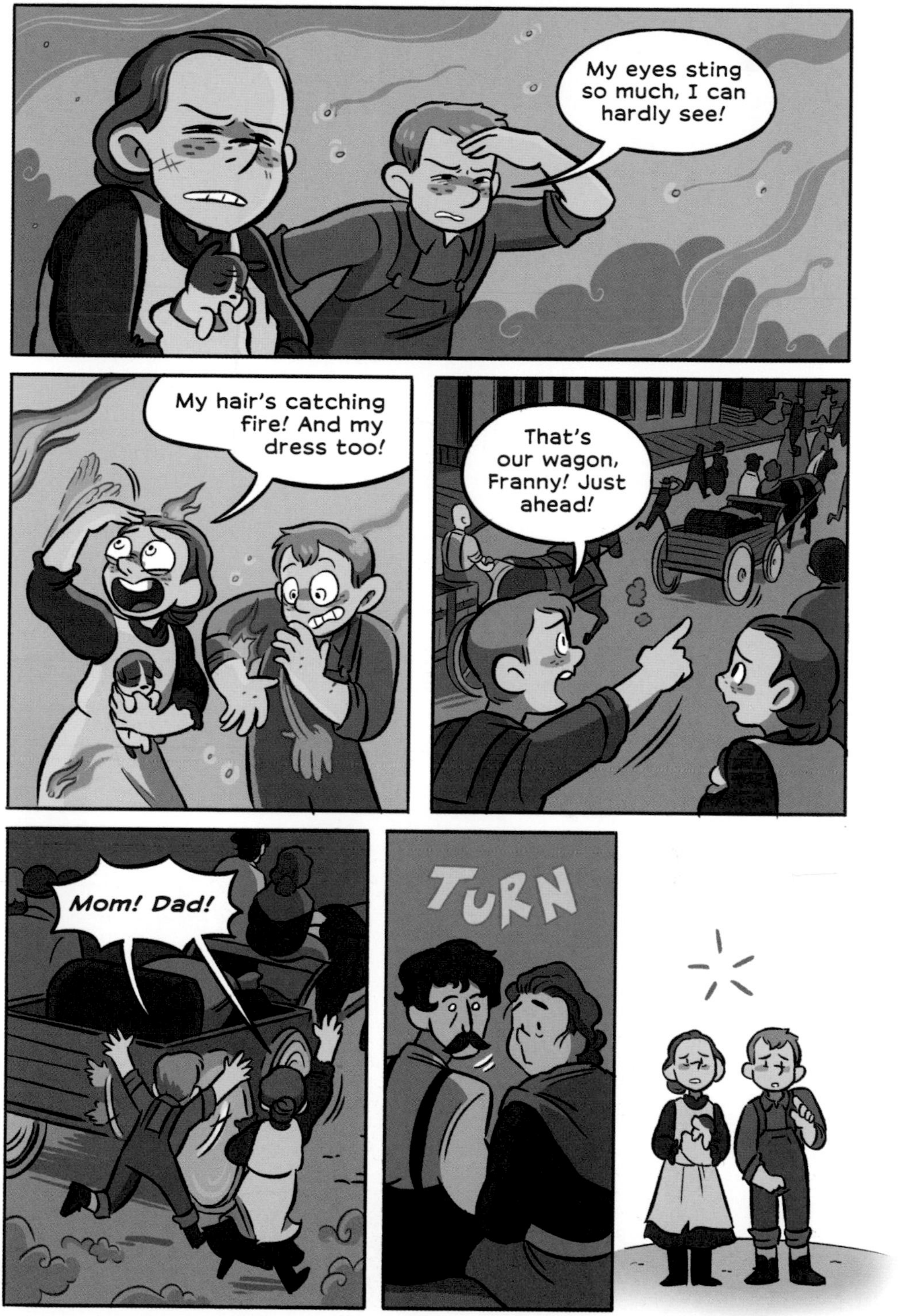
My eyes sting so much, I can hardly see!
My hair's catching fire! And my dress too!
That's our wagon, Franny! Just ahead!
Mom! Dad!
TURN

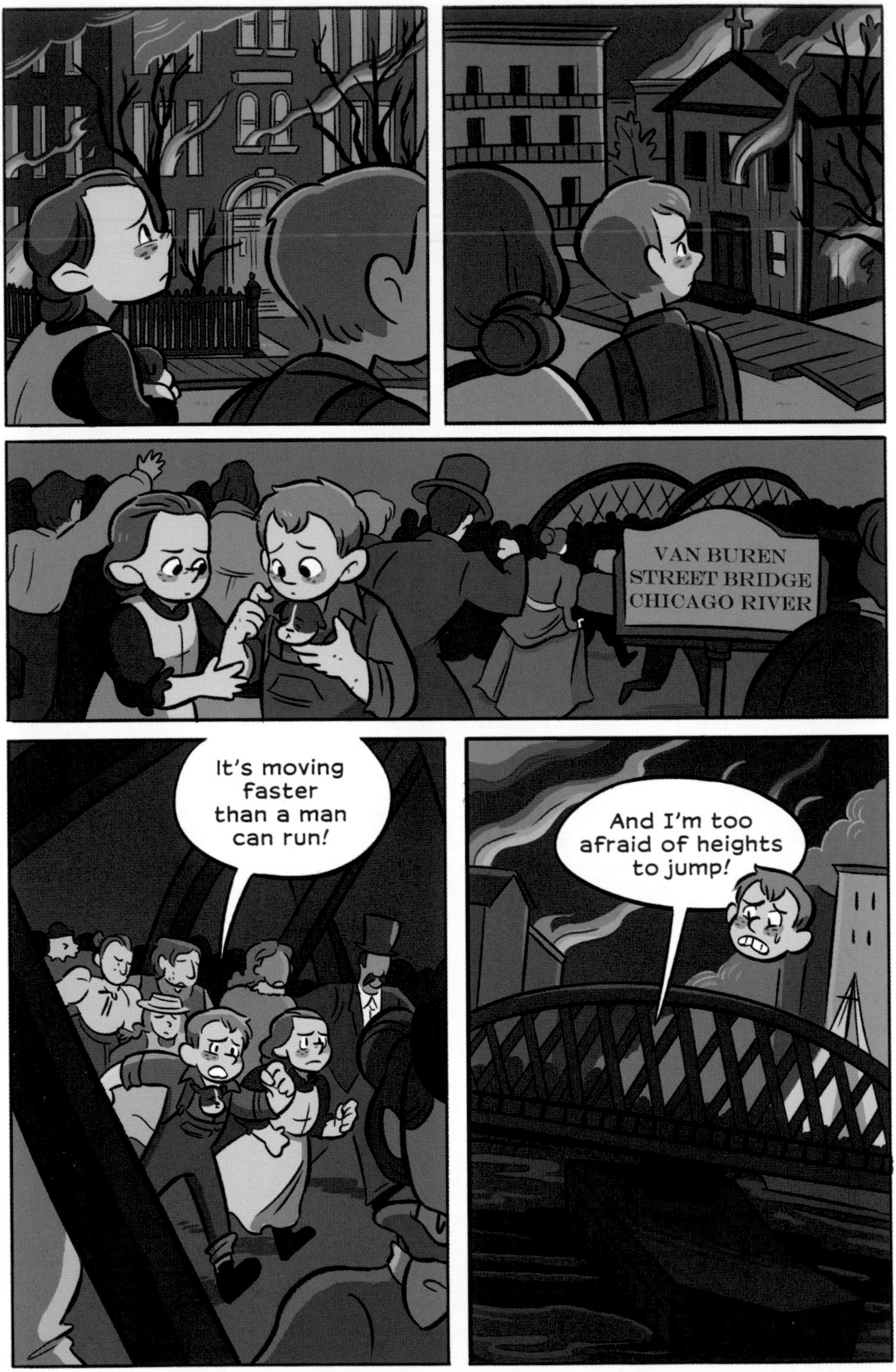
VAN BUREN
STREET BRIDGE
CHICAGO RIVER
It's moving faster than a man can run!
And I'm too afraid of heights to jump!

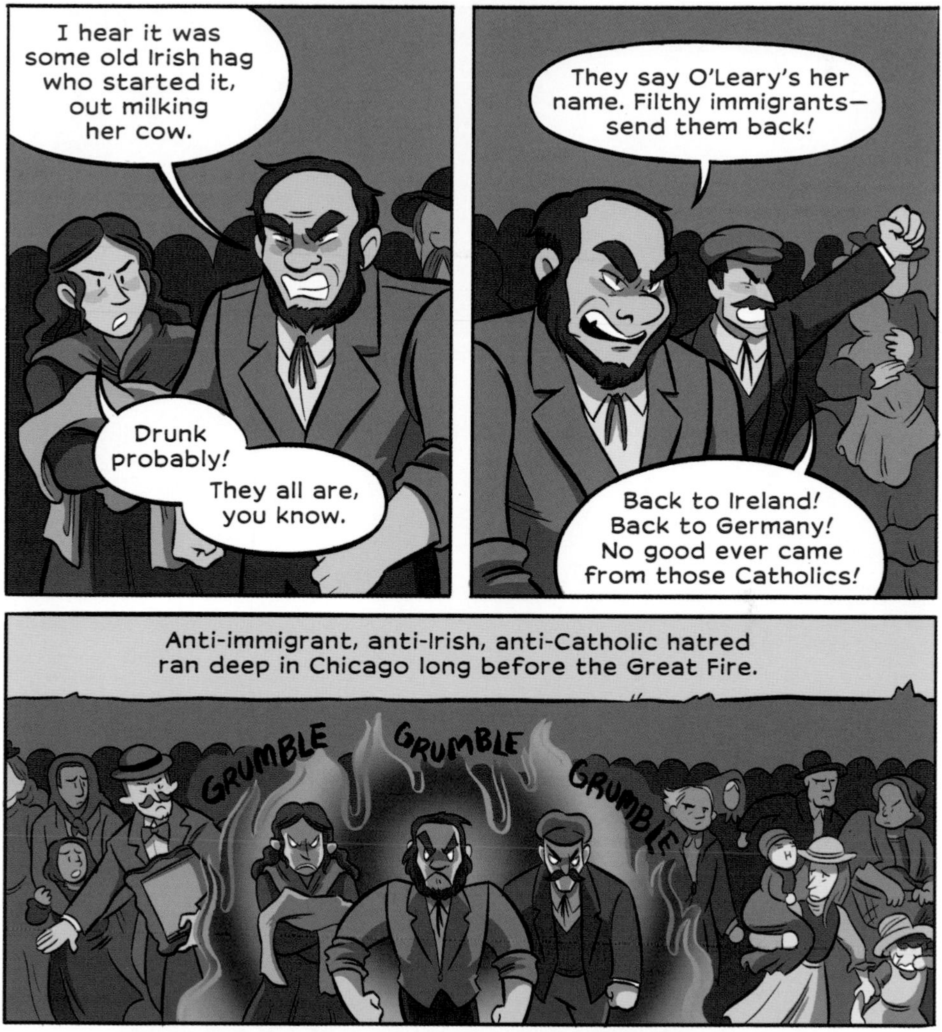
I hear it was some old Irish hag who started it, out milking her cow.
Drunk probably!
They all are, you know.
They say O'Leary's her name. Filthy immigrants— send them back!
Back to Ireland! Back to Germany! No good ever came from those Catholics!
Anti-immigrant, anti-Irish, anti-Catholic hatred ran deep in Chicago long before the Great Fire.
GRUMBLE
GRUMBLE
GRUMBLE

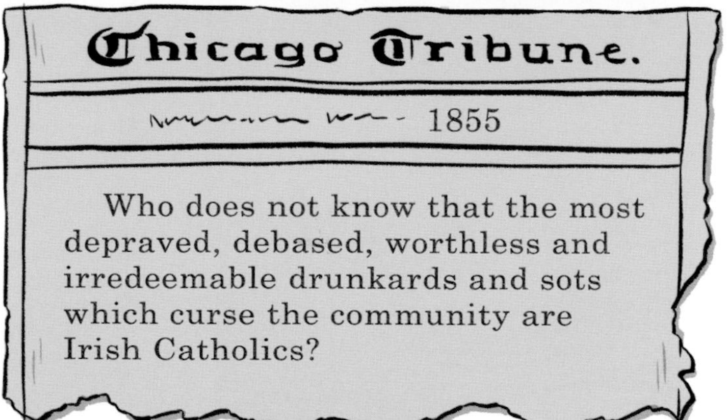
Chicago Tribune.

1855

Who does not know that the most depraved, debased, worthless and irredeemable drunkards and sots which curse the community are Irish Catholics?

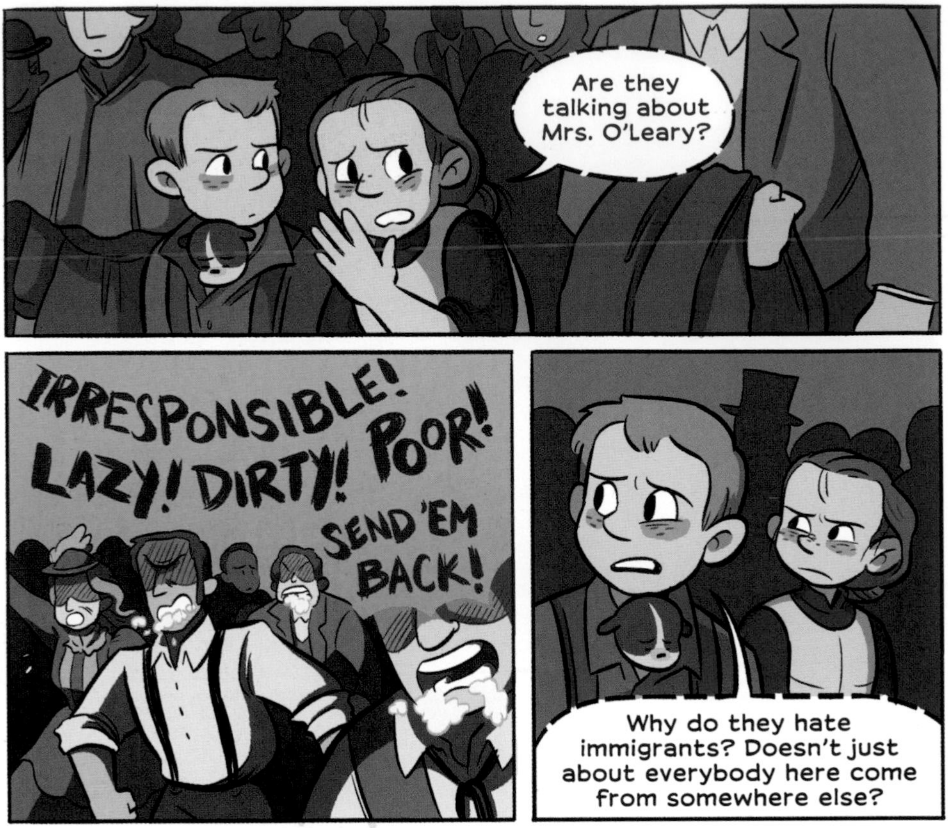
Are they talking about Mrs. O'Leary?
IRRESPONSIBLE! LAZY! DIRTY! POOR!
SEND 'EM BACK!
Why do they hate immigrants? Doesn't just about everybody here come from somewhere else?

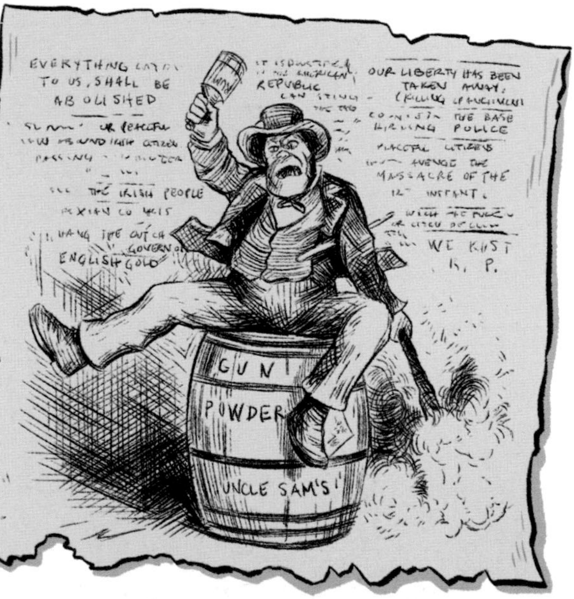
OUR LIBERTY HAS BEEN TAKEN AWAY
THE IRISH PEOPLE
ENGLISH GOLD
GUN POWDER
UNCLE SAM'S

Because hatred of Irish immigrants ran high both nationally and in Chicago, as depicted in this offensive political cartoon that ran in *Harper's Weekly* national magazine just one month before the fire, people were ready to believe the story about Mrs. O'Leary, and she became the Great Fire's "scapegoat"—someone blamed for the mistakes of others.

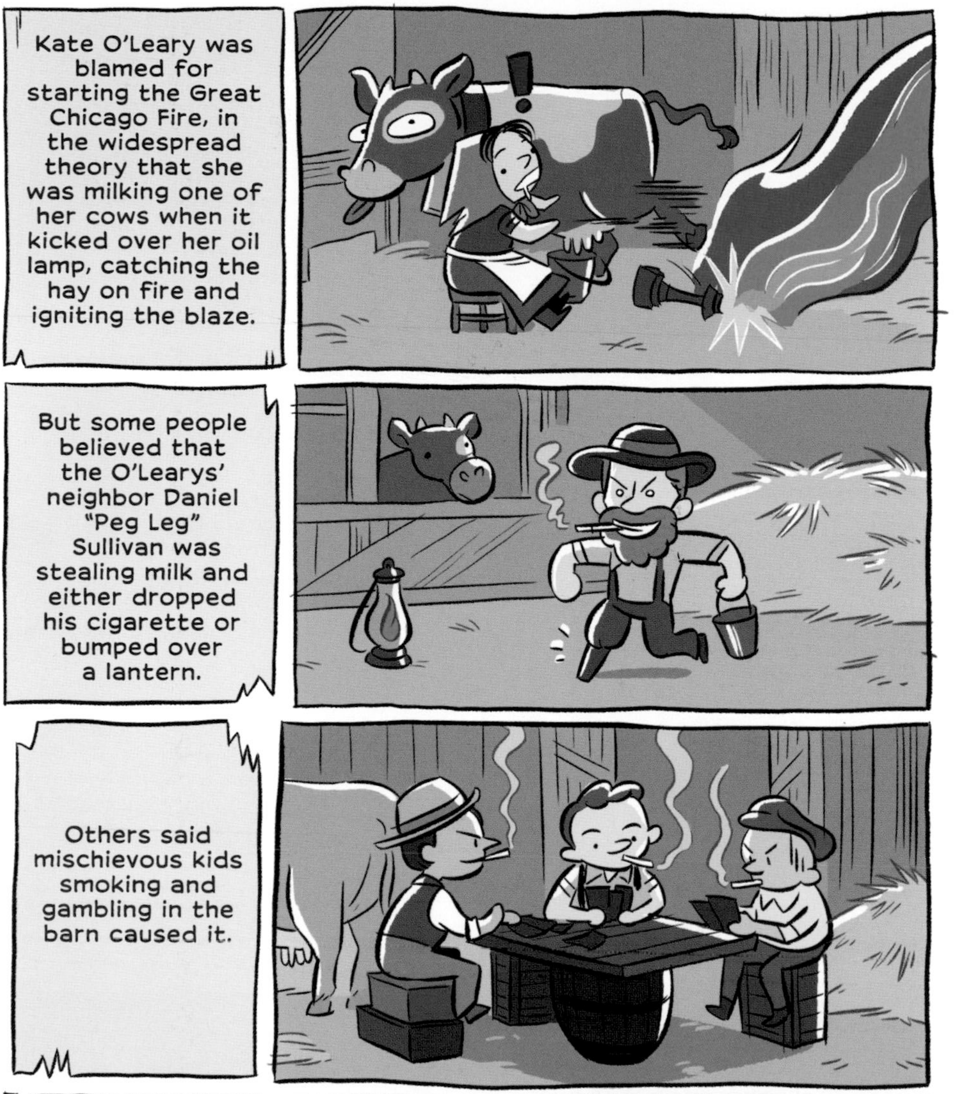
Kate O'Leary was blamed for starting the Great Chicago Fire, in the widespread theory that she was milking one of her cows when it kicked over her oil lamp, catching the hay on fire and igniting the blaze.
But some people believed that the O'Learys' neighbor Daniel "Peg Leg" Sullivan was stealing milk and either dropped his cigarette or bumped over a lantern.
Others said mischievous kids smoking and gambling in the barn caused it.
And still others thought that a meteor shower started the Chicago blaze—as well as fires that burned the same night in Peshtigo, Wisconsin, and Holland, Michigan.
Peshtigo
WISCONSIN
MICHIGAN
Holland
Chicago
ILLINOIS

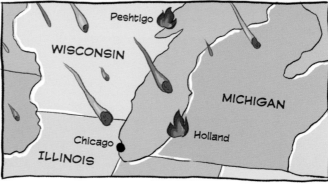

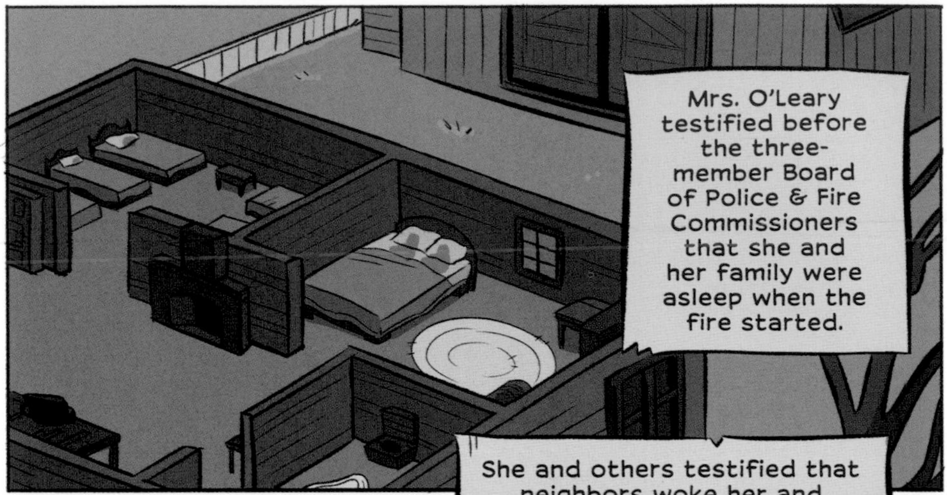
Mrs. O'Leary testified before the three-member Board of Police & Fire Commissioners that she and her family were asleep when the fire started.
She and others testified that neighbors woke her and Patrick O'Leary, hollering that their barn was on fire.

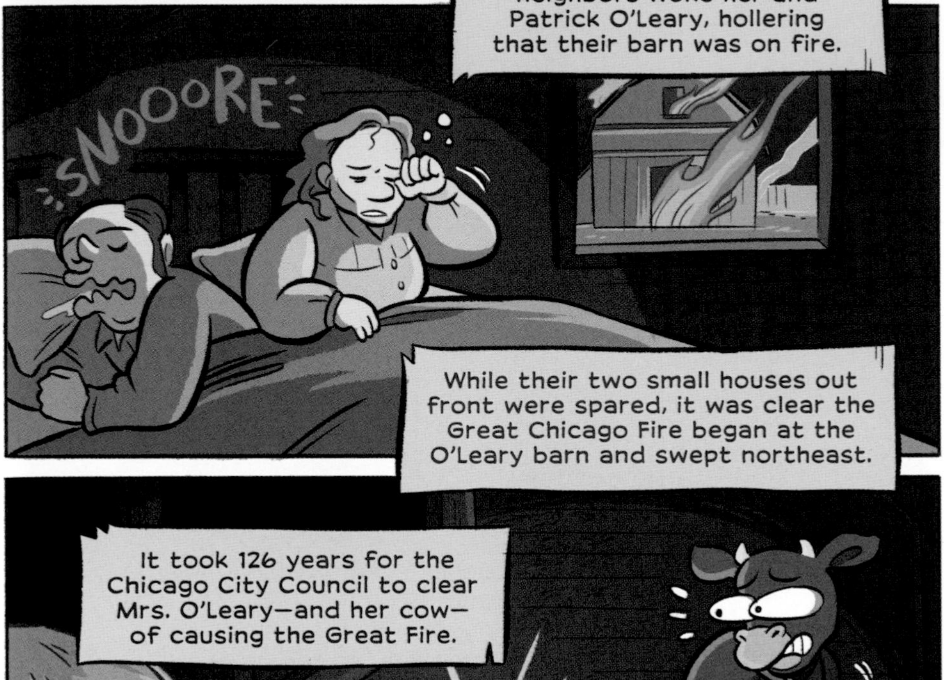
SNOOORE
While their two small houses out front were spared, it was clear the Great Chicago Fire began at the O'Leary barn and swept northeast.

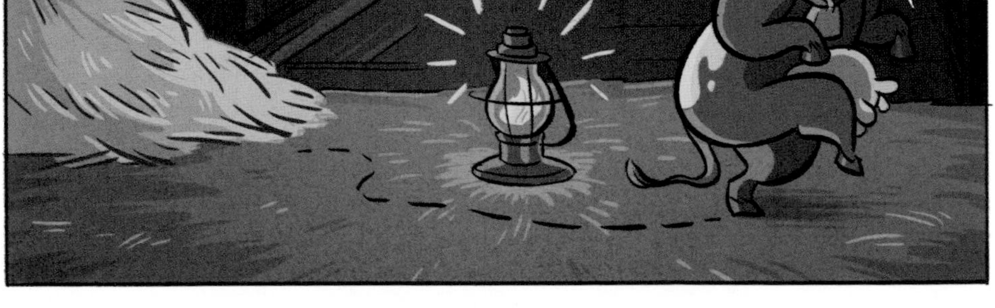
It took 126 years for the Chicago City Council to clear Mrs. O'Leary—and her cow—of causing the Great Fire.

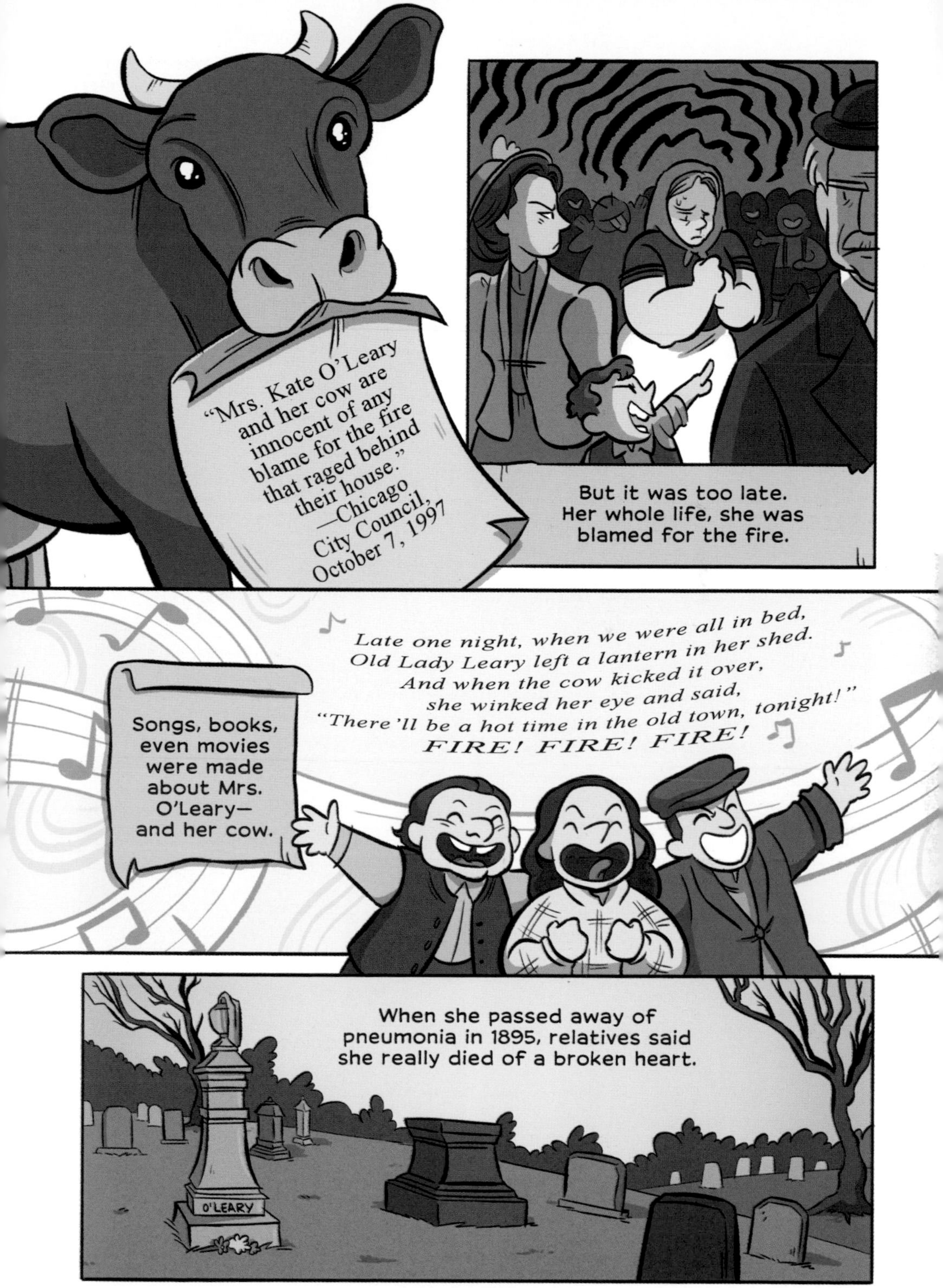
"Mrs. Kate O'Leary and her cow are innocent of any blame for the fire that raged behind their house." —Chicago City Council, October 7, 1997
But it was too late. Her whole life, she was blamed for the fire.
Songs, books, even movies were made about Mrs. O'Leary— and her cow.
Late one night, when we were all in bed,
Old Lady Leary left a lantern in her shed.
And when the cow kicked it over,
she winked her eye and said,
"There'll be a hot time in the old town, tonight!"
FIRE! FIRE! FIRE!
When she passed away of pneumonia in 1895, relatives said she really died of a broken heart.
O'LEARY

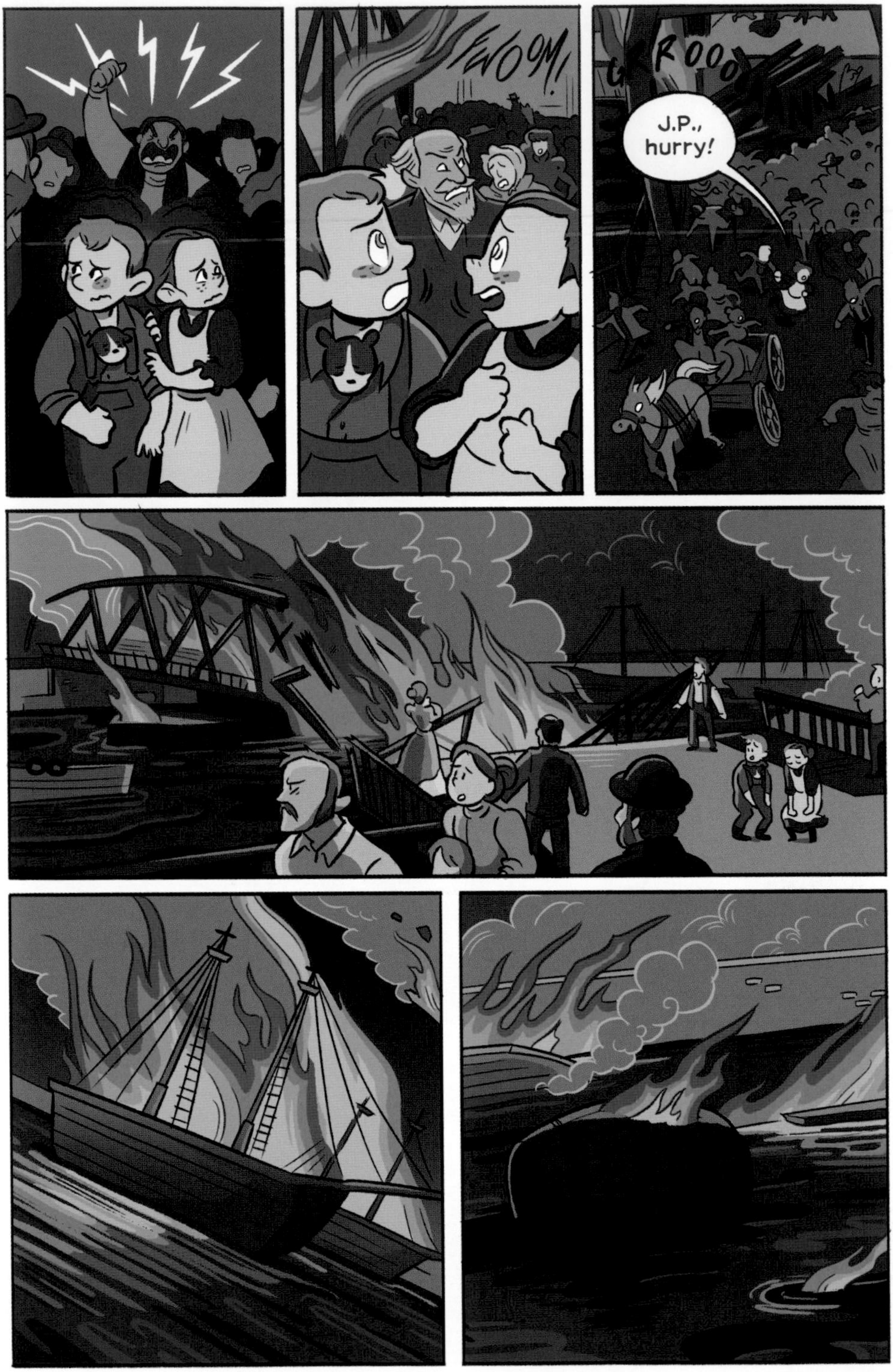
FWOOM!
J.P., hurry!

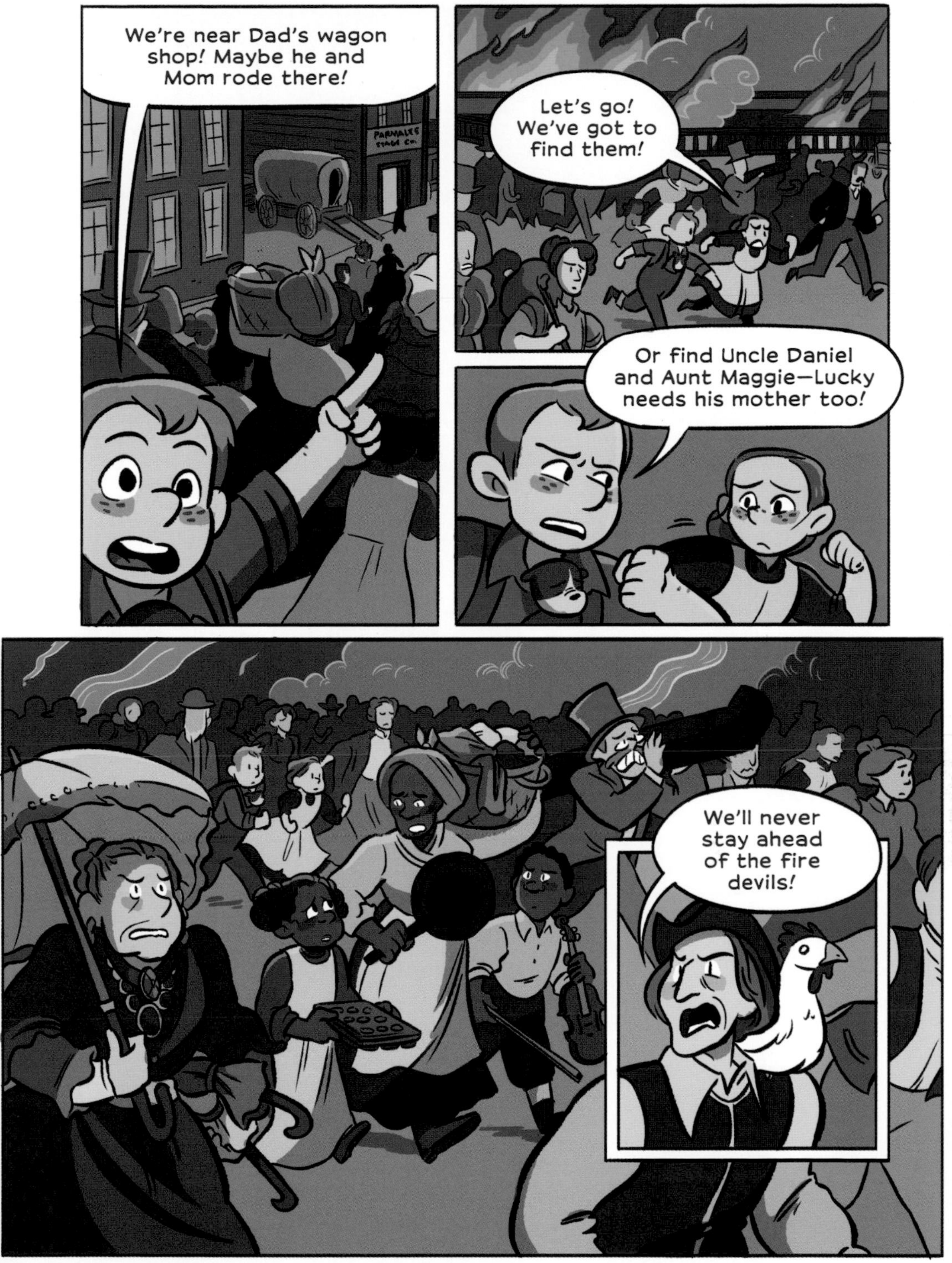
We're near Dad's wagon shop! Maybe he and Mom rode there!
PARMALEE'S STAGE CO.
Let's go! We've got to find them!
Or find Uncle Daniel and Aunt Maggie—Lucky needs his mother too!
We'll never stay ahead of the fire devils!

"Fire devils" referred to whirling pockets of flames fueled by gas and windy conditions.

Look, J.P.! The fire's jumping the river!

I thought that was impossible.

It's as if this fire is chasing us!

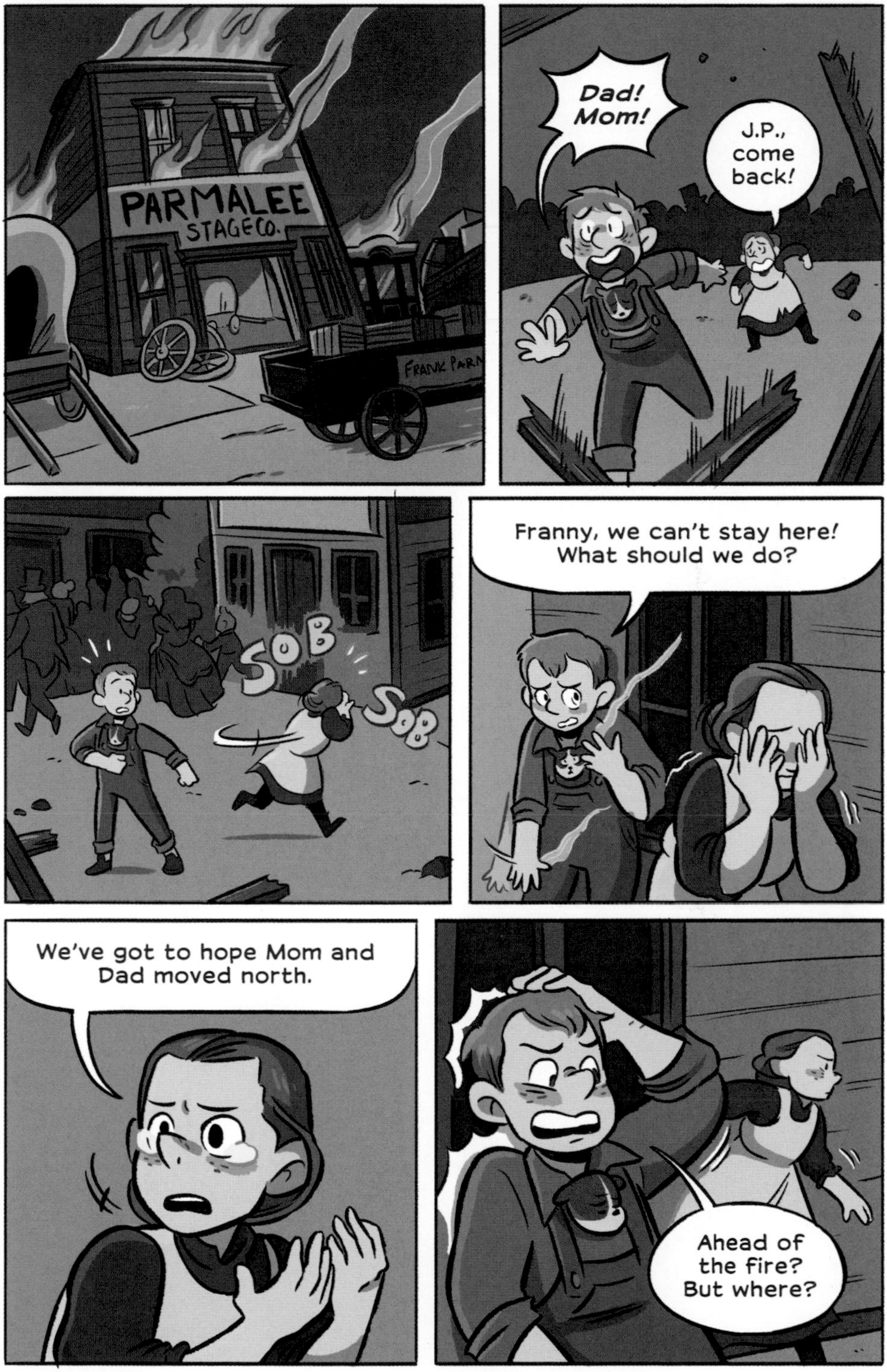
PARMALEE
STAGE CO.
FRANK PARM
Dad! Mom!
J.P., come back!
SOB
SOB
Franny, we can't stay here! What should we do?
We've got to hope Mom and Dad moved north.
Ahead of the fire? But where?

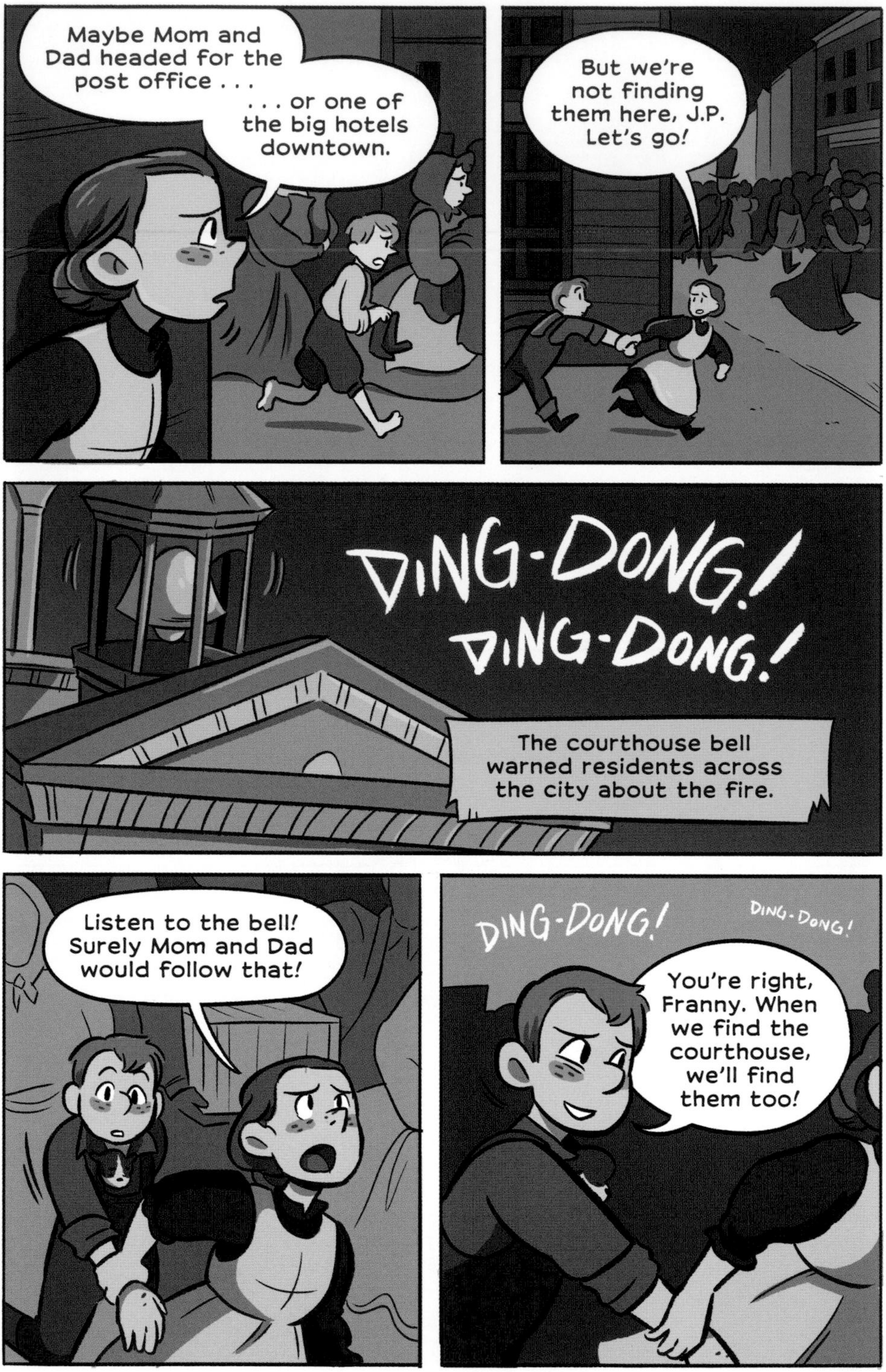

Maybe Mom and Dad headed for the post office . . .
. . . or one of the big hotels downtown.
But we're not finding them here, J.P. Let's go!
DING-DONG! DING-DONG!
The courthouse bell warned residents across the city about the fire.
Listen to the bell! Surely Mom and Dad would follow that!
DING-DONG!
DING-DONG!
You're right, Franny. When we find the courthouse, we'll find them too!

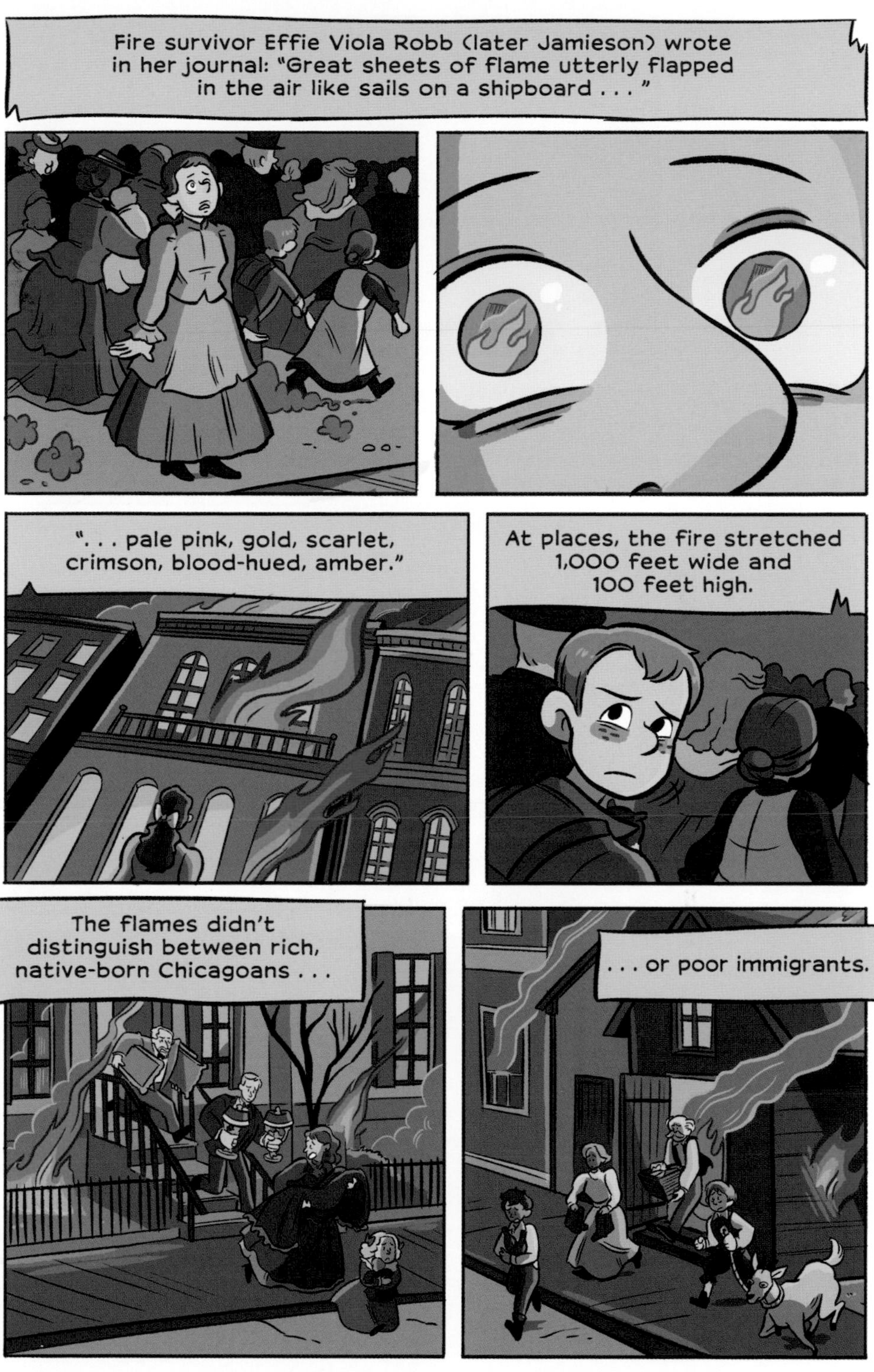
Fire survivor Effie Viola Robb (later Jamieson) wrote in her journal: "Great sheets of flame utterly flapped in the air like sails on a shipboard . . . "
". . . pale pink, gold, scarlet, crimson, blood-hued, amber."
At places, the fire stretched 1,000 feet wide and 100 feet high.
The flames didn't distinguish between rich, native-born Chicagoans . . .
. . . or poor immigrants.

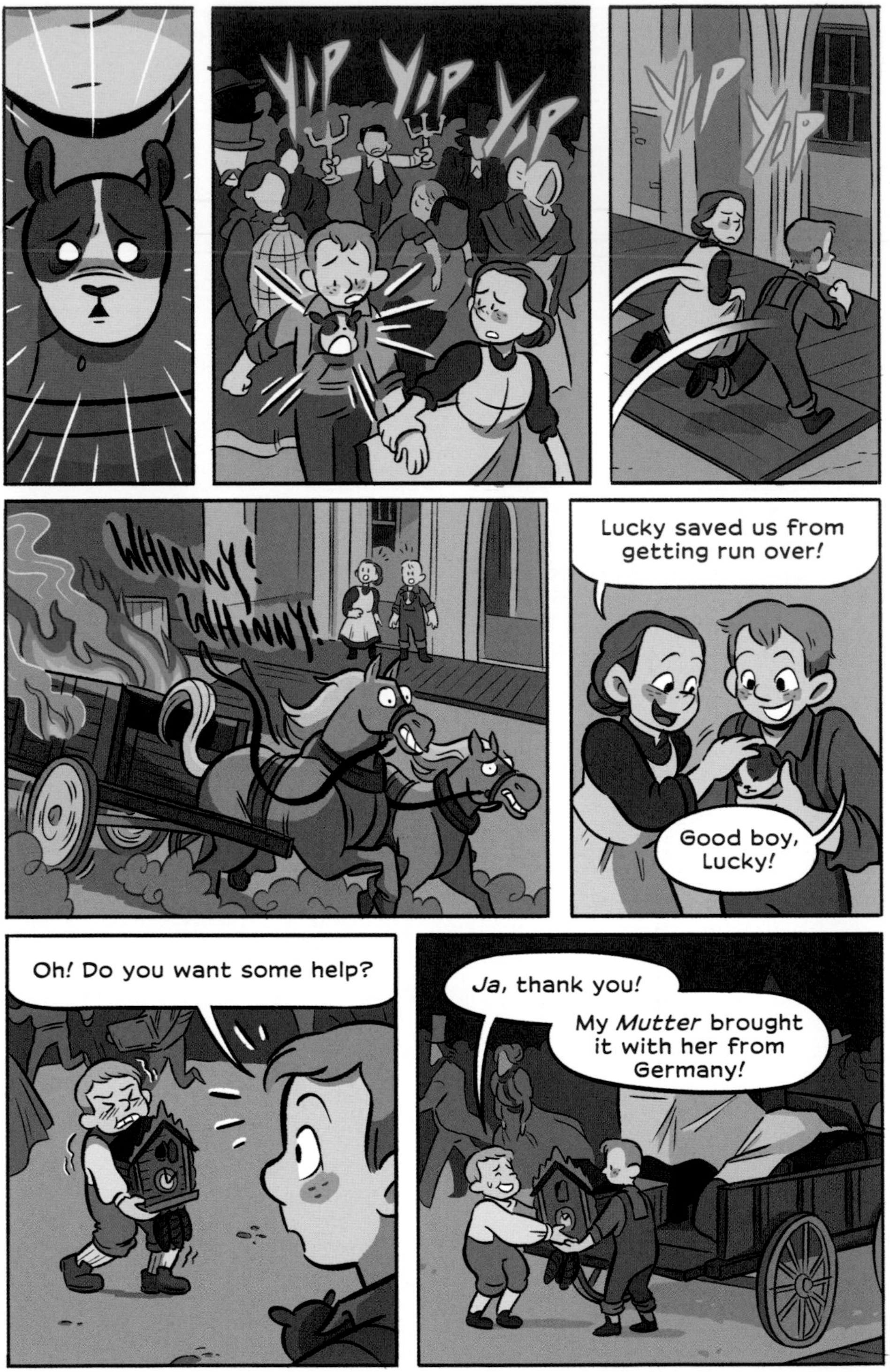
YIP YIP YIP
YIP YIP
WHINNY! WHINNY!
Lucky saved us from getting run over!
Good boy, Lucky!
Oh! Do you want some help?
Ja, thank you!
My *Mutter* brought it with her from Germany!

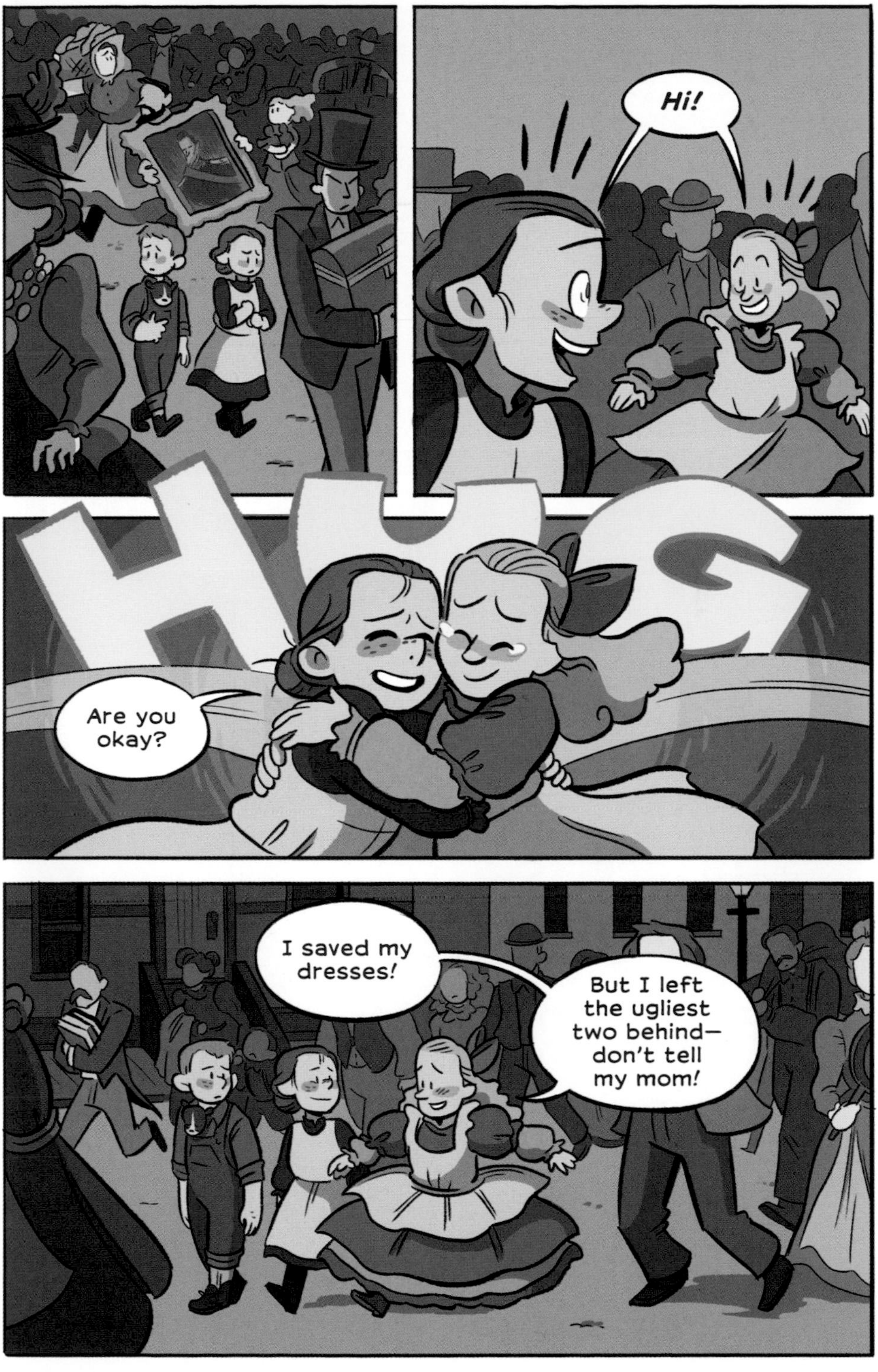
Hi!
HUG
Are you okay?
I saved my dresses!
But I left the ugliest two behind—don't tell my mom!

KA-BOOM!!!

When flames reached the gasworks, a holding tank exploded . . .

FLICKER

. . . cutting off the city's gas supply and plunging the streets into darkness.

FWOOSH

Look at the lamps—they've gone out! The city's in darkness now.

Except for the fire.

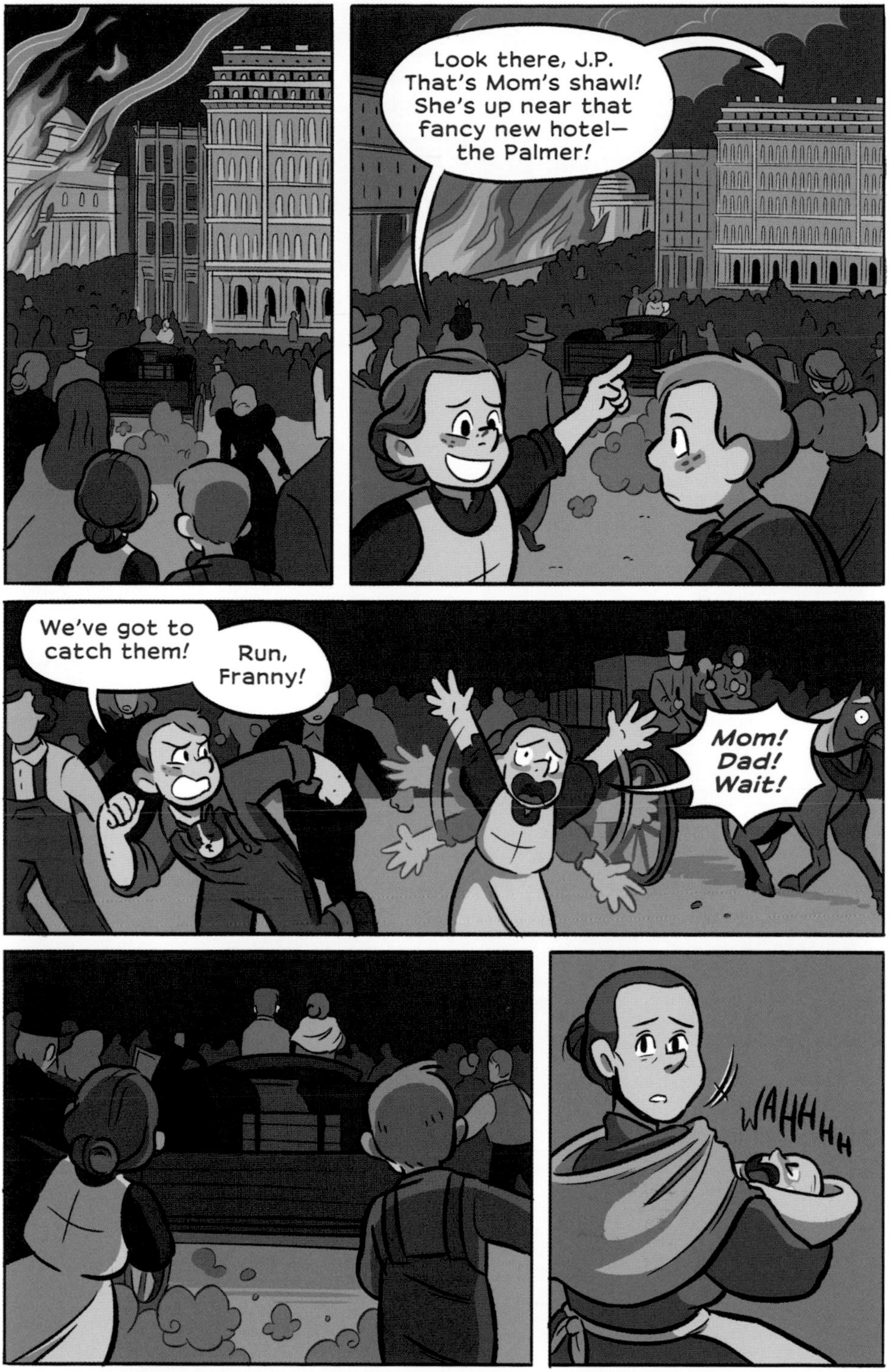
Look there, J.P. That's Mom's shawl! She's up near that fancy new hotel— the Palmer!
We've got to catch them!
Run, Franny!
Mom! Dad! Wait!
WAHHHH

Potter Palmer's luxurious new hotel had been open only 13 days.

Let him through, let him pass!

I'm the architect! I've got to save my plans!

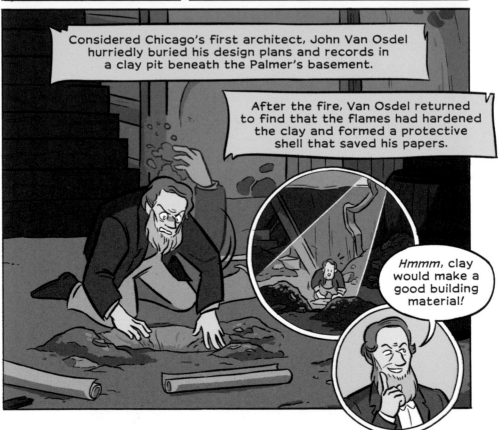

Considered Chicago's first architect, John Van Osdel hurriedly buried his design plans and records in a clay pit beneath the Palmer's basement.

After the fire, Van Osdel returned to find that the flames had hardened the clay and formed a protective shell that saved his papers.

Hmmm, clay would make a good building material!

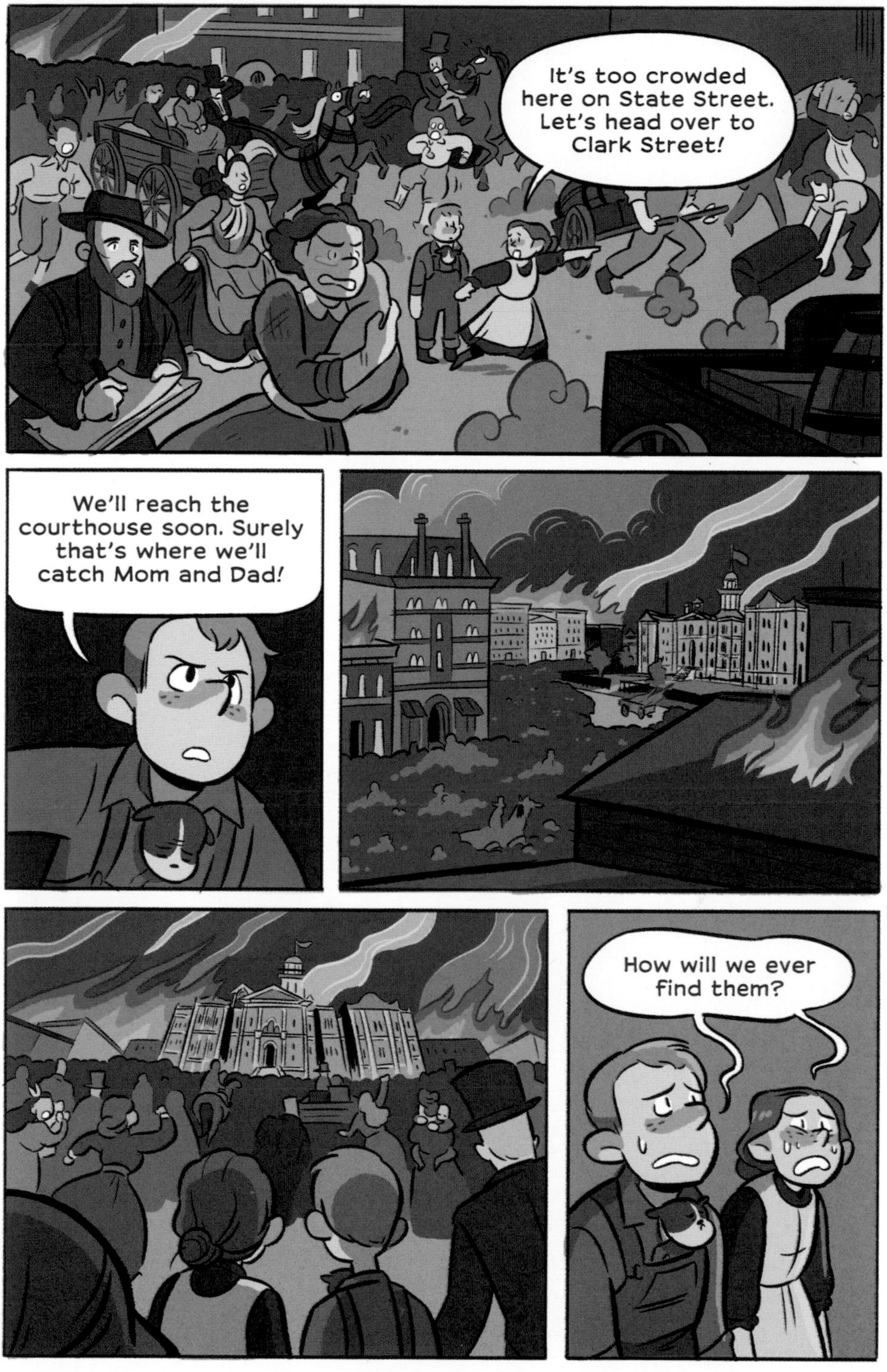
It's too crowded here on State Street. Let's head over to Clark Street!
We'll reach the courthouse soon. Surely that's where we'll catch Mom and Dad!
How will we ever find them?

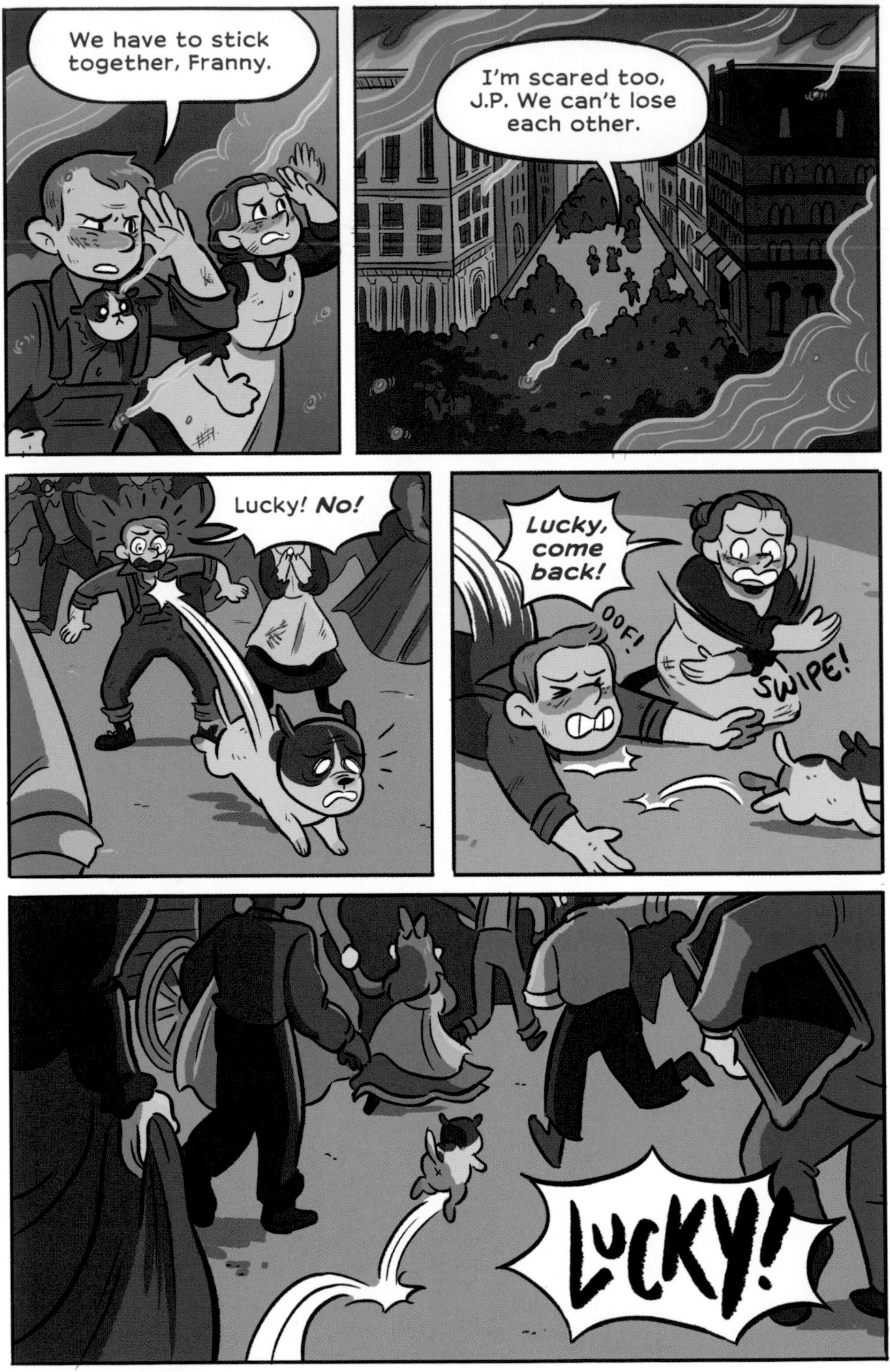

We have to stick together, Franny.
I'm scared too, J.P. We can't lose each other.
Lucky! *No!*
Lucky, come back!
OOF!
SWIPE!
LUCKY!

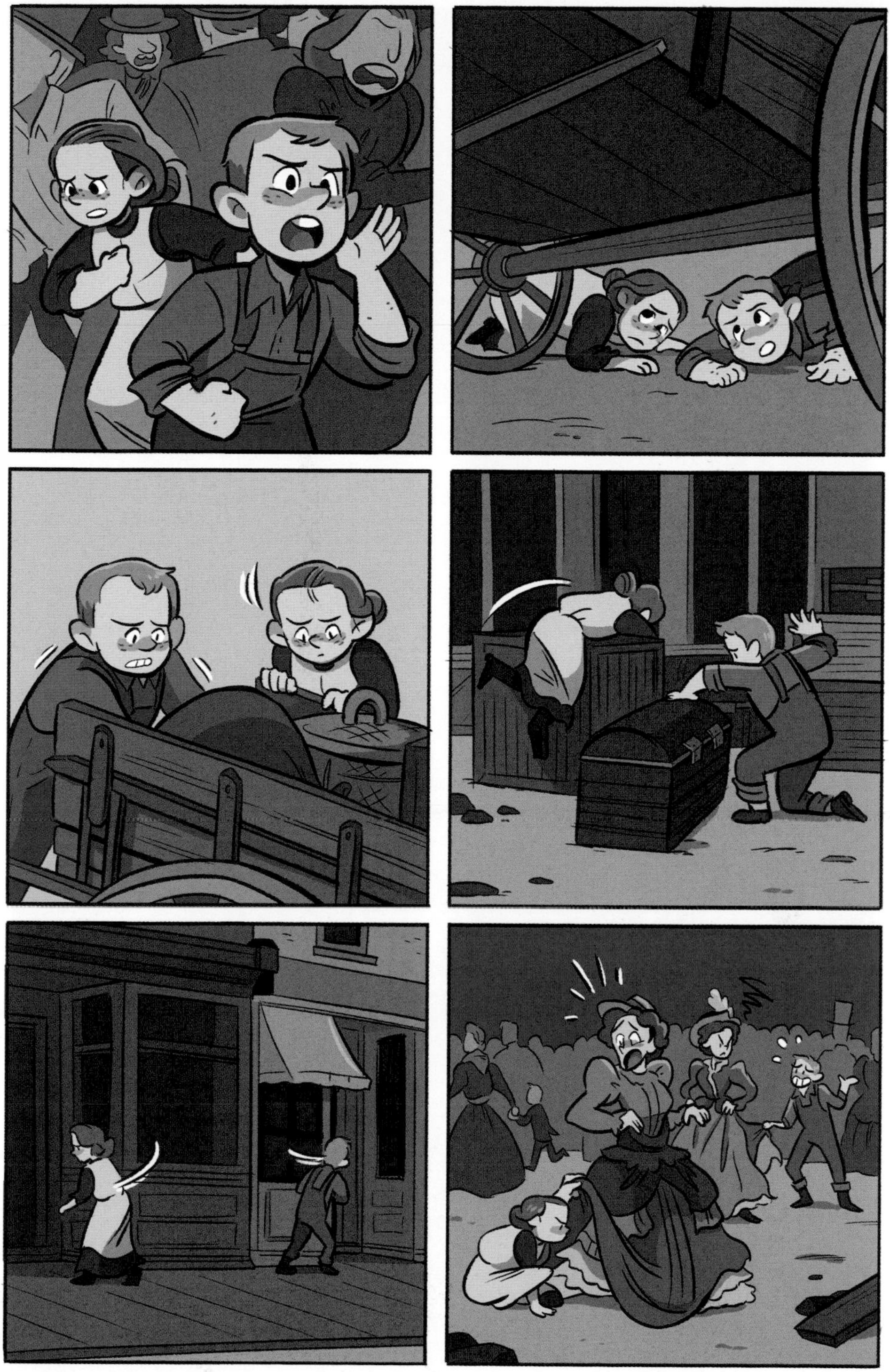

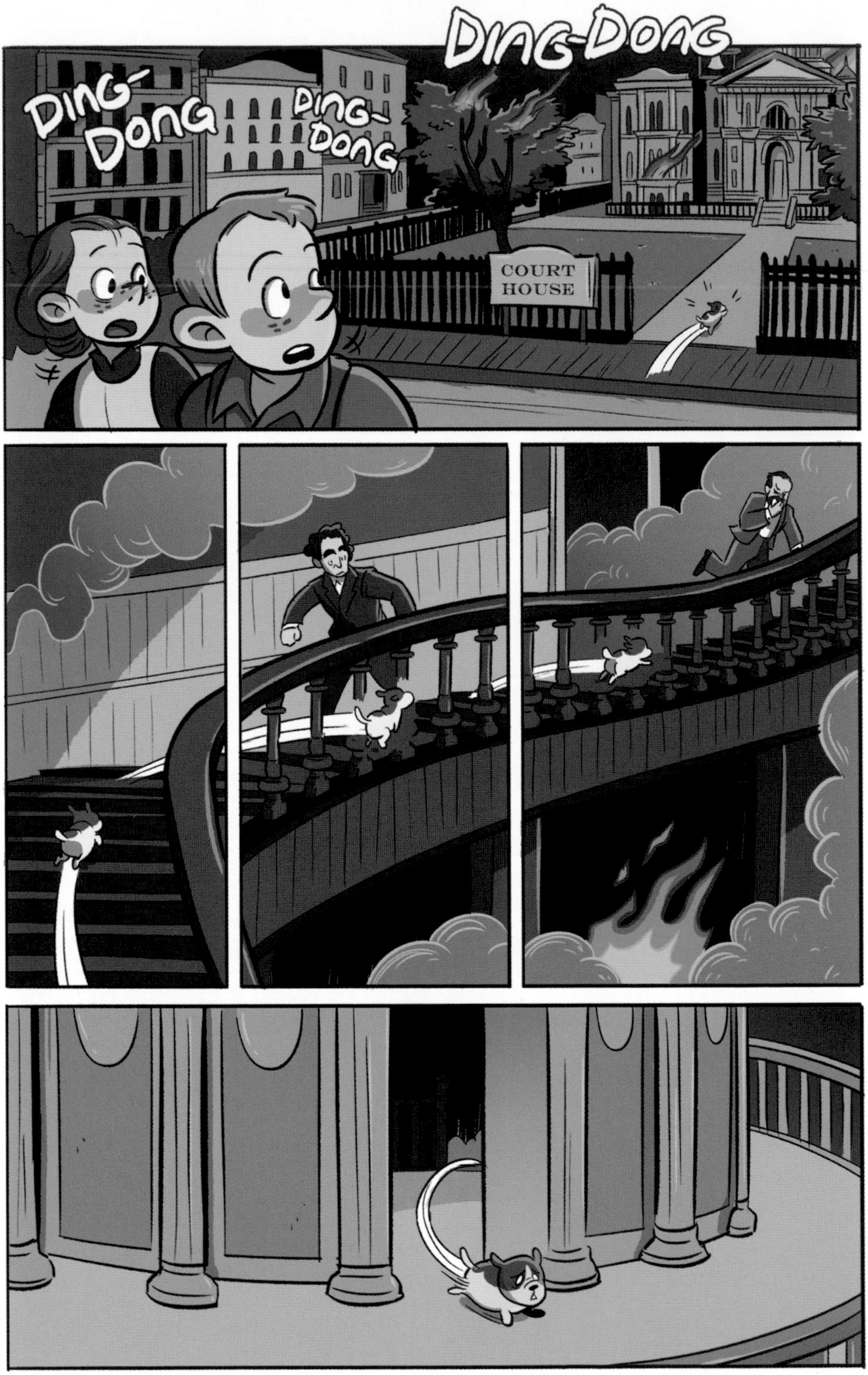
DING-DONG
DING-DONG
DING-DONG
COURT HOUSE

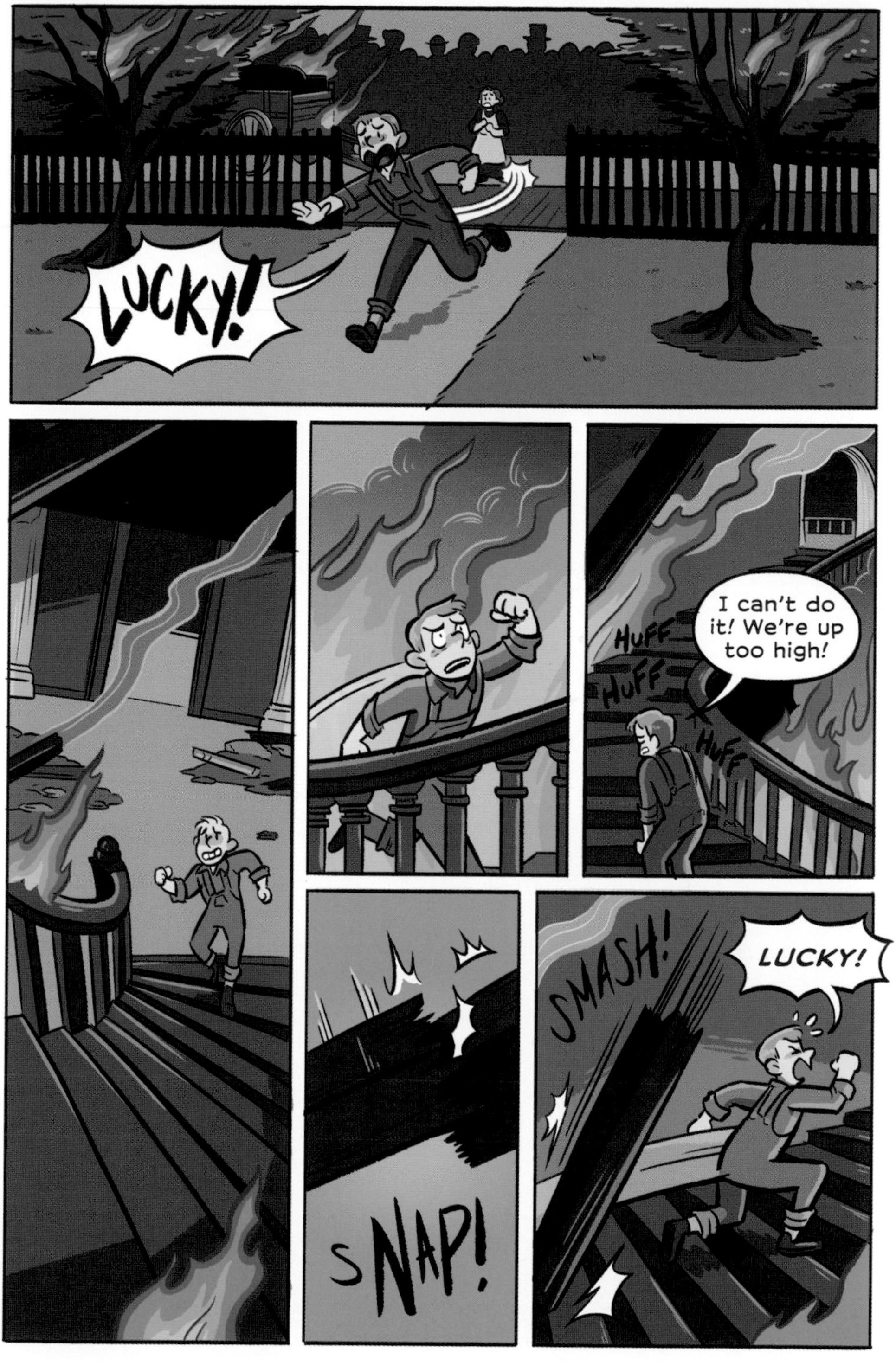
LUCKY!
HUFF
HUFF
HUFF
I can't do it! We're up too high!
SNAP!
SMASH!
LUCKY!

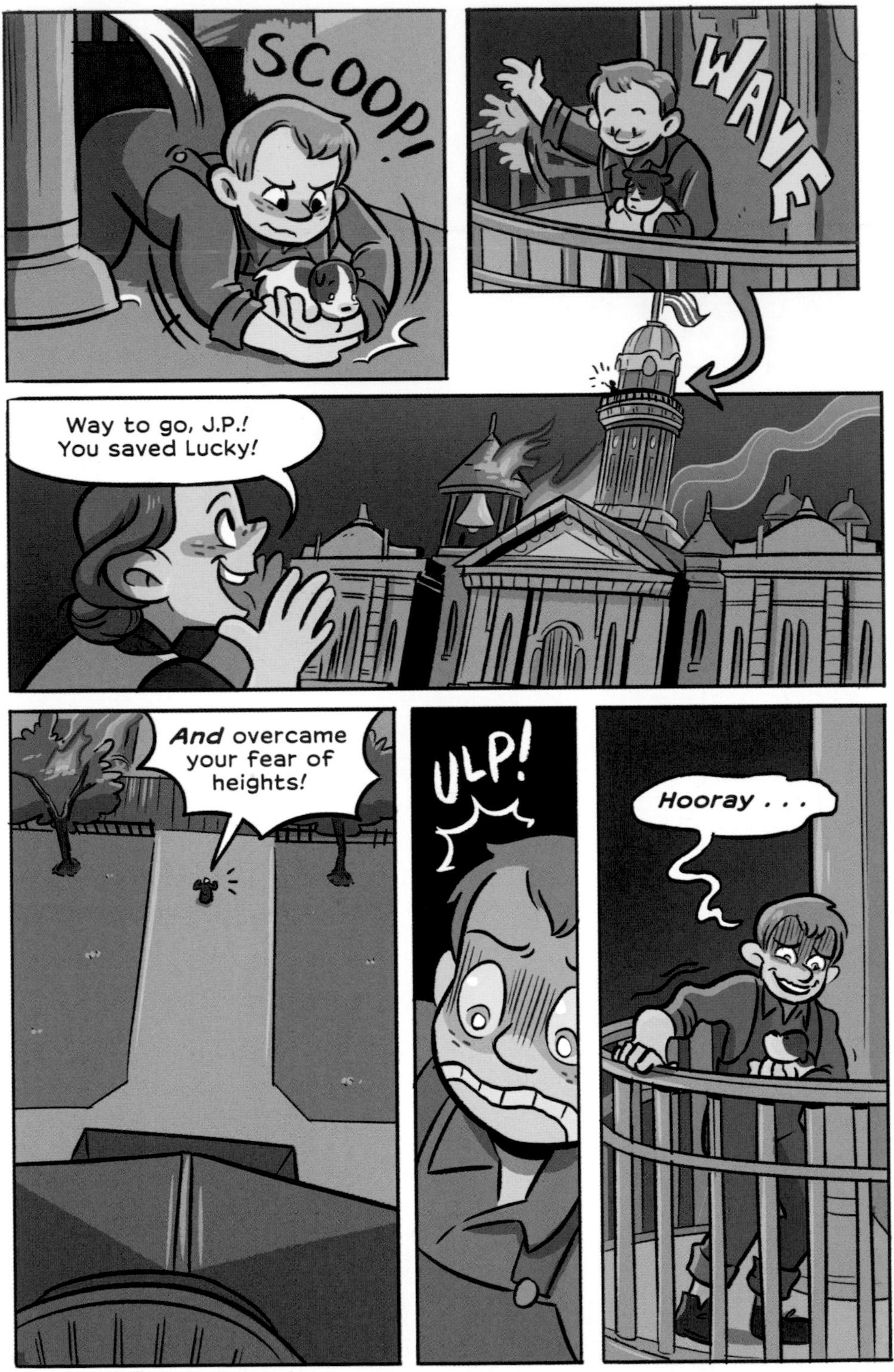
SCOOP!
WAVE
Way to go, J.P.! You saved Lucky!
And overcame your fear of heights!
ULP!
Hooray . . .

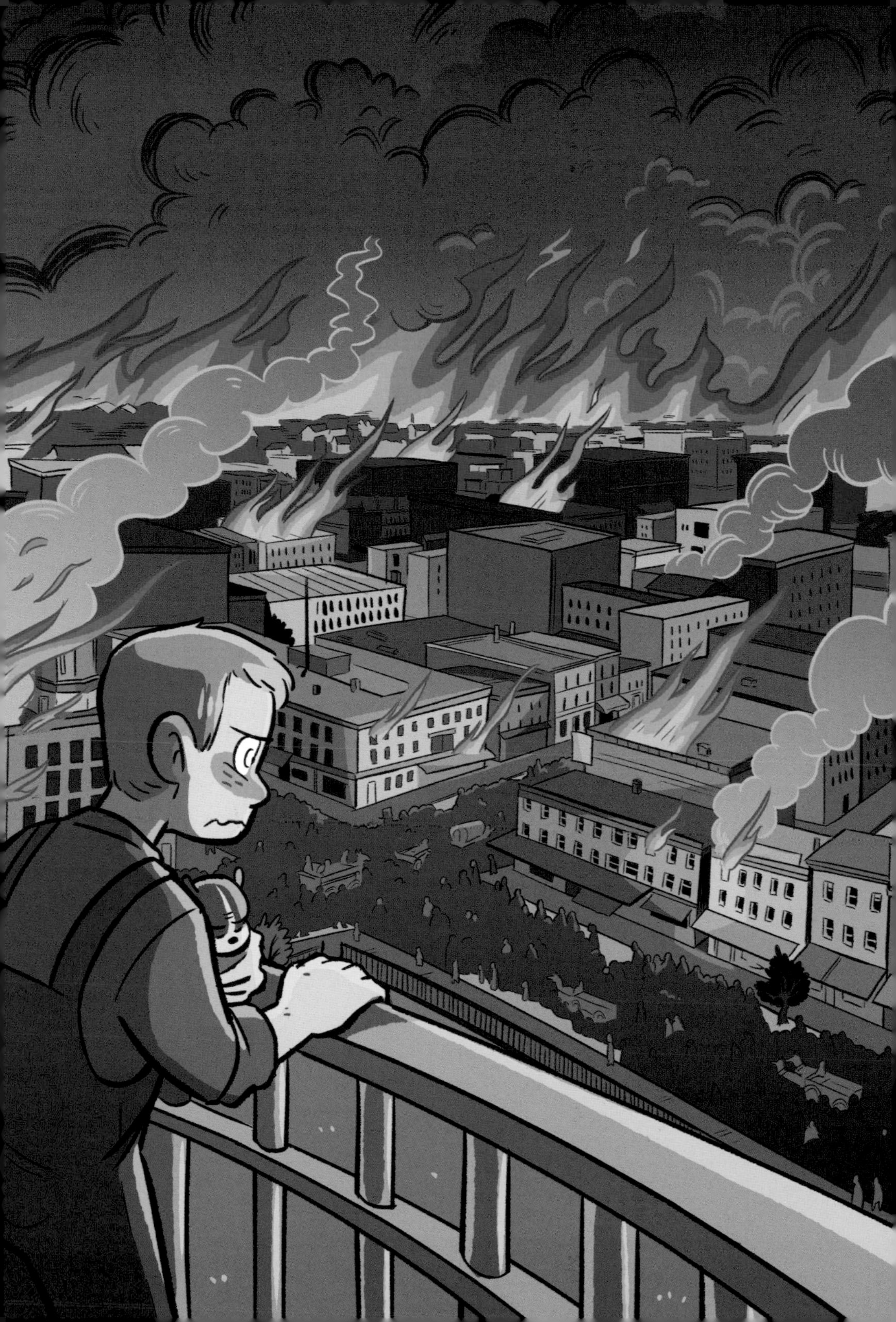

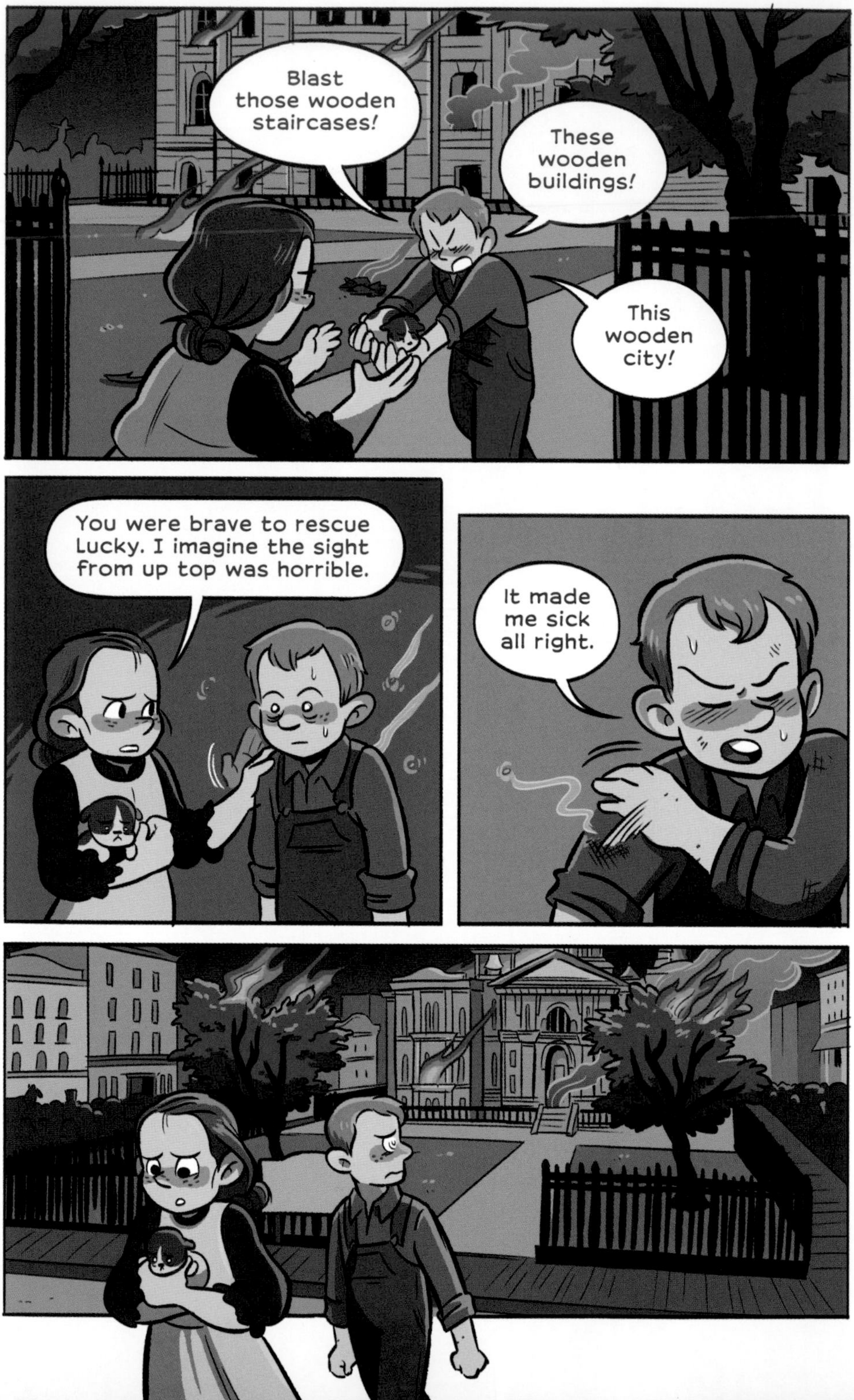
Blast those wooden staircases!
These wooden buildings!
This wooden city!
You were brave to rescue Lucky. I imagine the sight from up top was horrible.
It made me sick all right.

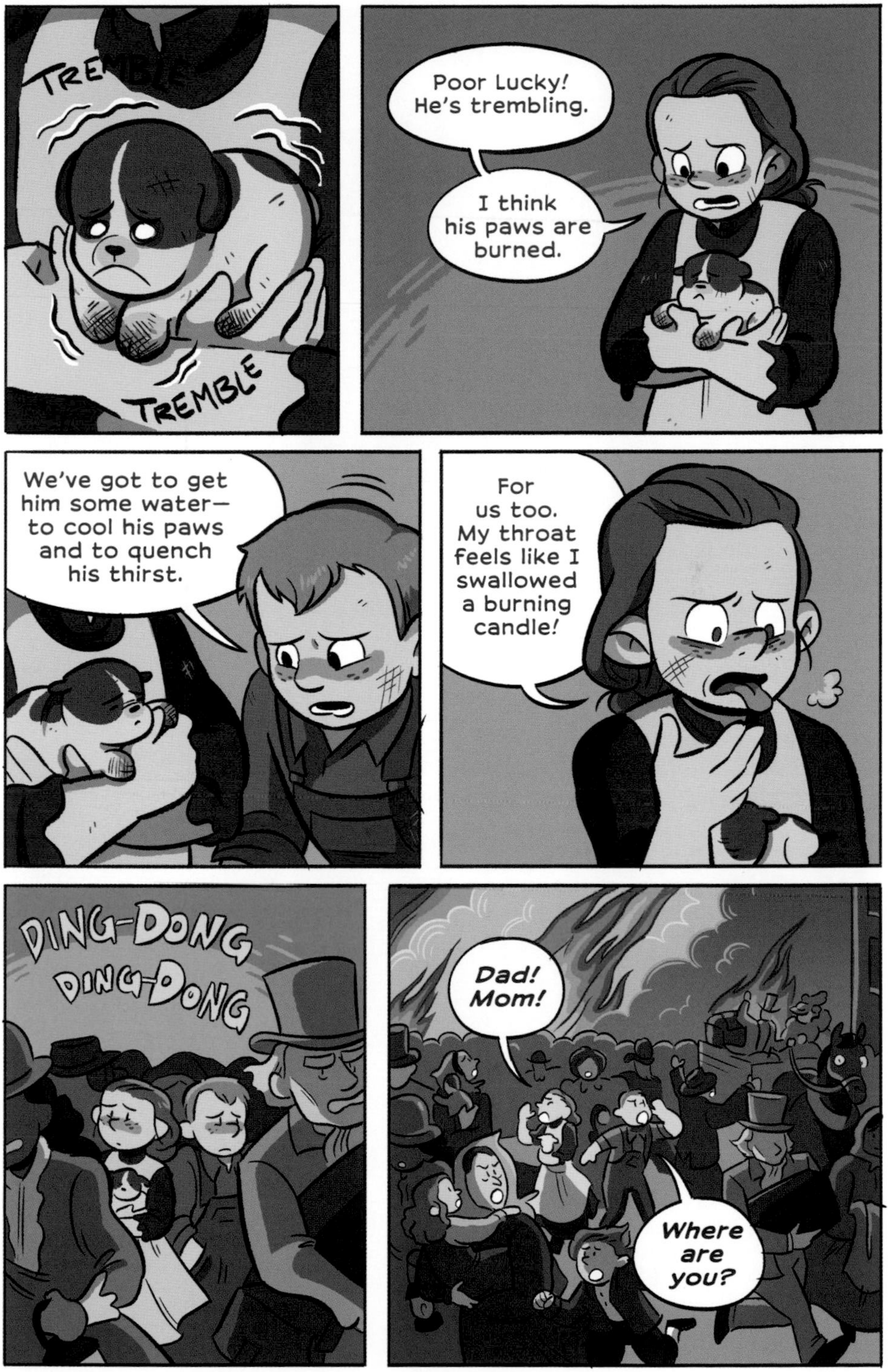
TREMBLE
TREMBLE
Poor Lucky! He's trembling.
I think his paws are burned.
We've got to get him some water—to cool his paws and to quench his thirst.
For us too. My throat feels like I swallowed a burning candle!
DING-DONG
DING-DONG
Dad! Mom!
Where are you?

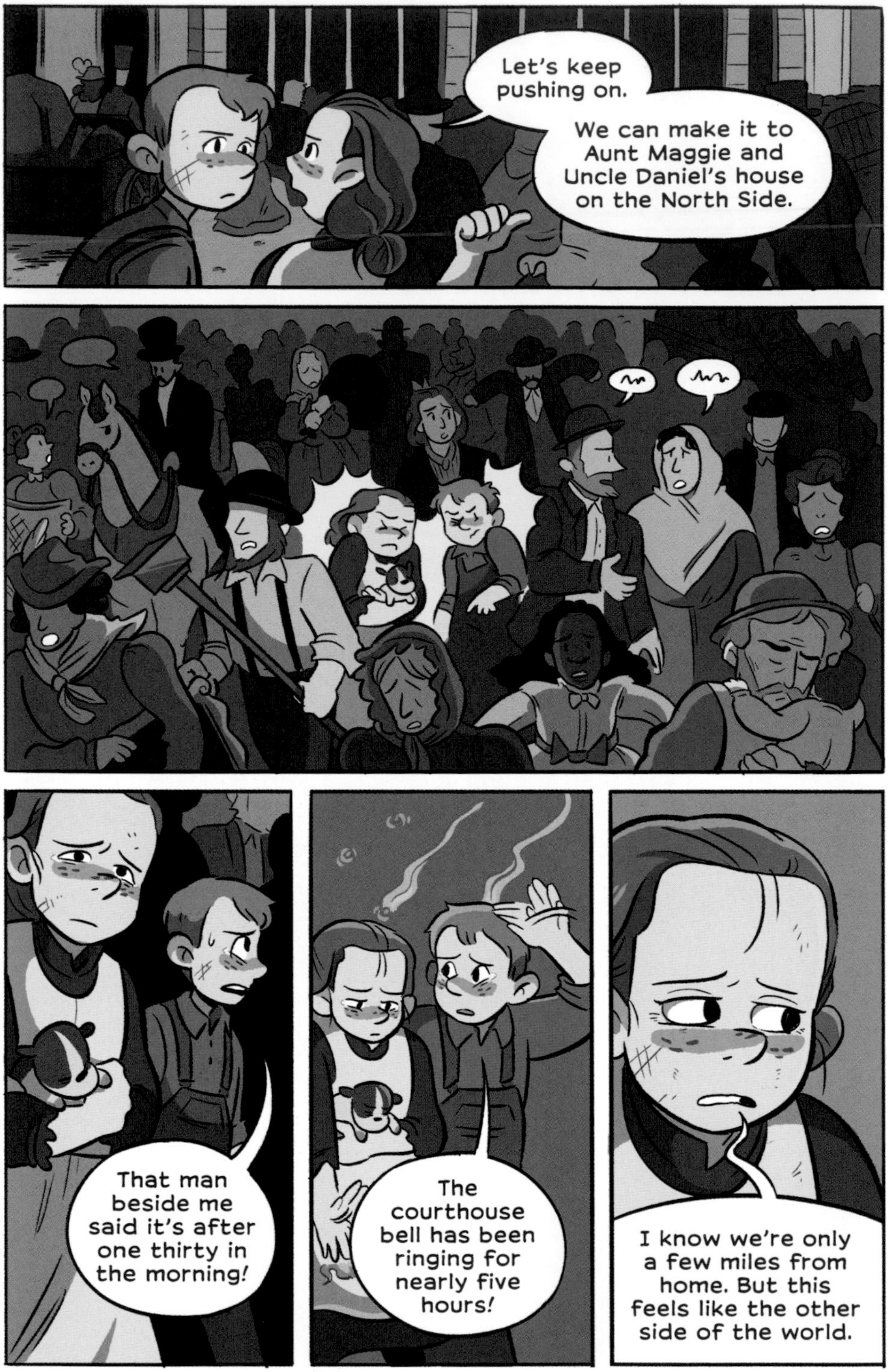

Let's keep pushing on.
We can make it to Aunt Maggie and Uncle Daniel's house on the North Side.
That man beside me said it's after one thirty in the morning!
The courthouse bell has been ringing for nearly five hours!
I know we're only a few miles from home. But this feels like the other side of the world.

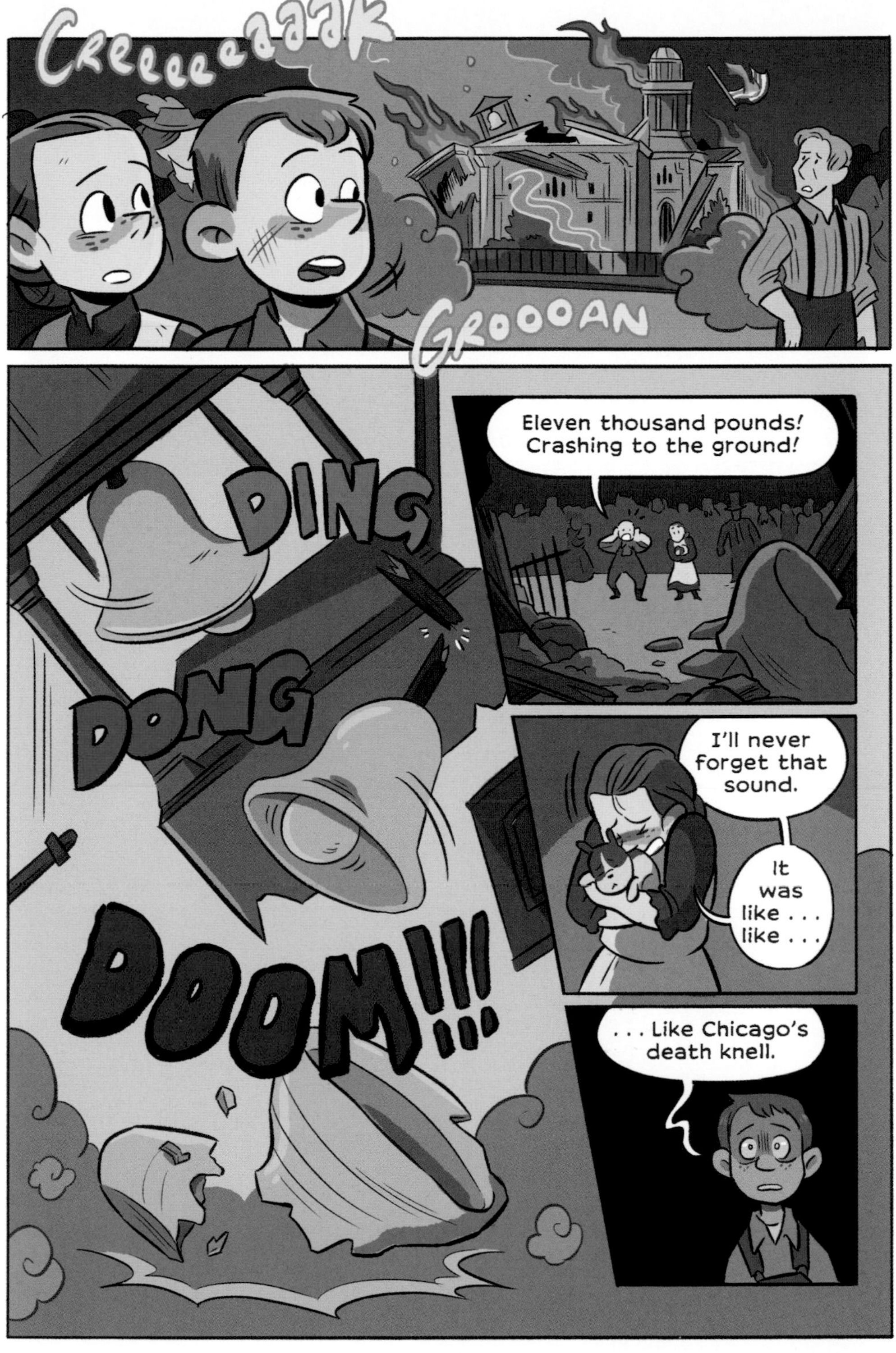
Creeeeeaaak
Grooan
Ding
Dong
DOOM!!!
Eleven thousand pounds! Crashing to the ground!
I'll never forget that sound.
It was like . . . like . . .
. . . Like Chicago's death knell.

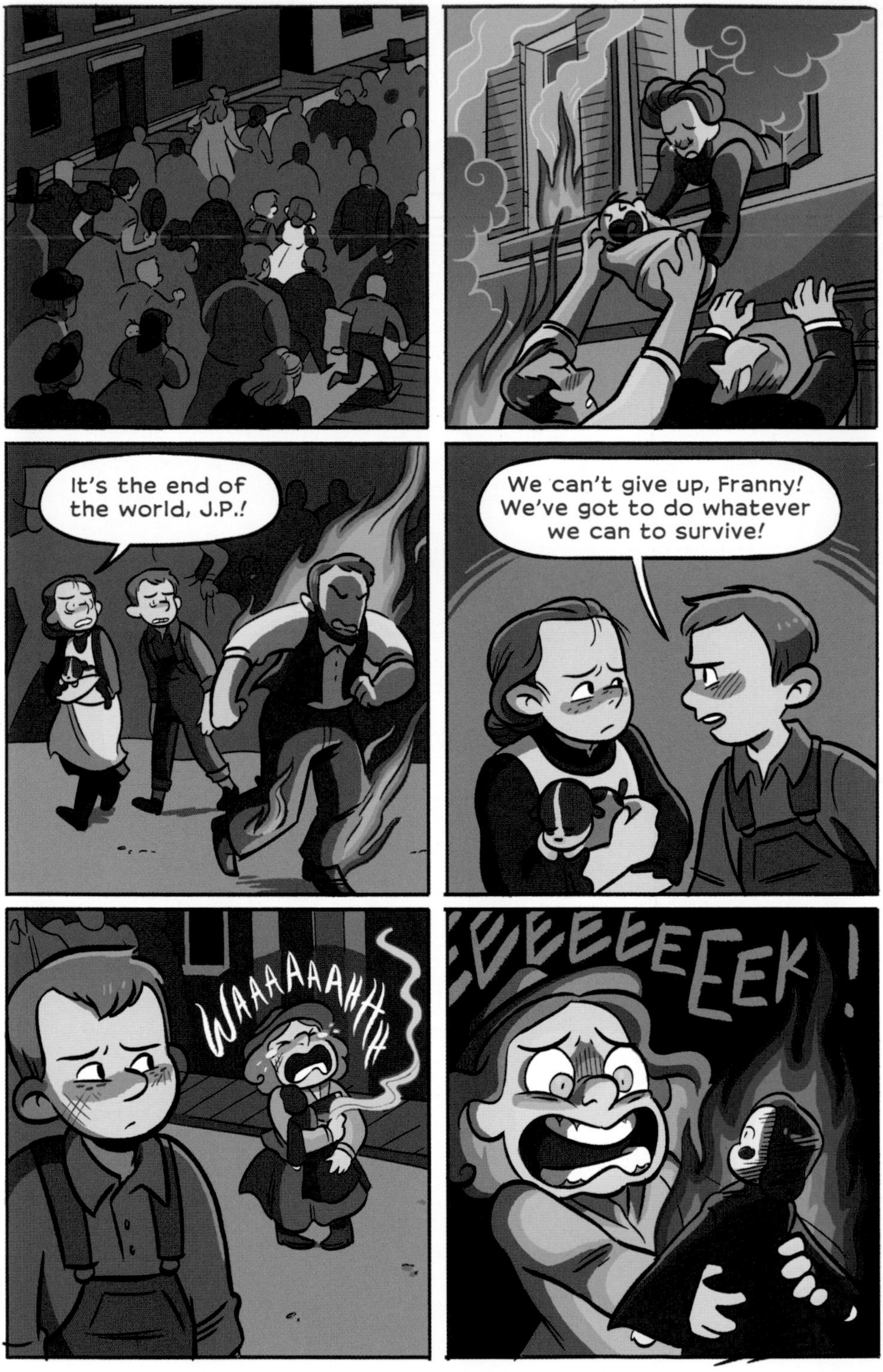
It's the end of the world, J.P.!
We can't give up, Franny! We've got to do whatever we can to survive!
WAAAAAAHHH
EEEEEEEEK!

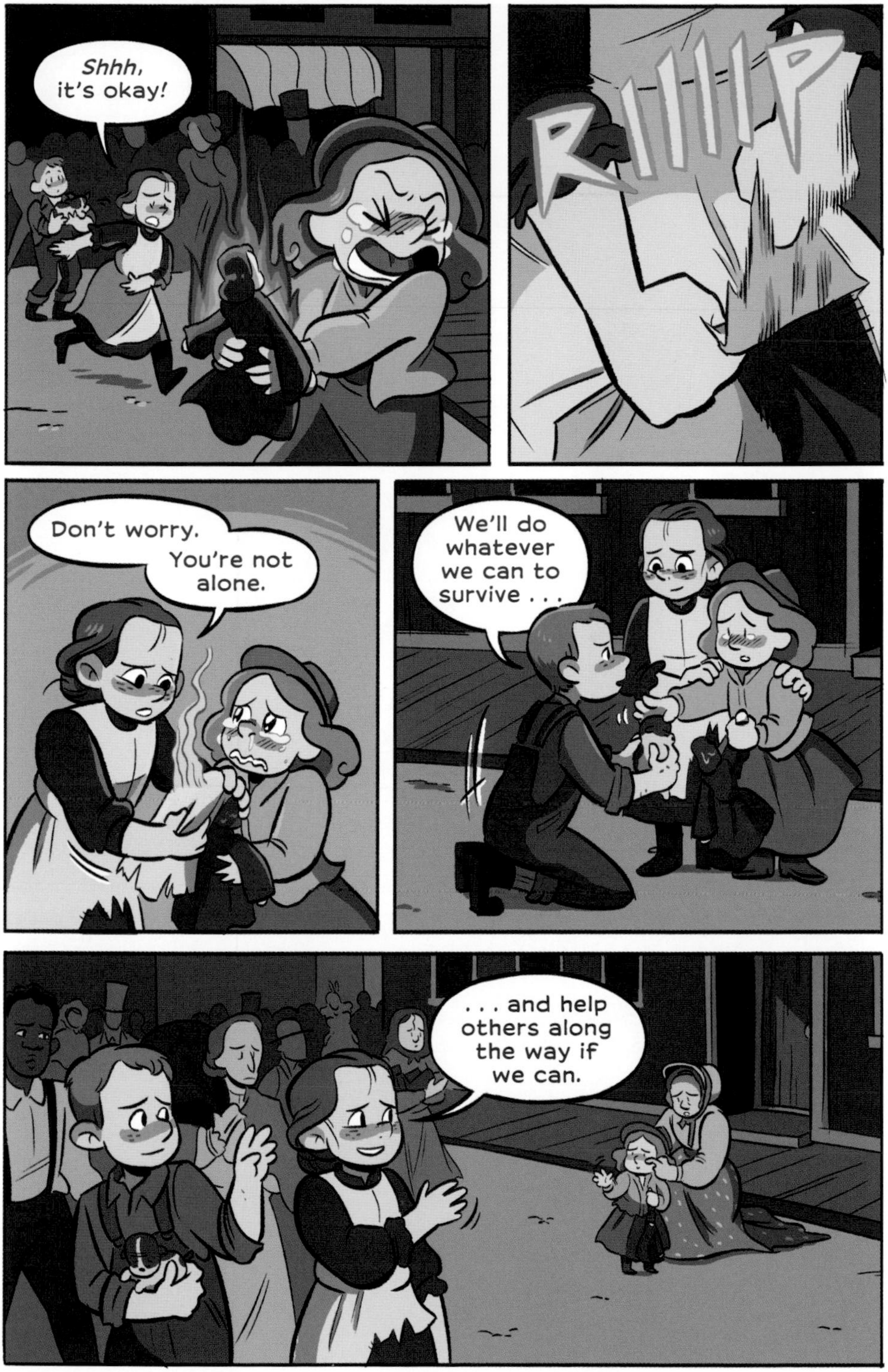
Shhh, it's okay!
RIIIIP
Don't worry.
You're not alone.
We'll do whatever we can to survive . . .
. . . and help others along the way if we can.

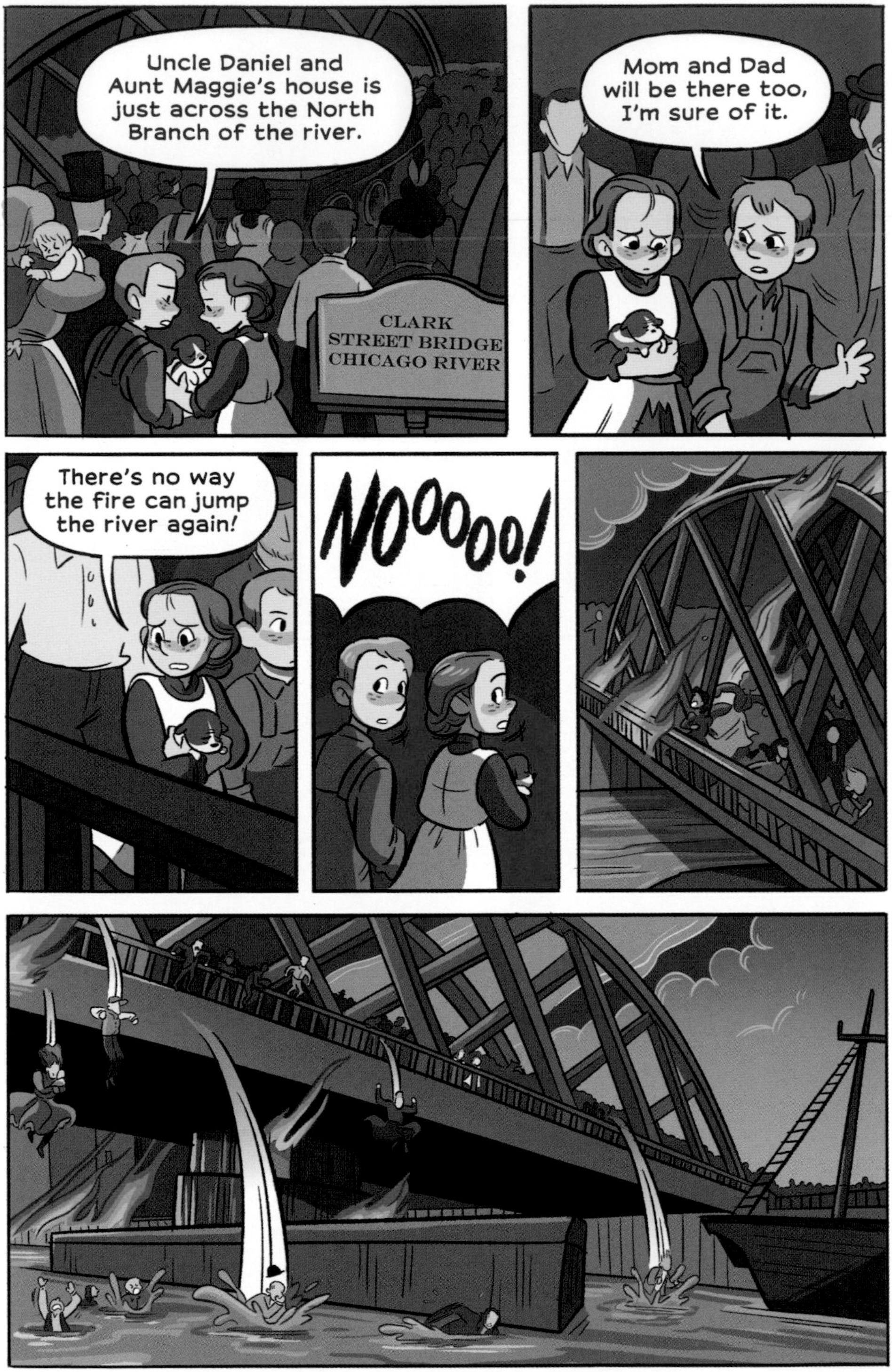

Uncle Daniel and Aunt Maggie's house is just across the North Branch of the river.
CLARK STREET BRIDGE CHICAGO RIVER
Mom and Dad will be there too, I'm sure of it.
There's no way the fire can jump the river again!
NOOOOO!

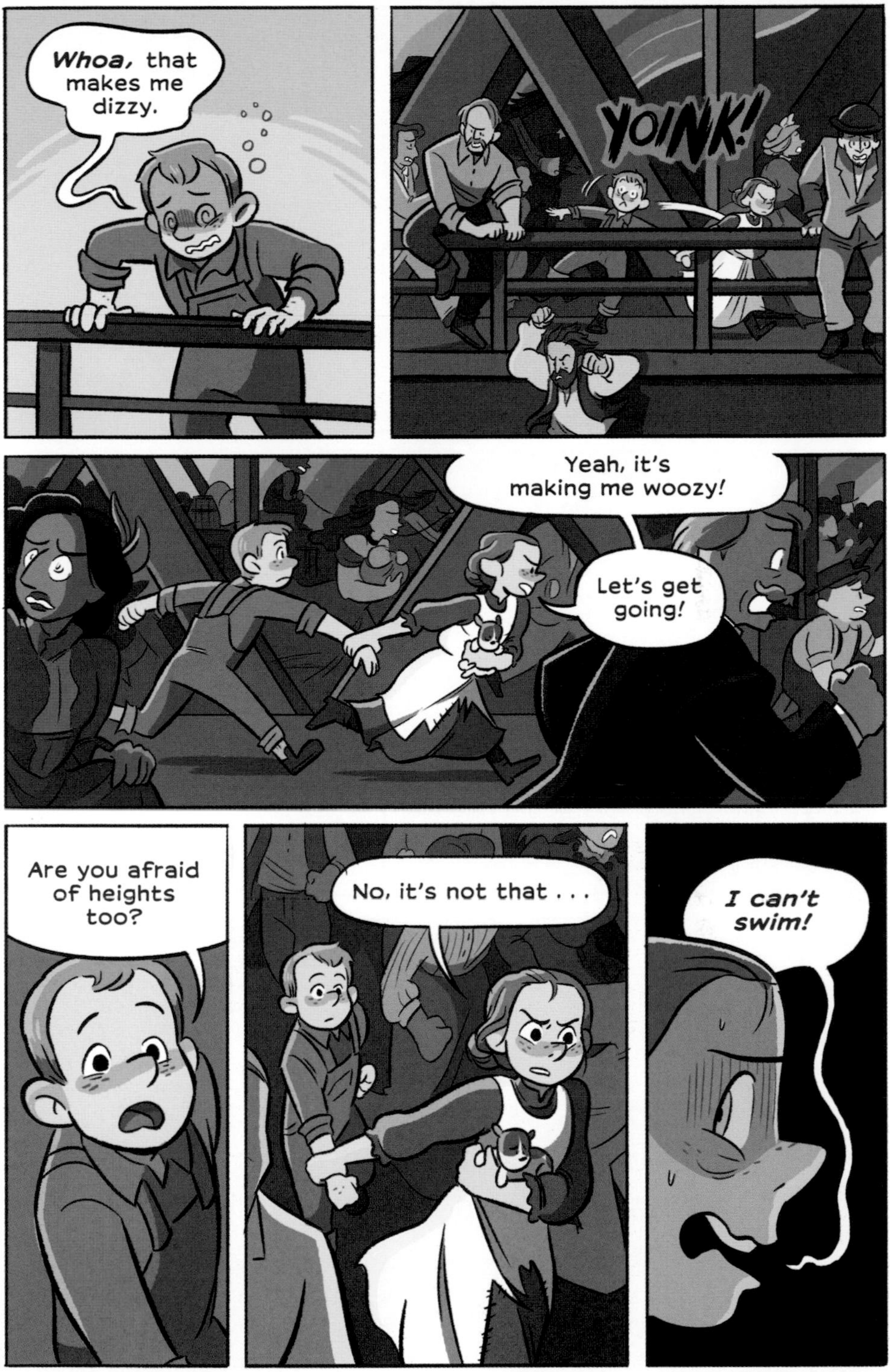
Whoa, that makes me dizzy.
YOINK!
Yeah, it's making me woozy!
Let's get going!
Are you afraid of heights too?
No, it's not that . . .
I can't swim!

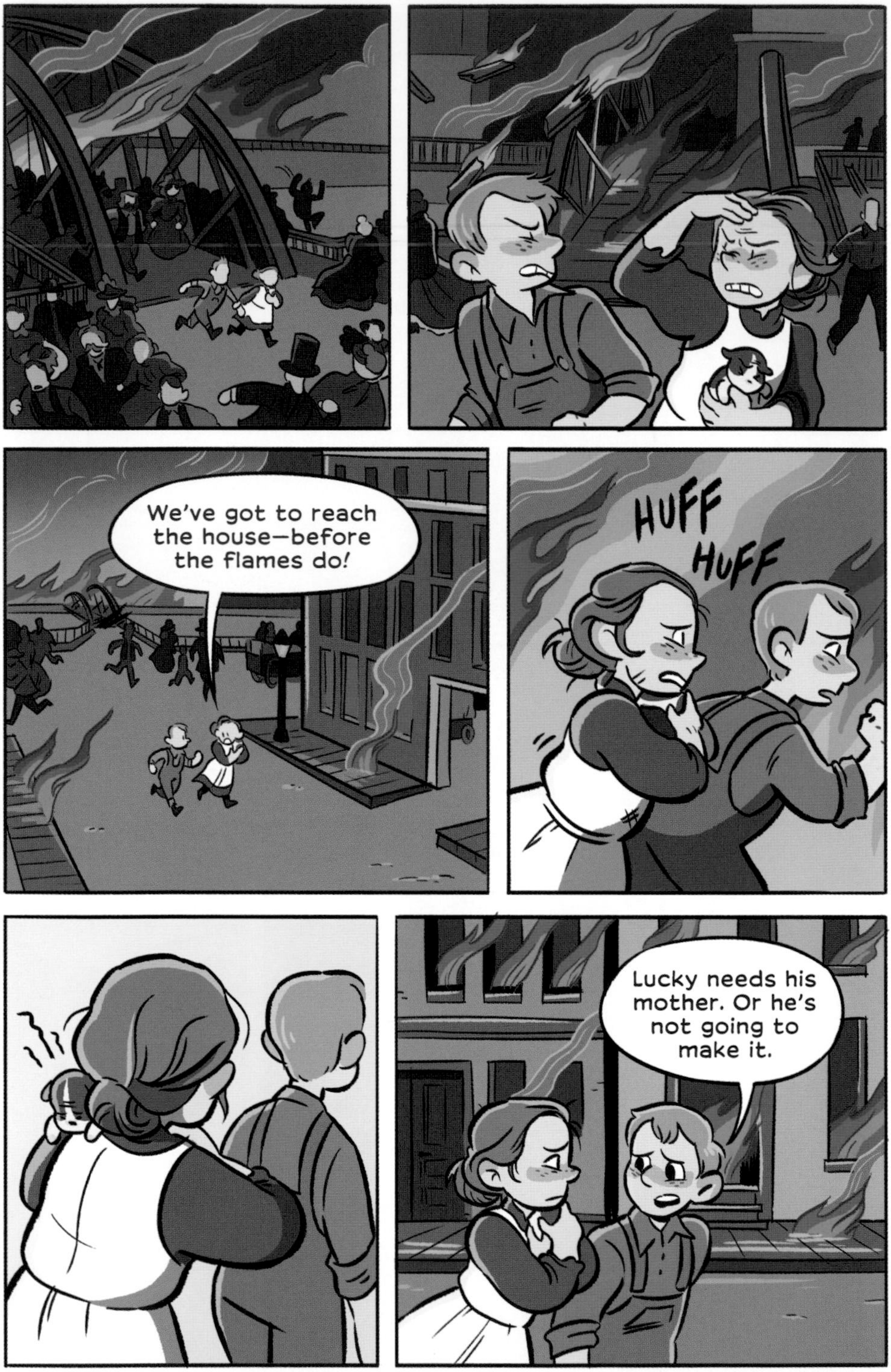
We've got to reach the house—before the flames do!
HUFF
HUFF
Lucky needs his mother. Or he's not going to make it.

Look, Franny! Water!

This will help you, Lucky boy.

It's dried up! The water's out!

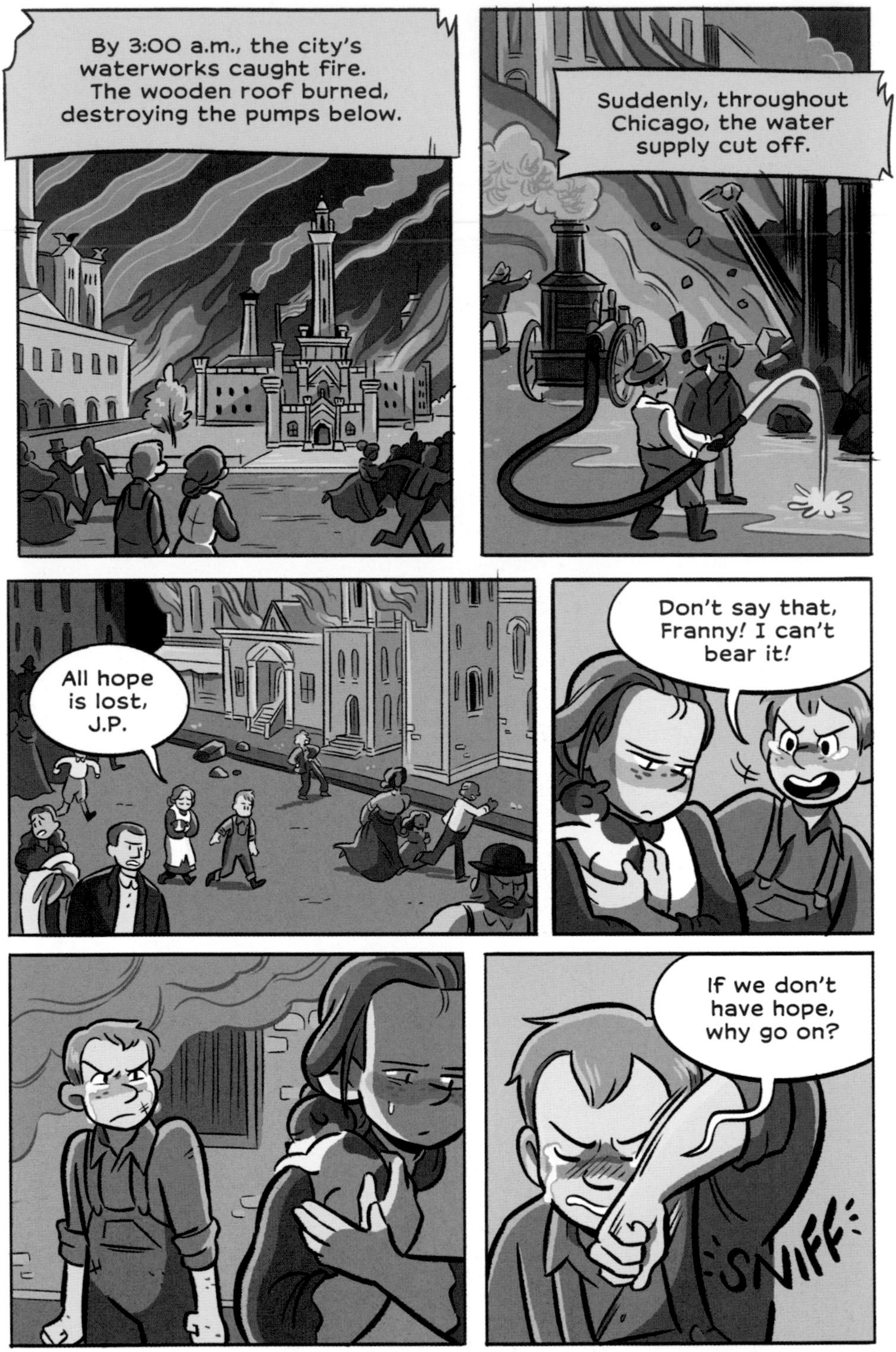

By 3:00 a.m., the city's waterworks caught fire. The wooden roof burned, destroying the pumps below.
Suddenly, throughout Chicago, the water supply cut off.
All hope is lost, J.P.
Don't say that, Franny! I can't bear it!
If we don't have hope, why go on?
SNIFF

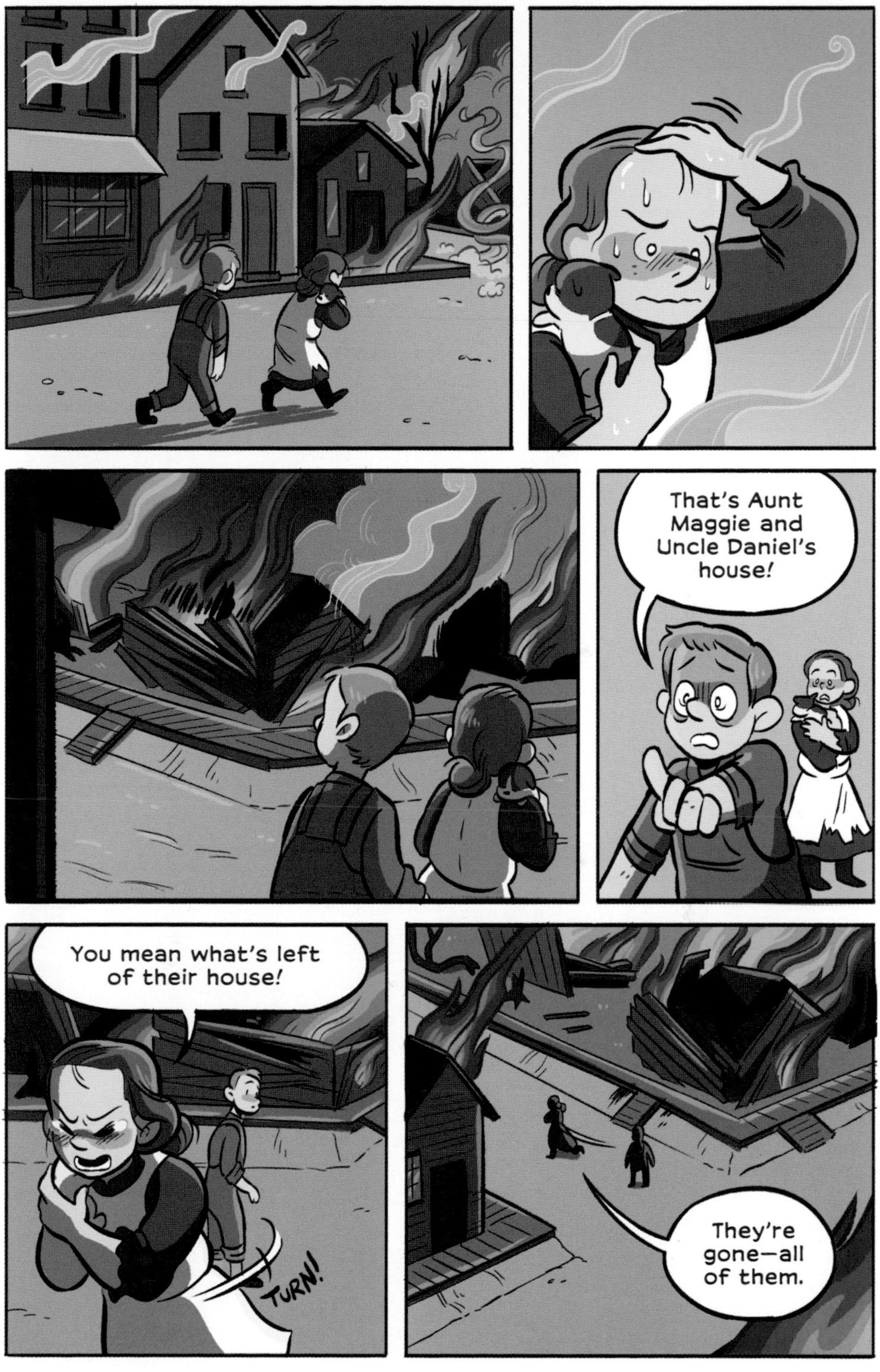

That's Aunt Maggie and Uncle Daniel's house!
You mean what's left of their house!
TURN!
They're gone—all of them.

Mrs. Higginson! You know our mom—her sister worked for you!

Have you seen our aunt Maggie? Or our mom?

Anna E. Higginson survived the Chicago Fire and shared memories in a November 1871 letter.

She grieved not for the money or home they lost, but rather for the treasured objects that were part of her family's history:

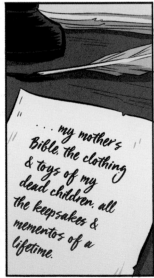

... my mother's Bible, the clothing & toys of my dead children, all the keepsakes & mementos of a lifetime.

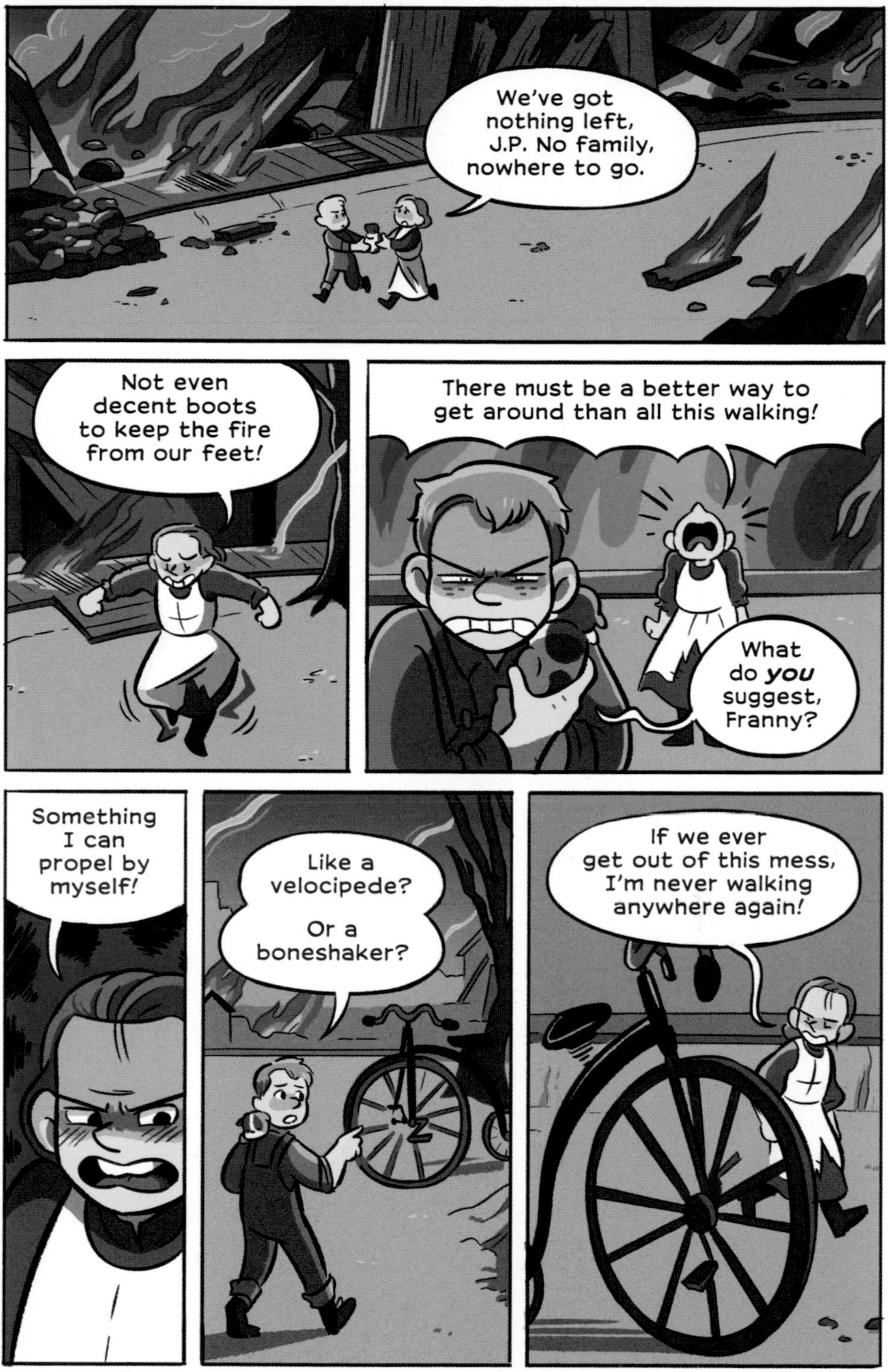
We've got nothing left, J.P. No family, nowhere to go.
Not even decent boots to keep the fire from our feet!
There must be a better way to get around than all this walking!
What do *you* suggest, Franny?
Something I can propel by myself!
Like a velocipede?
Or a boneshaker?
If we ever get out of this mess, I'm never walking anywhere again!

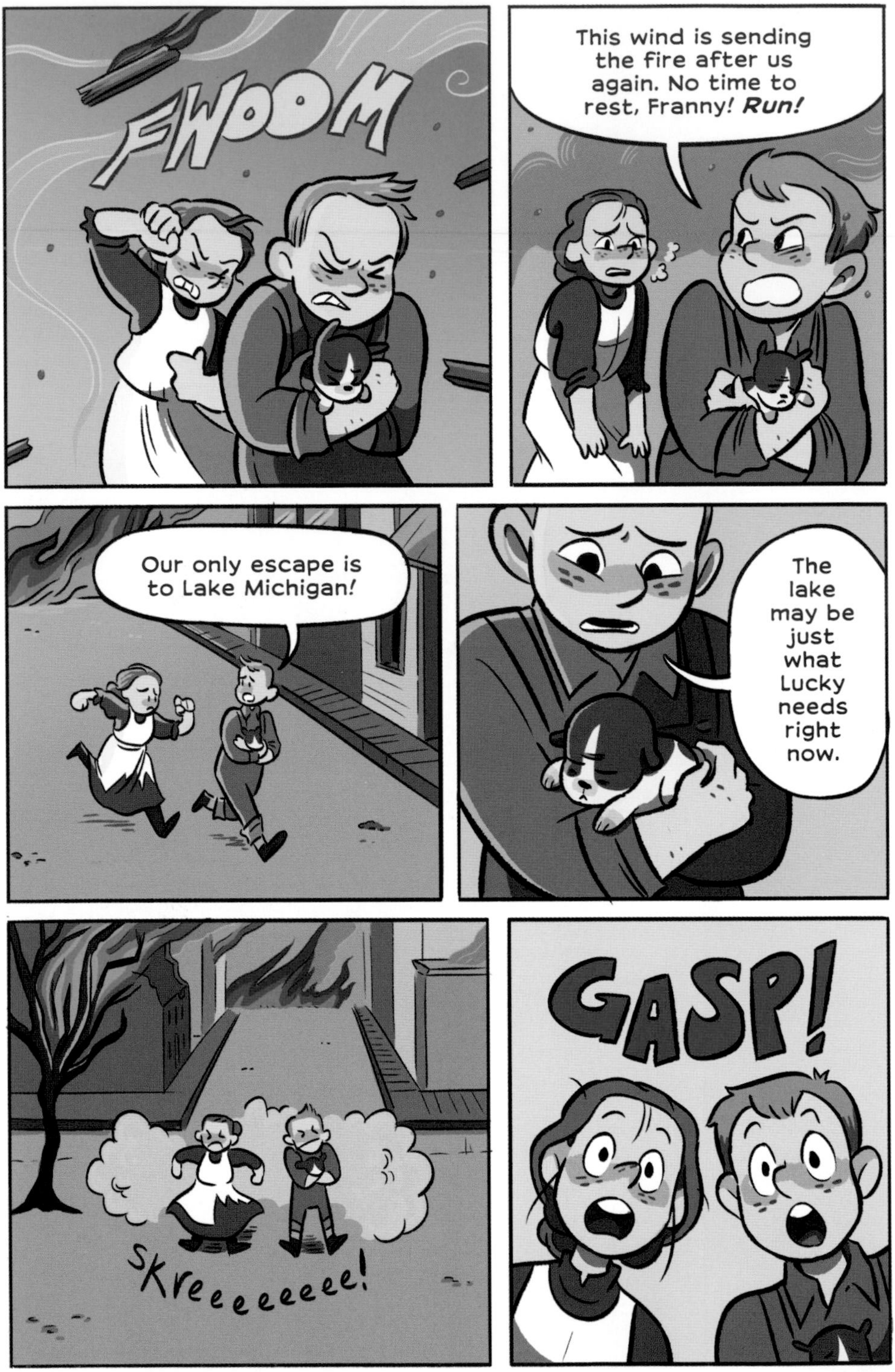
FWOOM
This wind is sending the fire after us again. No time to rest, Franny! *Run!*
Our only escape is to Lake Michigan!
The lake may be just what Lucky needs right now.
SKreeeeeeee!
GASP!

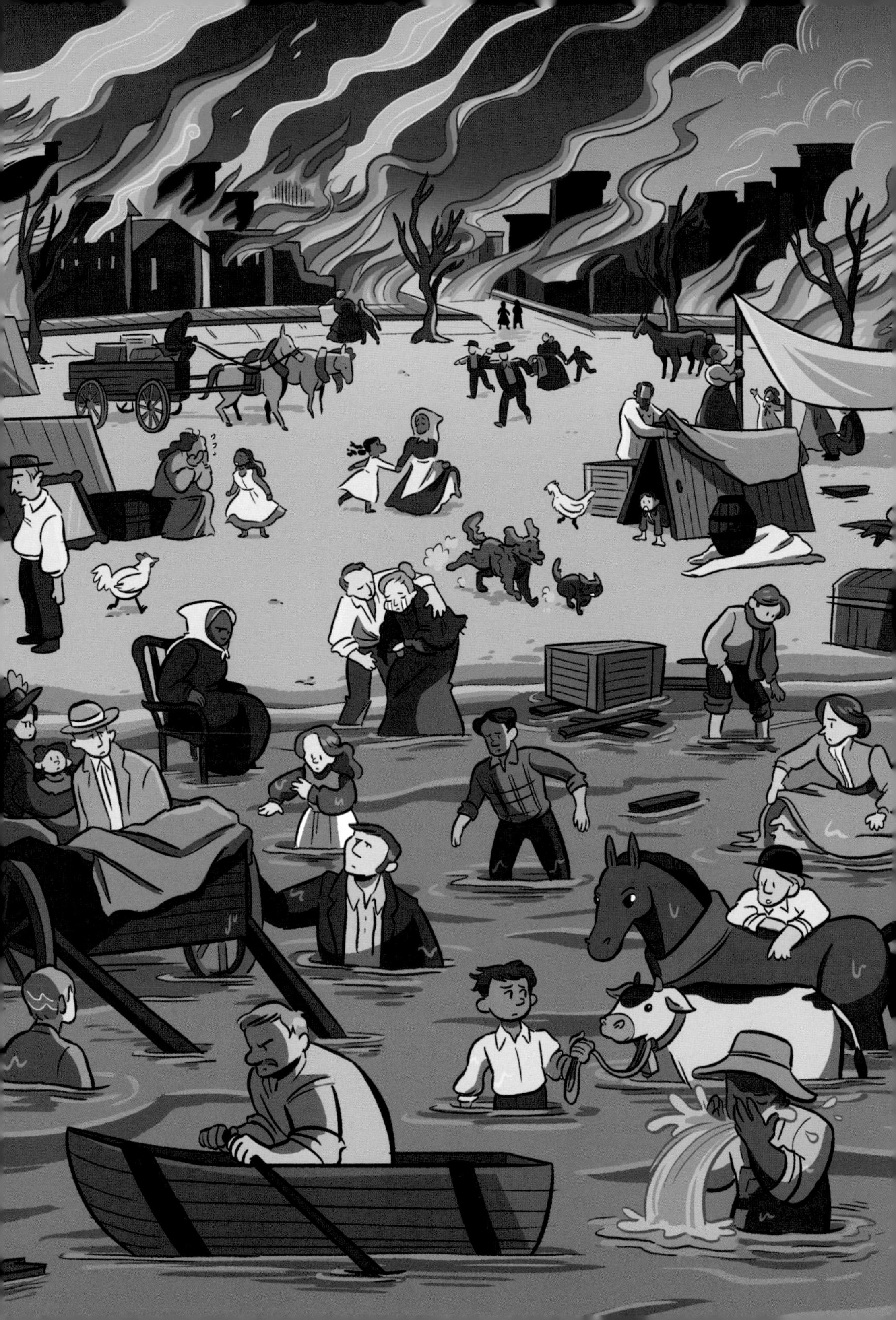

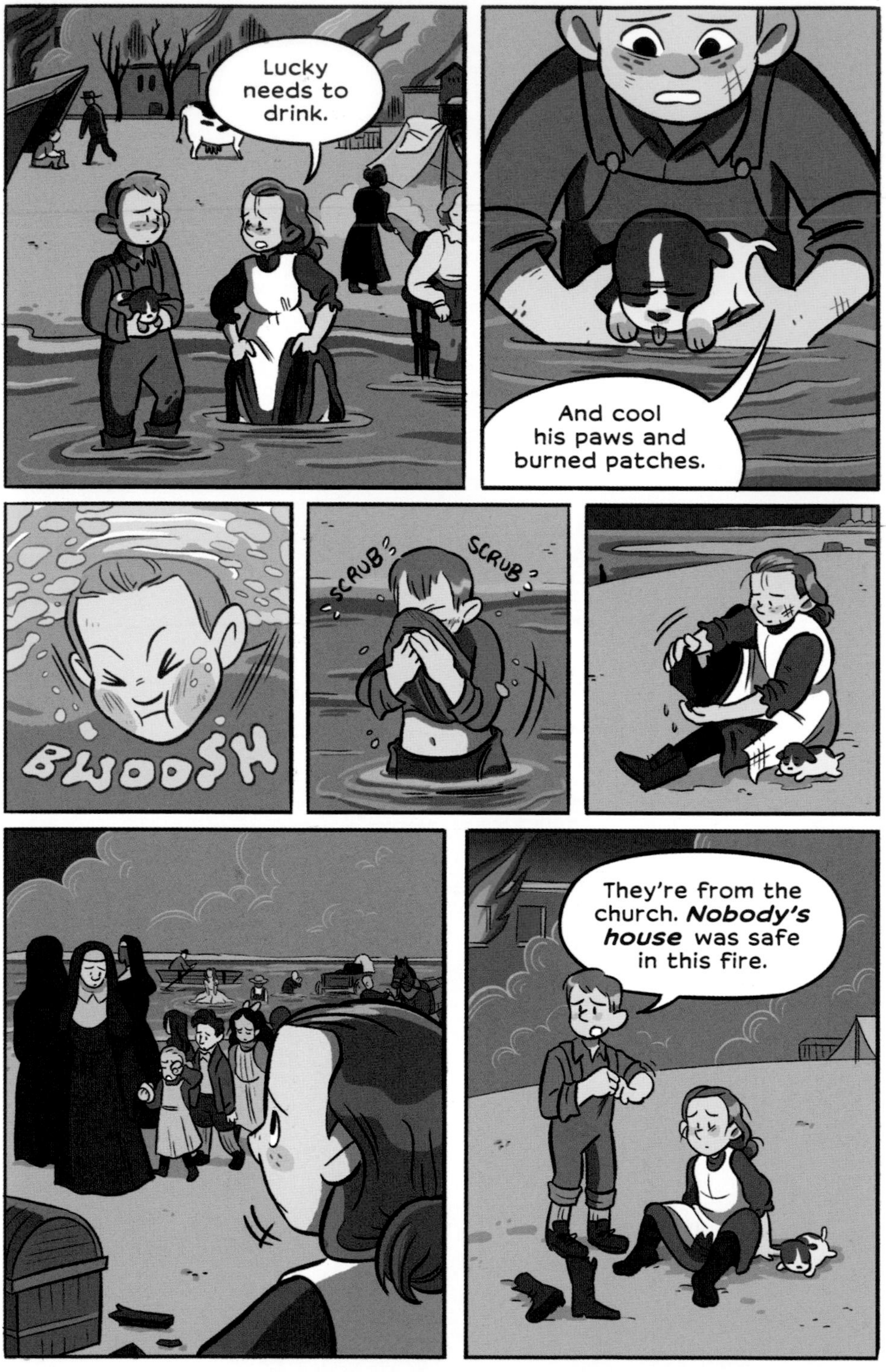
Lucky needs to drink.
And cool his paws and burned patches.
BWOOSH
SCRUB
SCRUB
They're from the church. ***Nobody's house*** was safe in this fire.

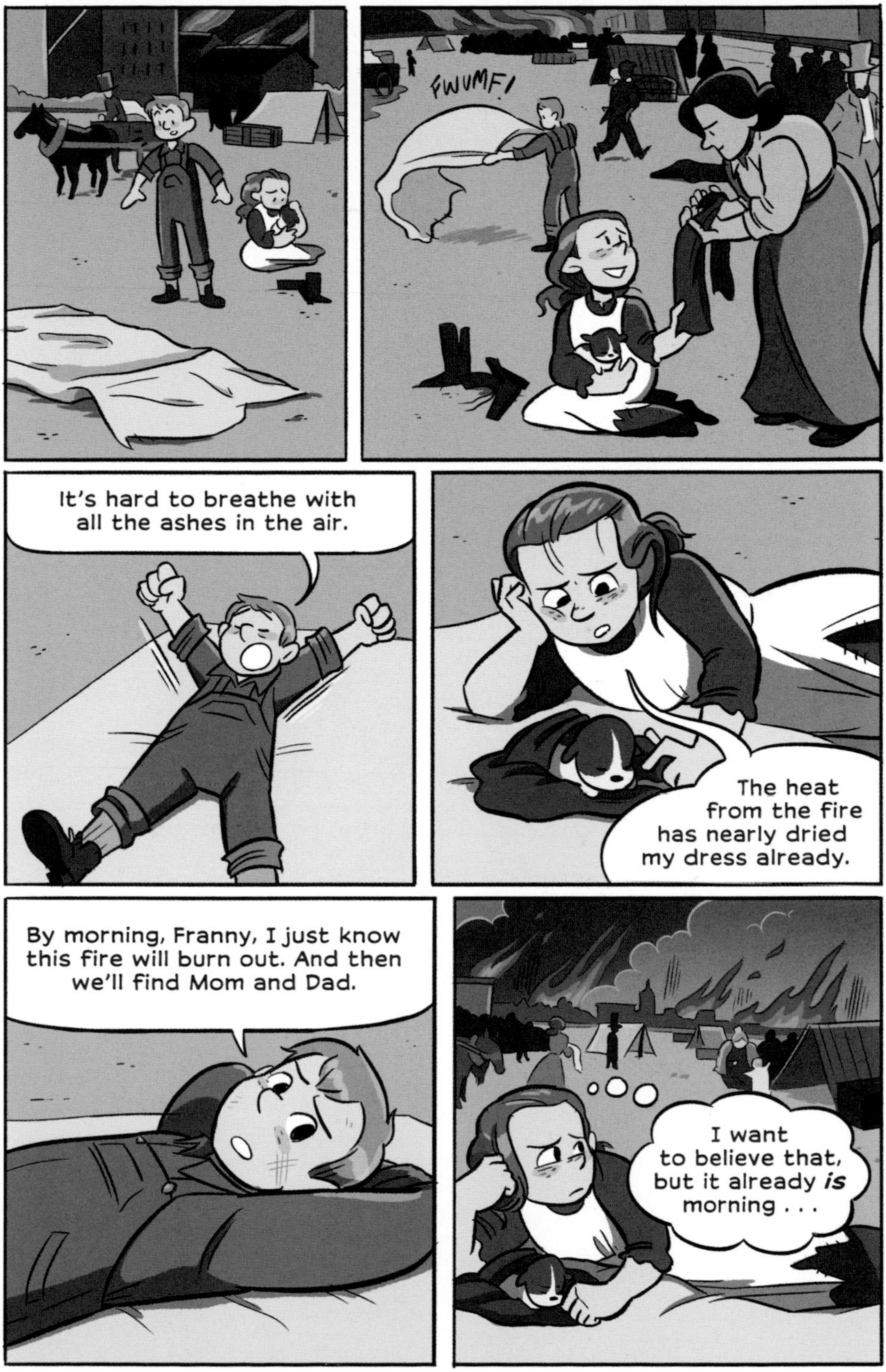
FWUMF!
It's hard to breathe with all the ashes in the air.
The heat from the fire has nearly dried my dress already.
By morning, Franny, I just know this fire will burn out. And then we'll find Mom and Dad.
I want to believe that, but it already *is* morning . . .

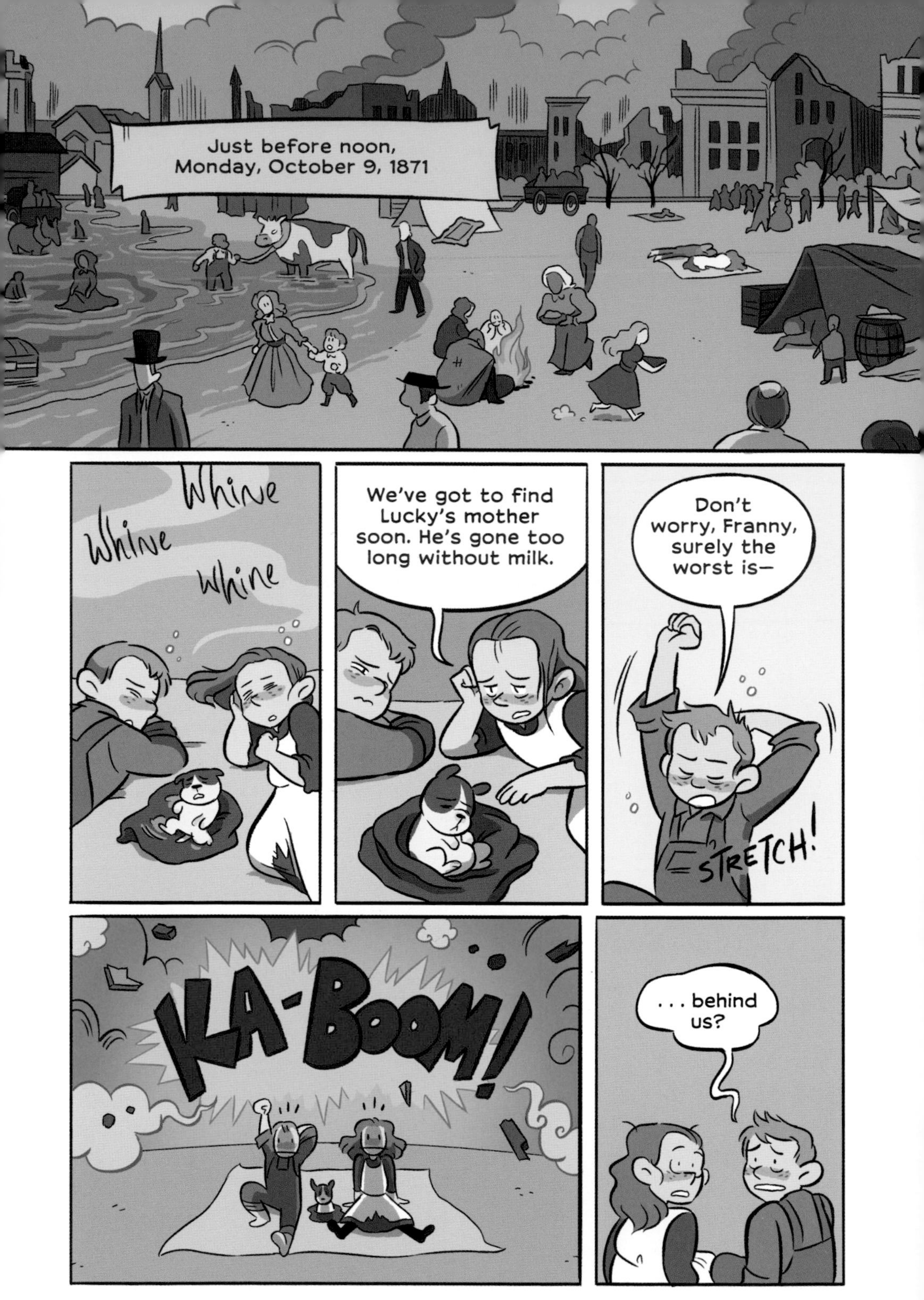
Just before noon,
Monday, October 9, 1871
Whine
Whine
Whine
We've got to find Lucky's mother soon. He's gone too long without milk.
Don't worry, Franny, surely the worst is—
STRETCH!
KA-BOOM!
. . . behind us?

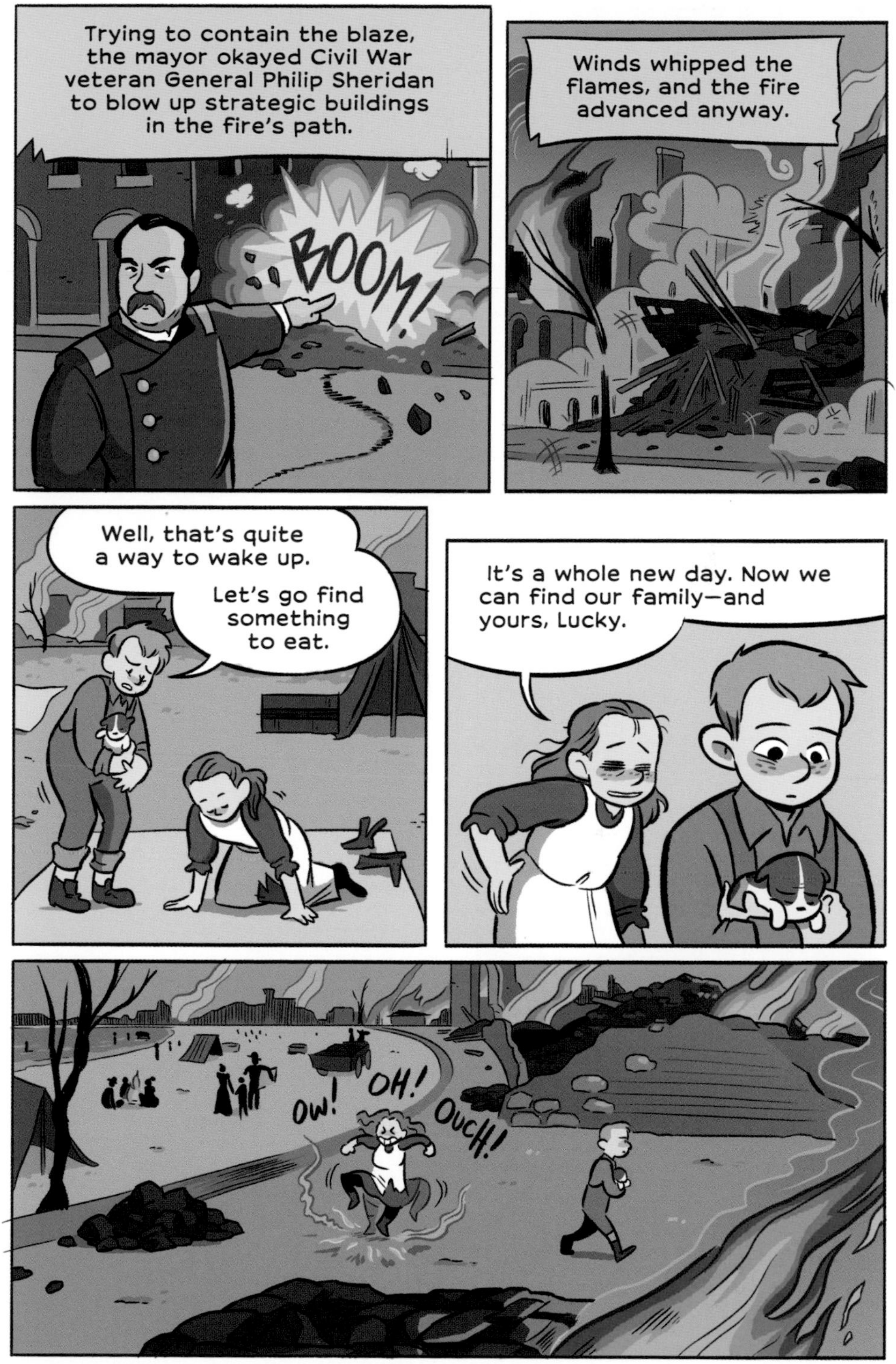
Trying to contain the blaze, the mayor okayed Civil War veteran General Philip Sheridan to blow up strategic buildings in the fire's path.
BOOM!
Winds whipped the flames, and the fire advanced anyway.
Well, that's quite a way to wake up.
Let's go find something to eat.
It's a whole new day. Now we can find our family—and yours, Lucky.
OW!
OH!
OUCH!

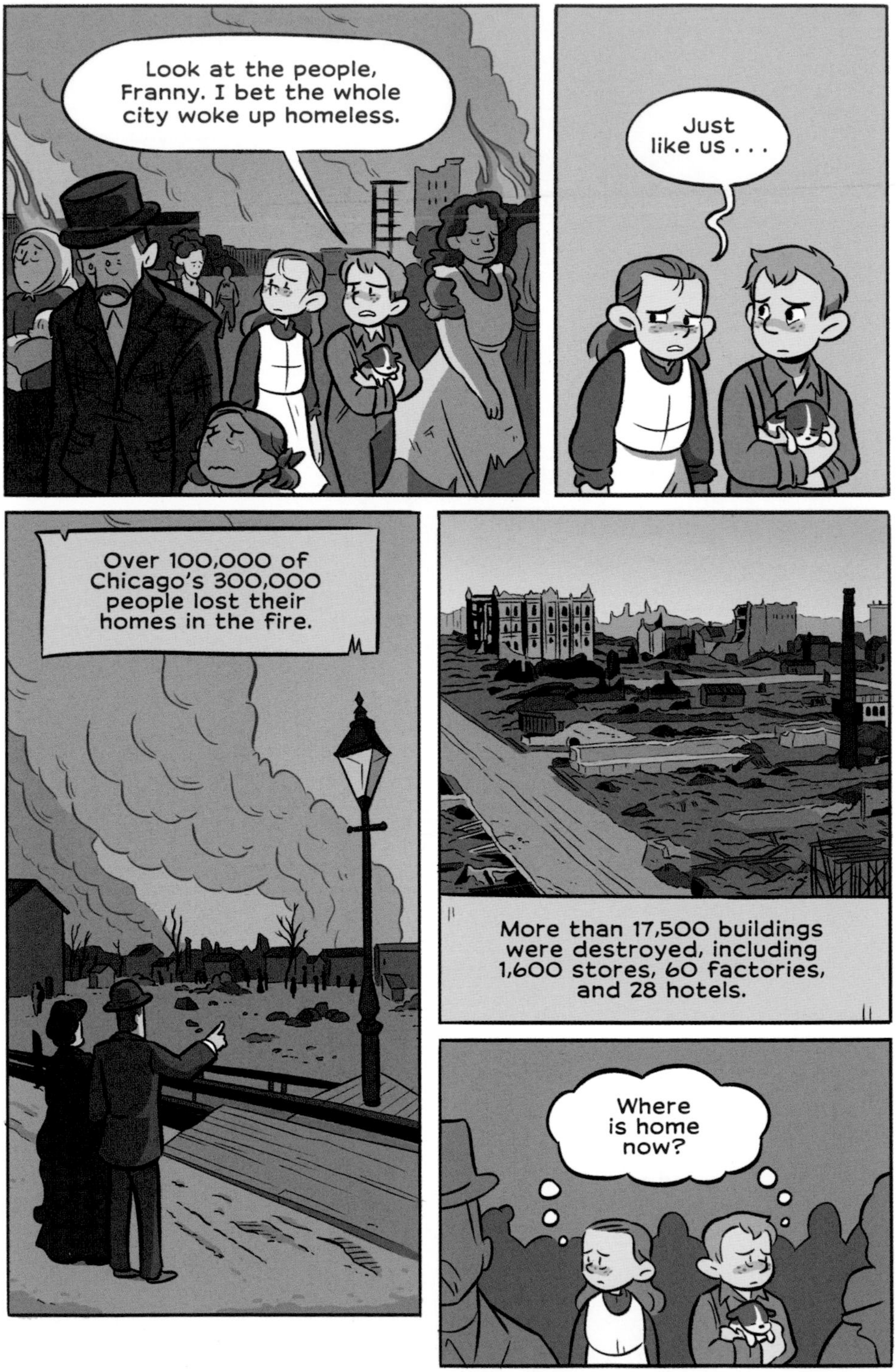
Look at the people, Franny. I bet the whole city woke up homeless.
Just like us . . .
Over 100,000 of Chicago's 300,000 people lost their homes in the fire.
More than 17,500 buildings were destroyed, including 1,600 stores, 60 factories, and 28 hotels.
Where is home now?

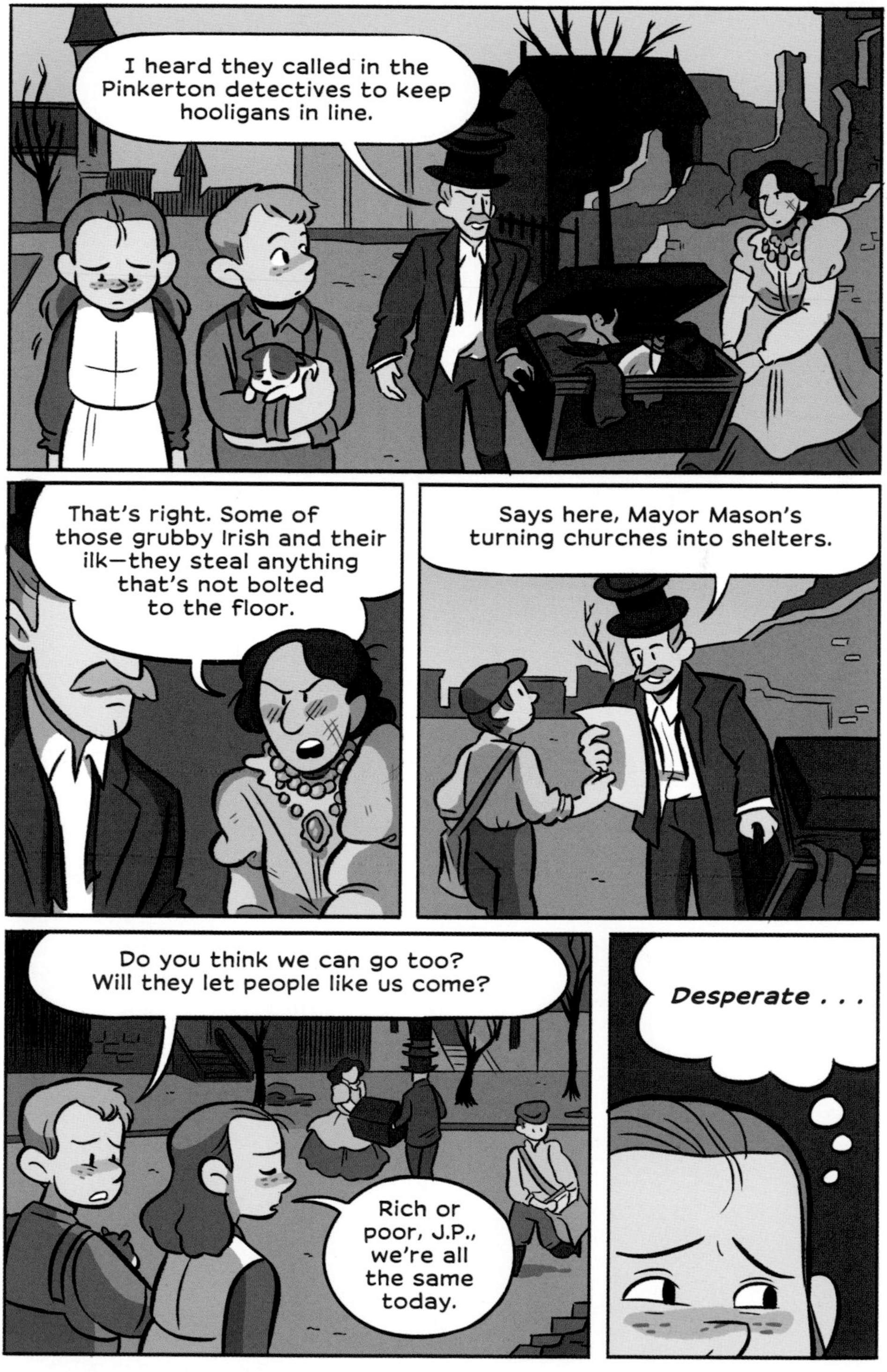
I heard they called in the Pinkerton detectives to keep hooligans in line.
That's right. Some of those grubby Irish and their ilk—they steal anything that's not bolted to the floor.
Says here, Mayor Mason's turning churches into shelters.
Do you think we can go too? Will they let people like us come?
Rich or poor, J.P., we're all the same today.
Desperate . . .

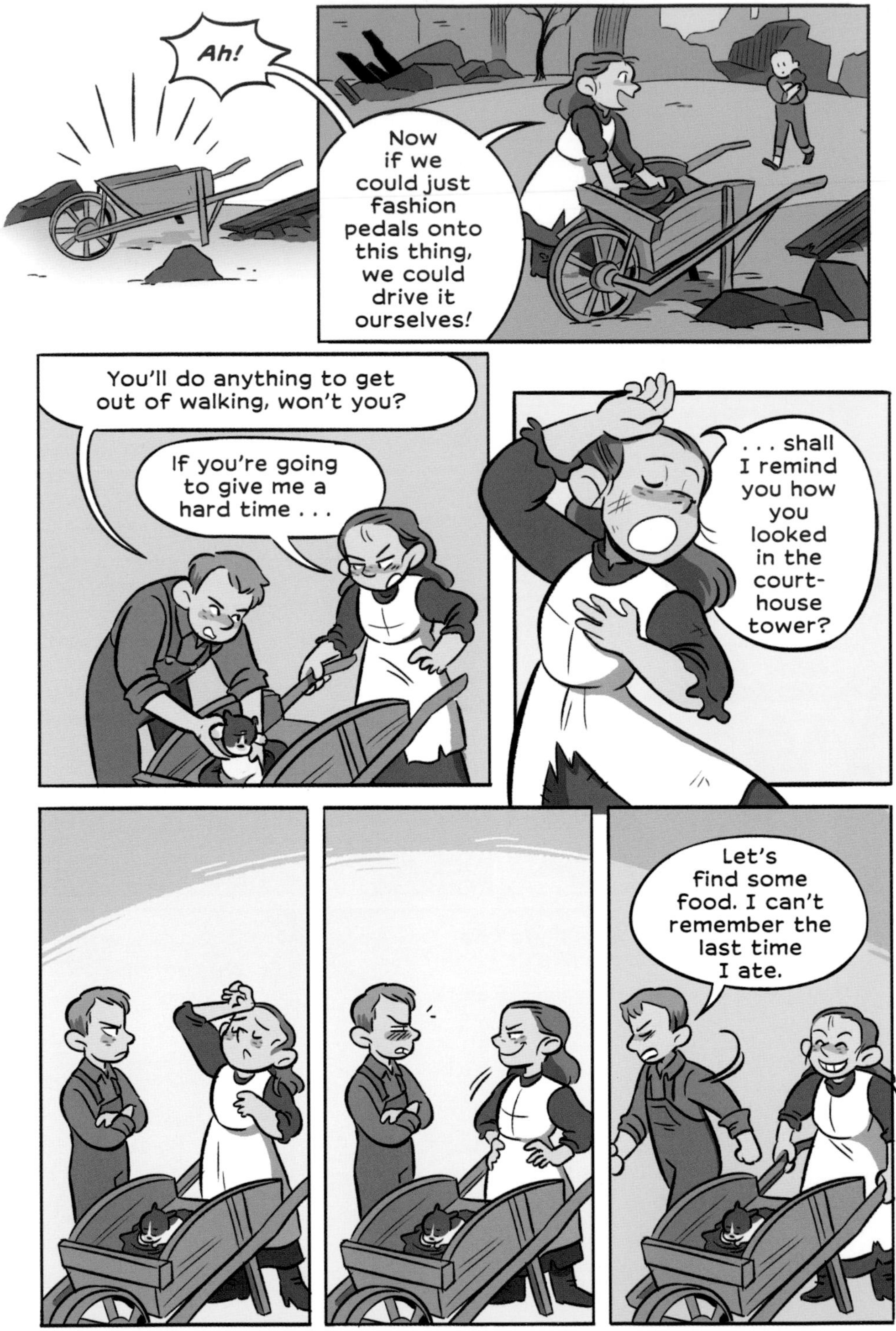
Ah!
Now if we could just fashion pedals onto this thing, we could drive it ourselves!
You'll do anything to get out of walking, won't you?
If you're going to give me a hard time . . .
. . . shall I remind you how you looked in the court-house tower?
Let's find some food. I can't remember the last time I ate.

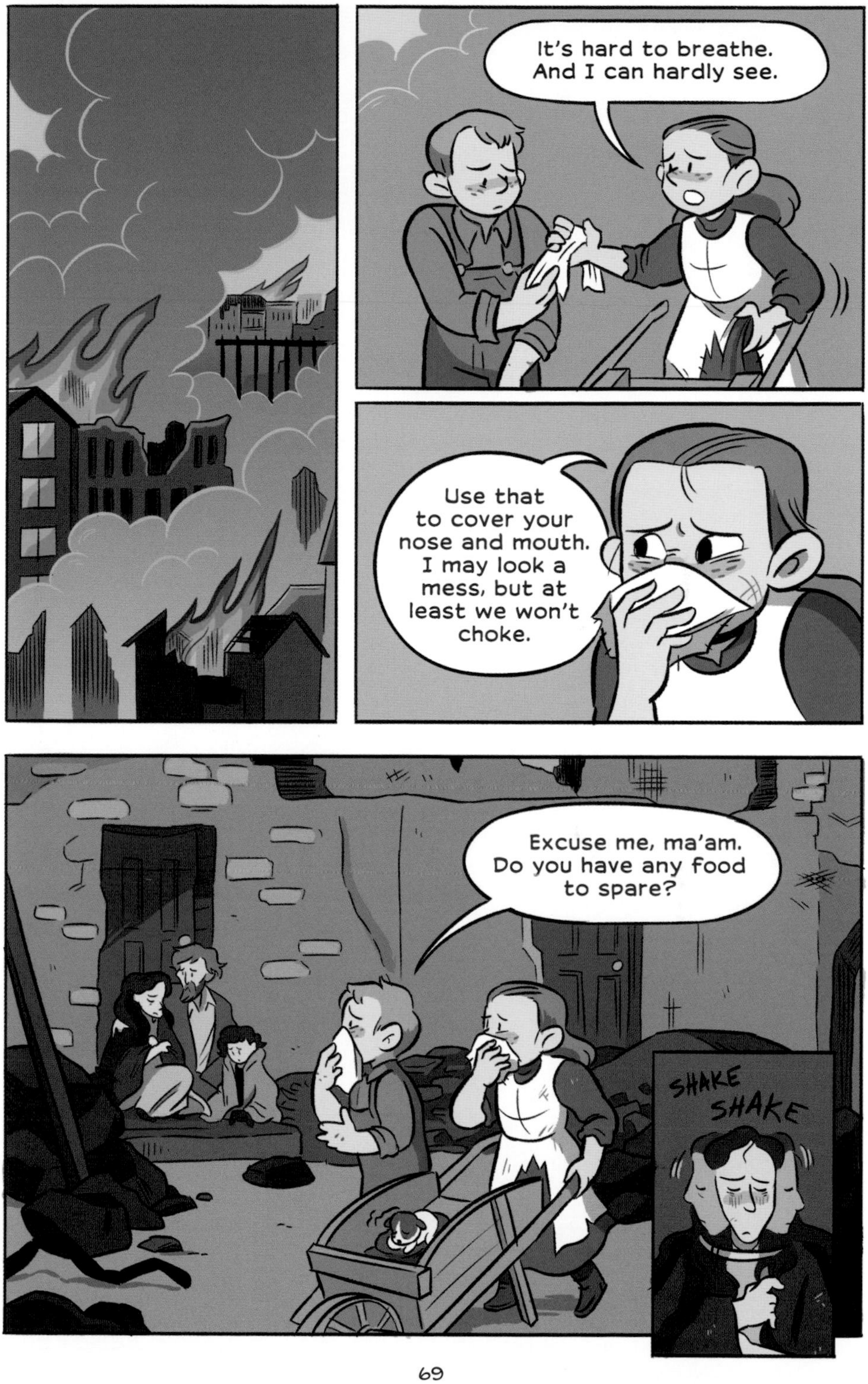
It's hard to breathe. And I can hardly see.
Use that to cover your nose and mouth. I may look a mess, but at least we won't choke.
Excuse me, ma'am. Do you have any food to spare?
SHAKE SHAKE

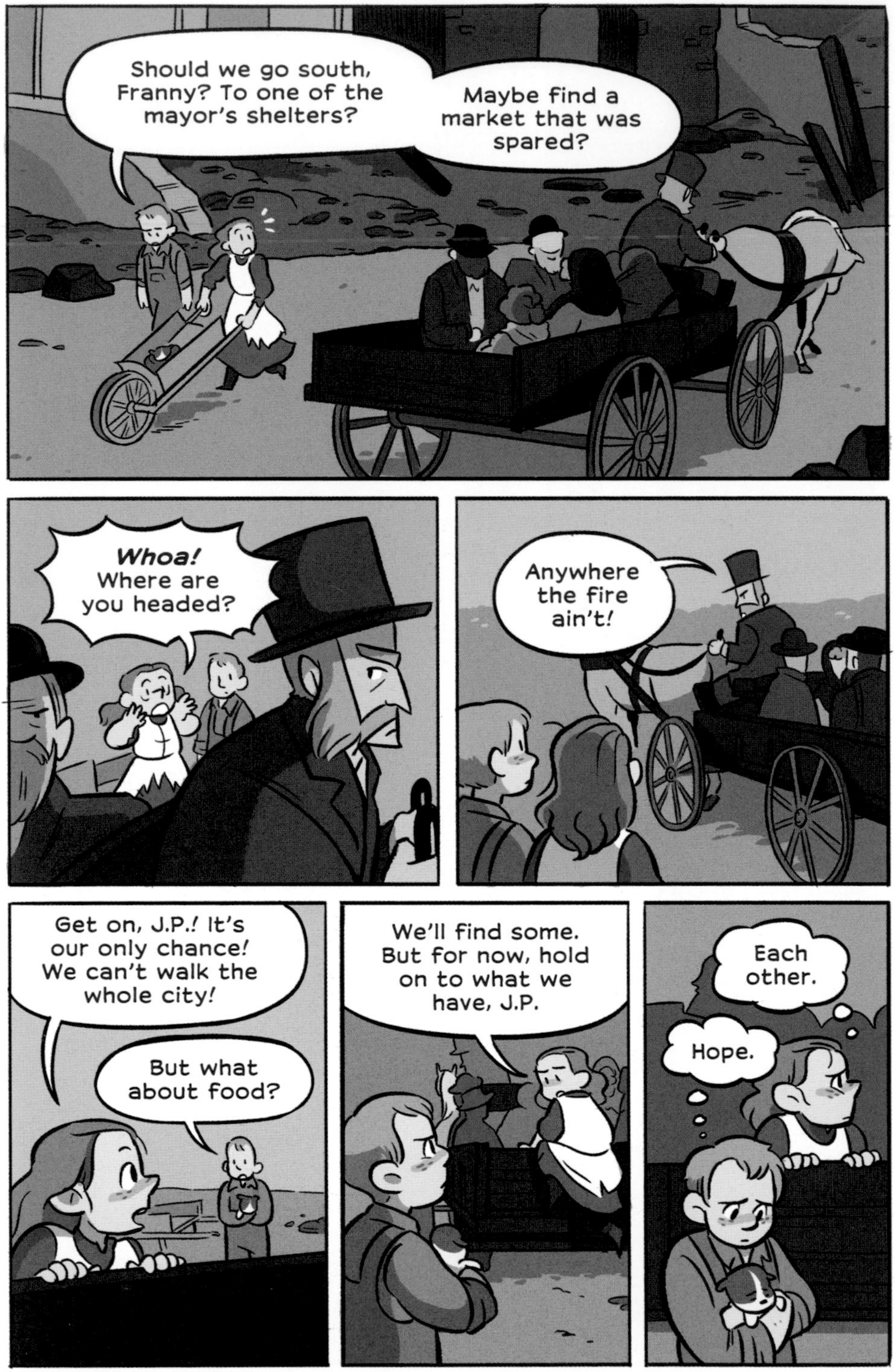
Should we go south, Franny? To one of the mayor's shelters?
Maybe find a market that was spared?
Whoa! Where are you headed?
Anywhere the fire ain't!
Get on, J.P.! It's our only chance! We can't walk the whole city!
But what about food?
We'll find some. But for now, hold on to what we have, J.P.
Hope.
Each other.

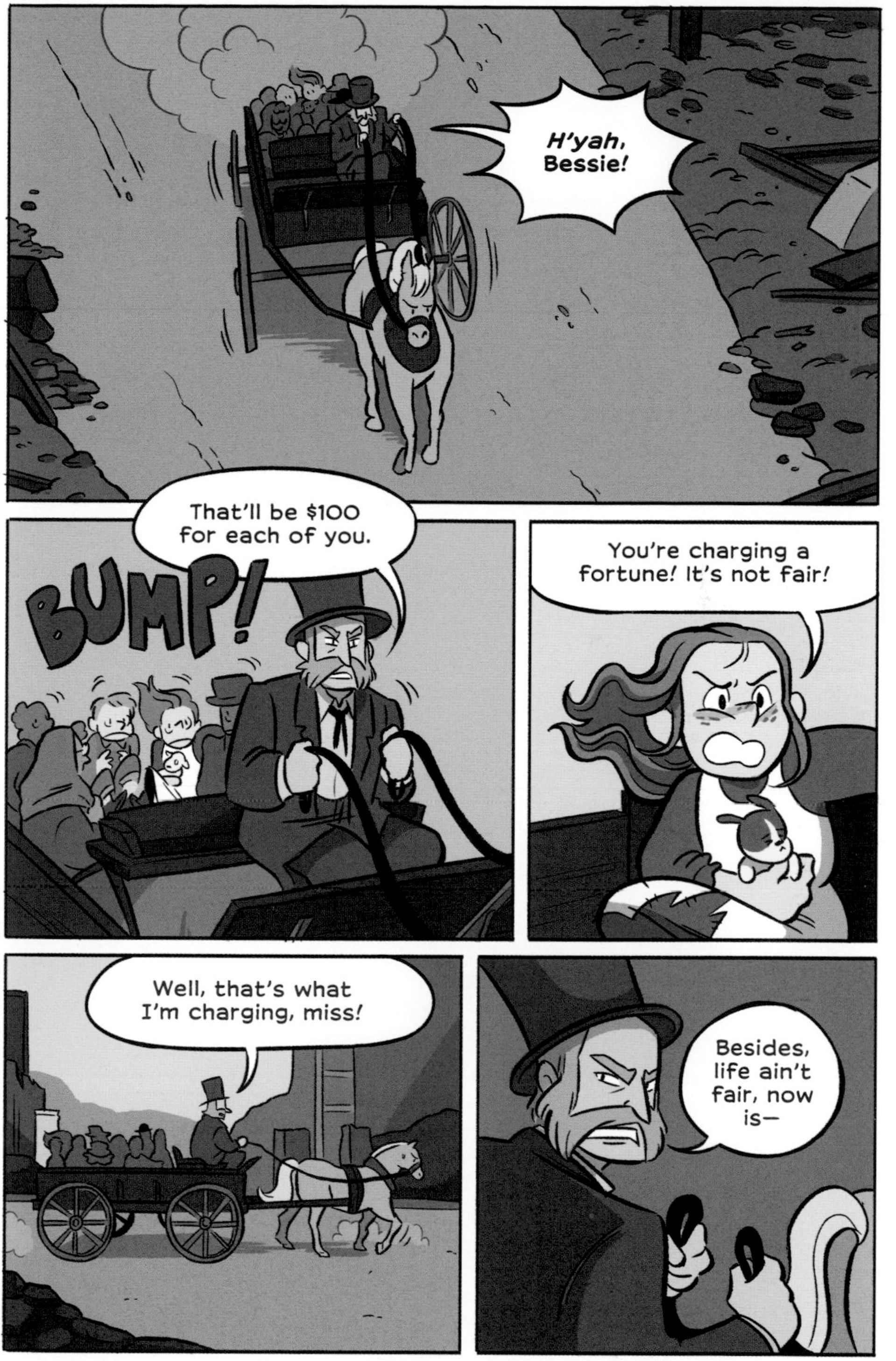

H'yah, Bessie!
That'll be $100 for each of you.
BUMP!
You're charging a fortune! It's not fair!
Well, that's what I'm charging, miss!
Besides, life ain't fair, now is—

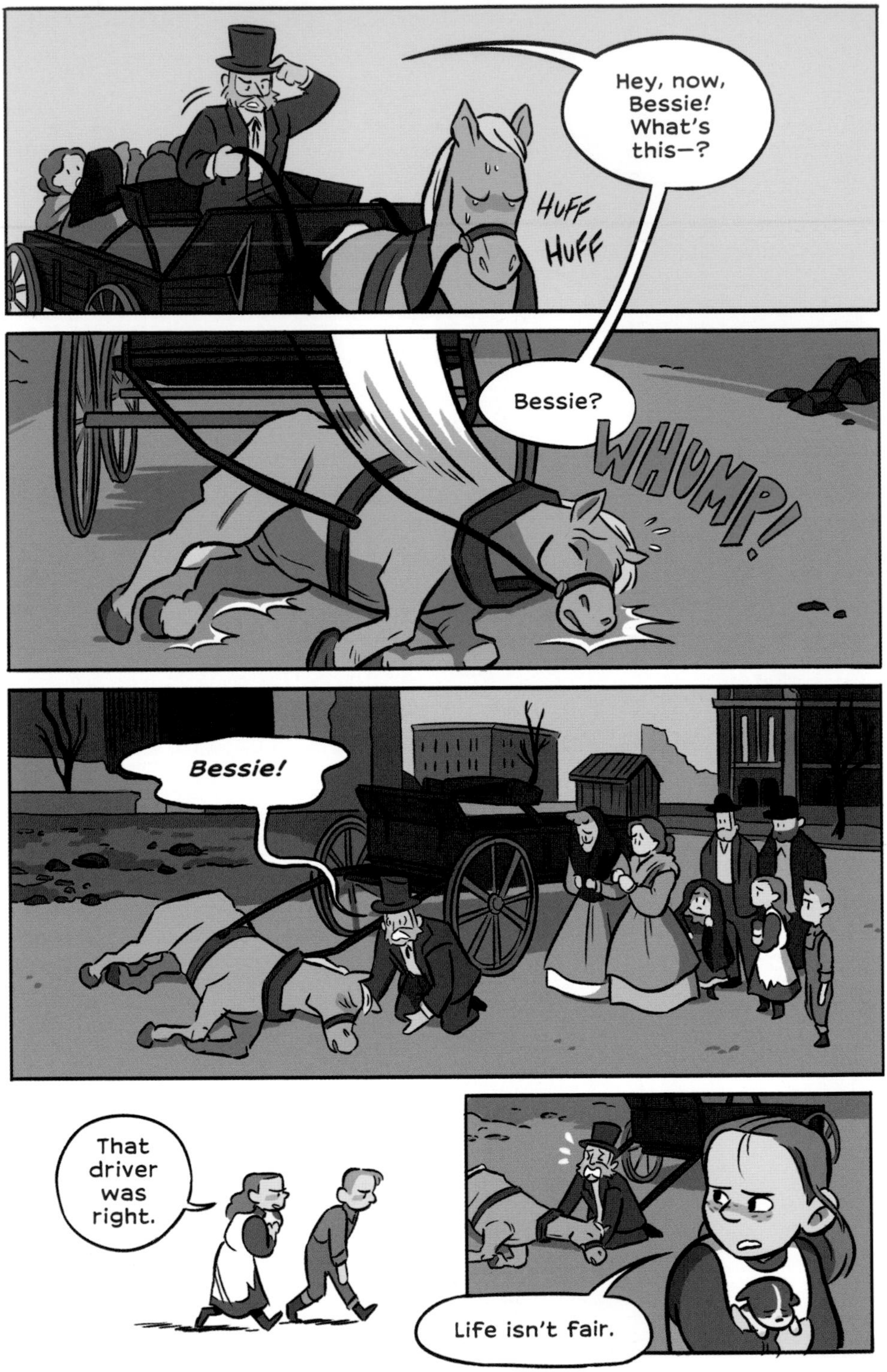
Hey, now, Bessie! What's this—?
HUFF HUFF
Bessie?
WHUMP!
Bessie!
That driver was right.
Life isn't fair.

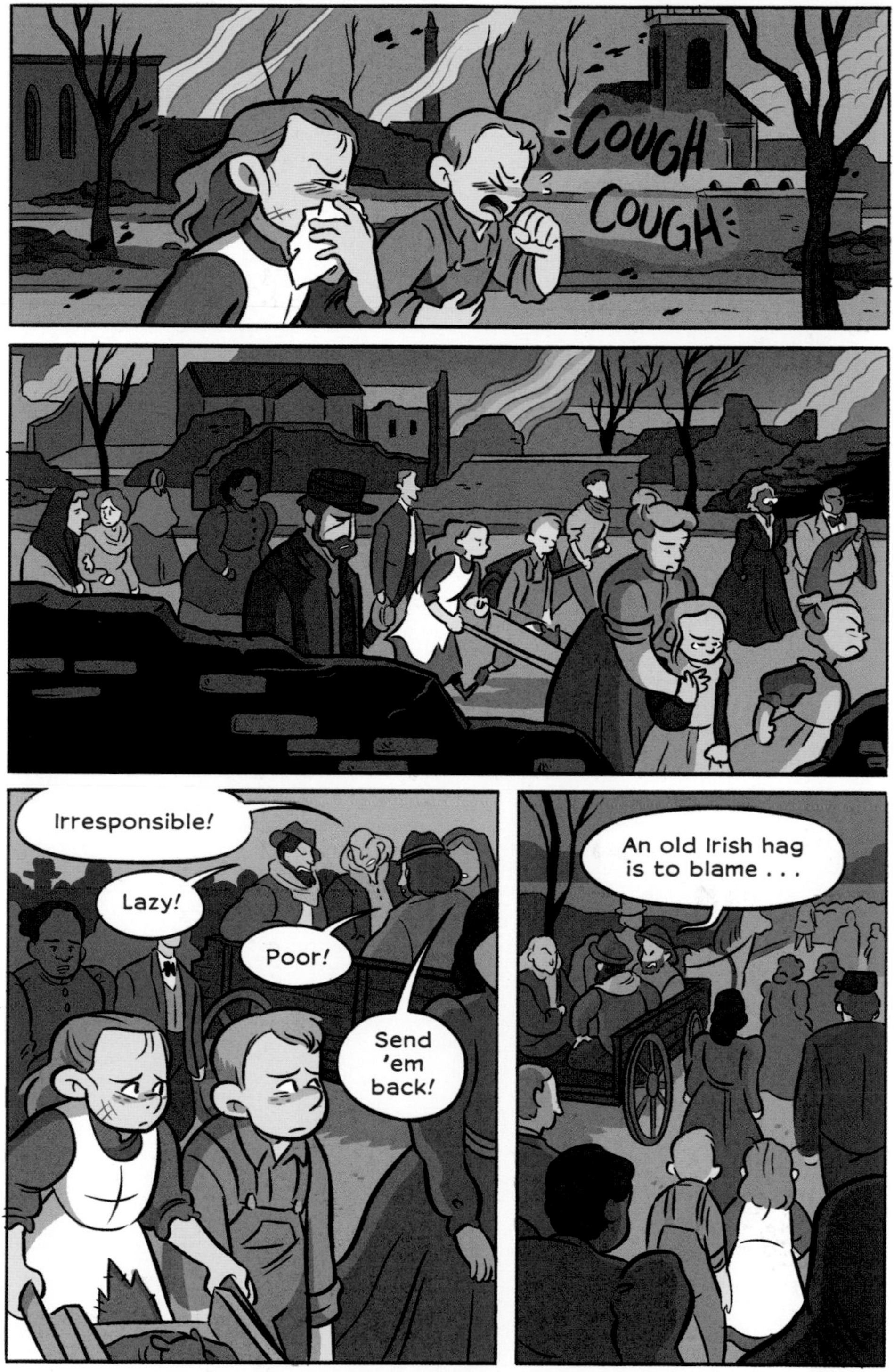
COUGH
COUGH
Irresponsible!
Lazy!
Poor!
Send 'em back!
An old Irish hag is to blame . . .

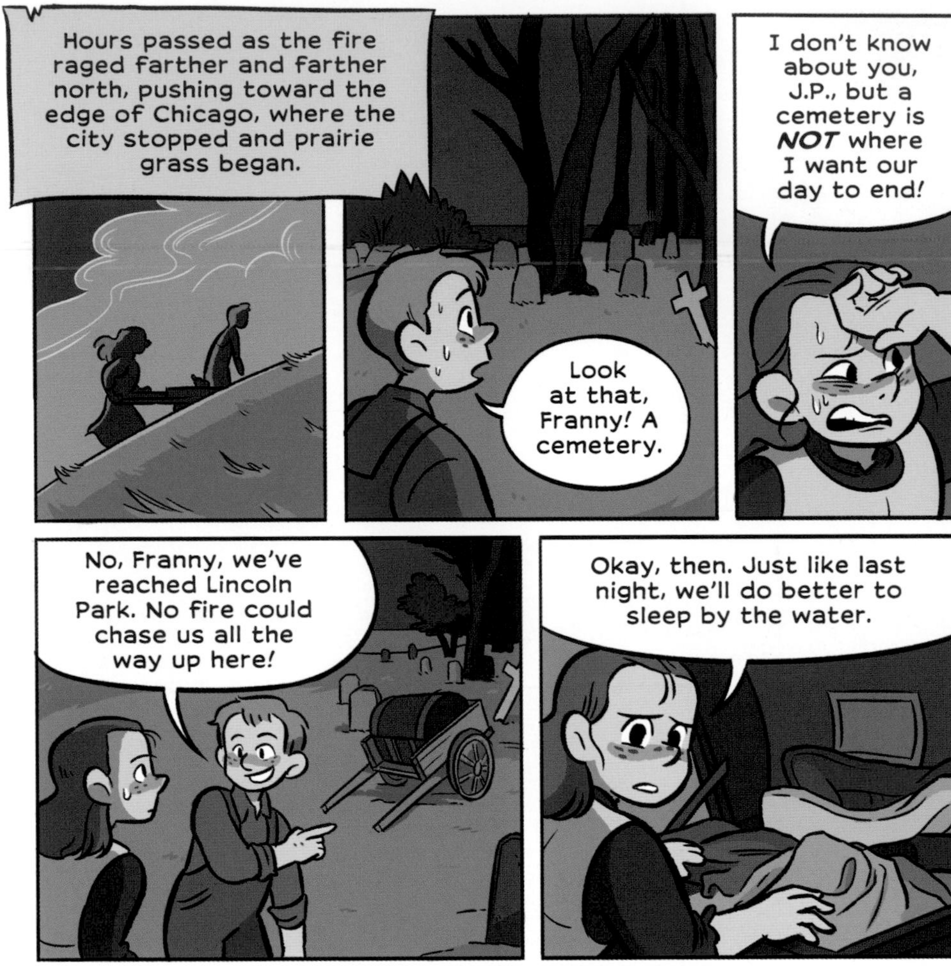
Hours passed as the fire raged farther and farther north, pushing toward the edge of Chicago, where the city stopped and prairie grass began.
Look at that, Franny! A cemetery.
I don't know about you, J.P., but a cemetery is **NOT** where I want our day to end!
No, Franny, we've reached Lincoln Park. No fire could chase us all the way up here!
Okay, then. Just like last night, we'll do better to sleep by the water.

"We saw poor women followed by their affrighted crying children . . . the tears washing the blackness from their faces, which were pictures of despair," wrote the *Prairie Farmer* on October 14, 1871.

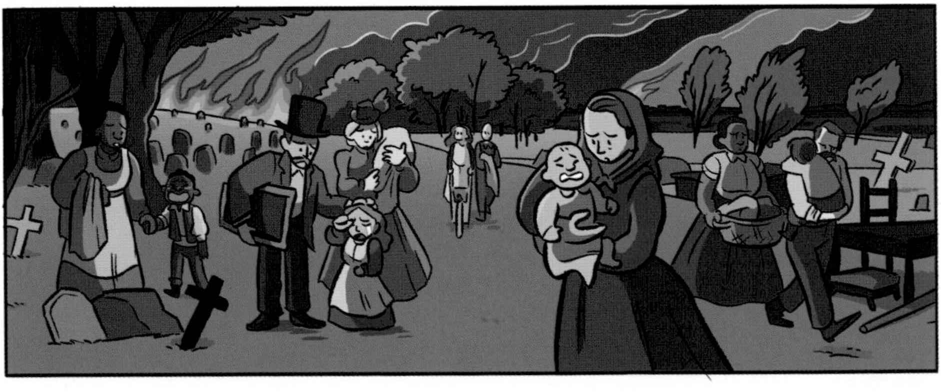

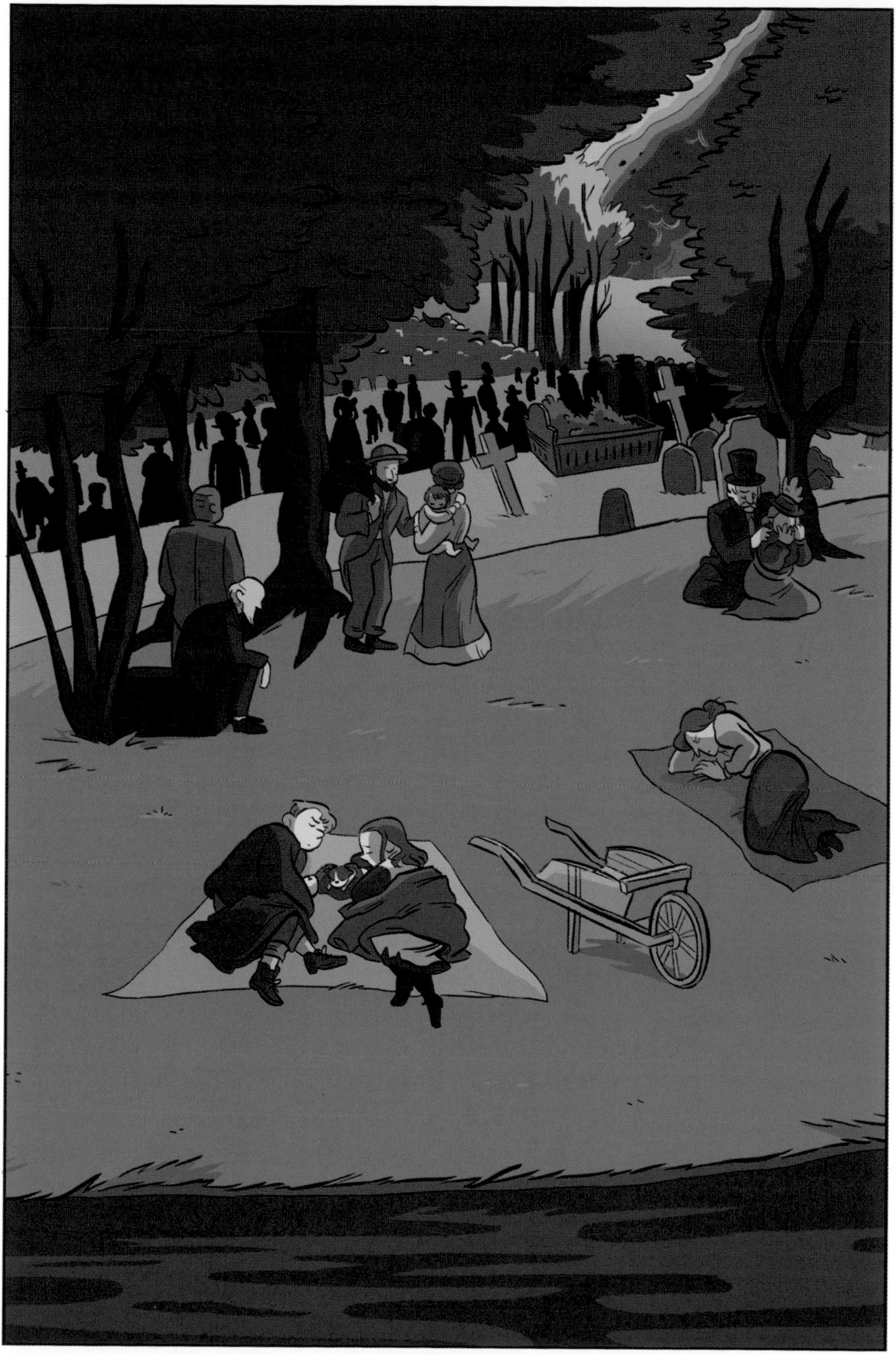

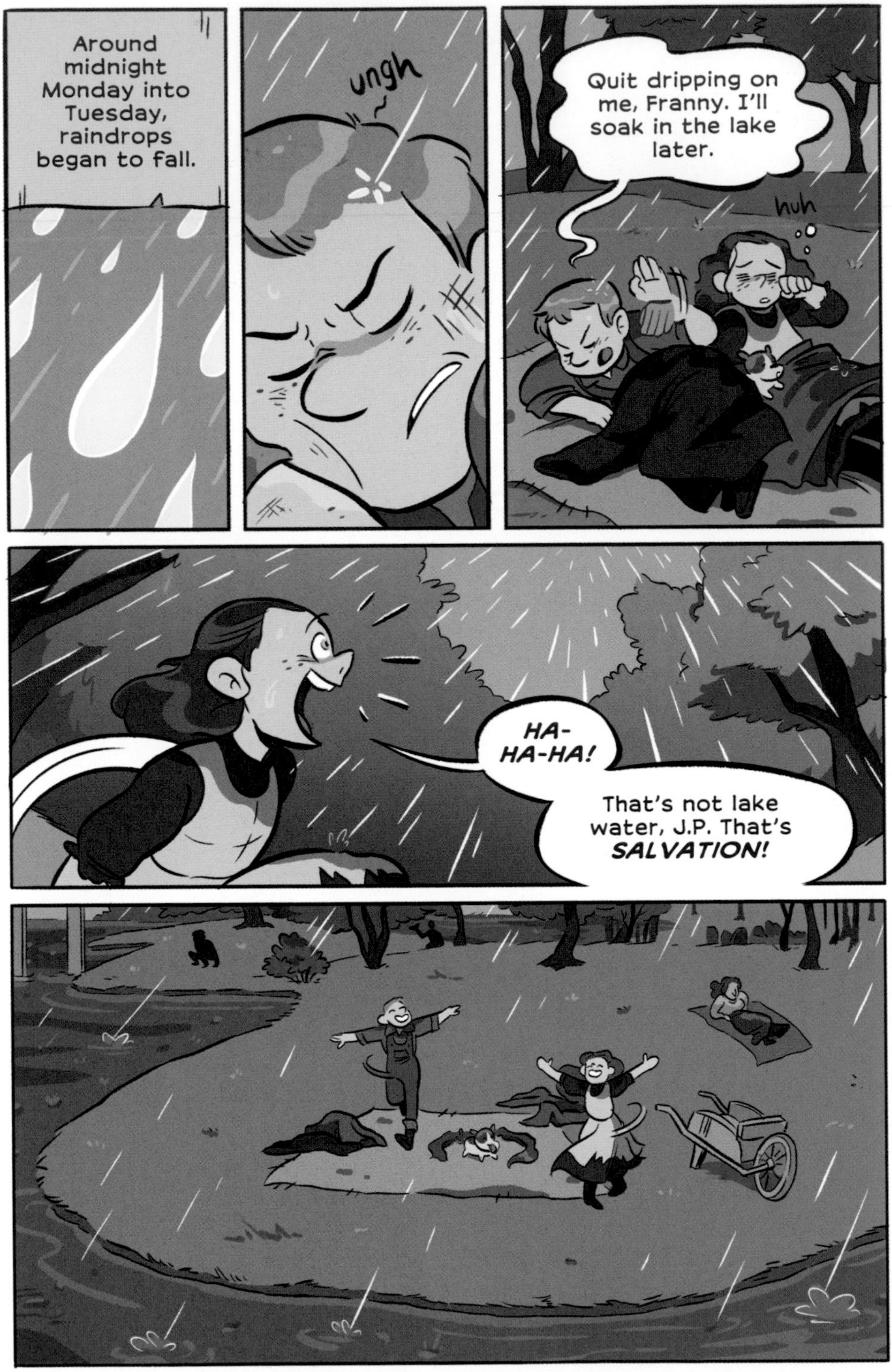
Around midnight Monday into Tuesday, raindrops began to fall.
ungh
Quit dripping on me, Franny. I'll soak in the lake later.
huh
HA-HA-HA!
That's not lake water, J.P. That's SALVATION!

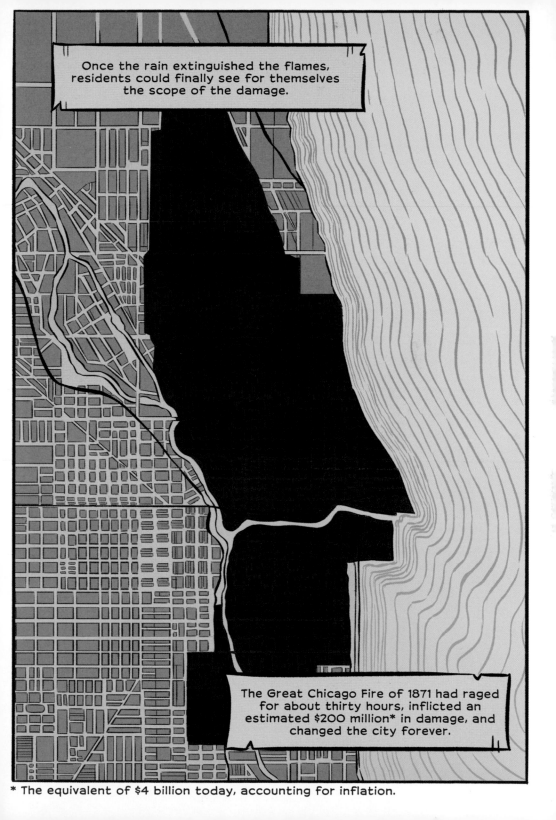

Once the rain extinguished the flames, residents could finally see for themselves the scope of the damage.

The Great Chicago Fire of 1871 had raged for about thirty hours, inflicted an estimated $200 million* in damage, and changed the city forever.

* The equivalent of $4 billion today, accounting for inflation.

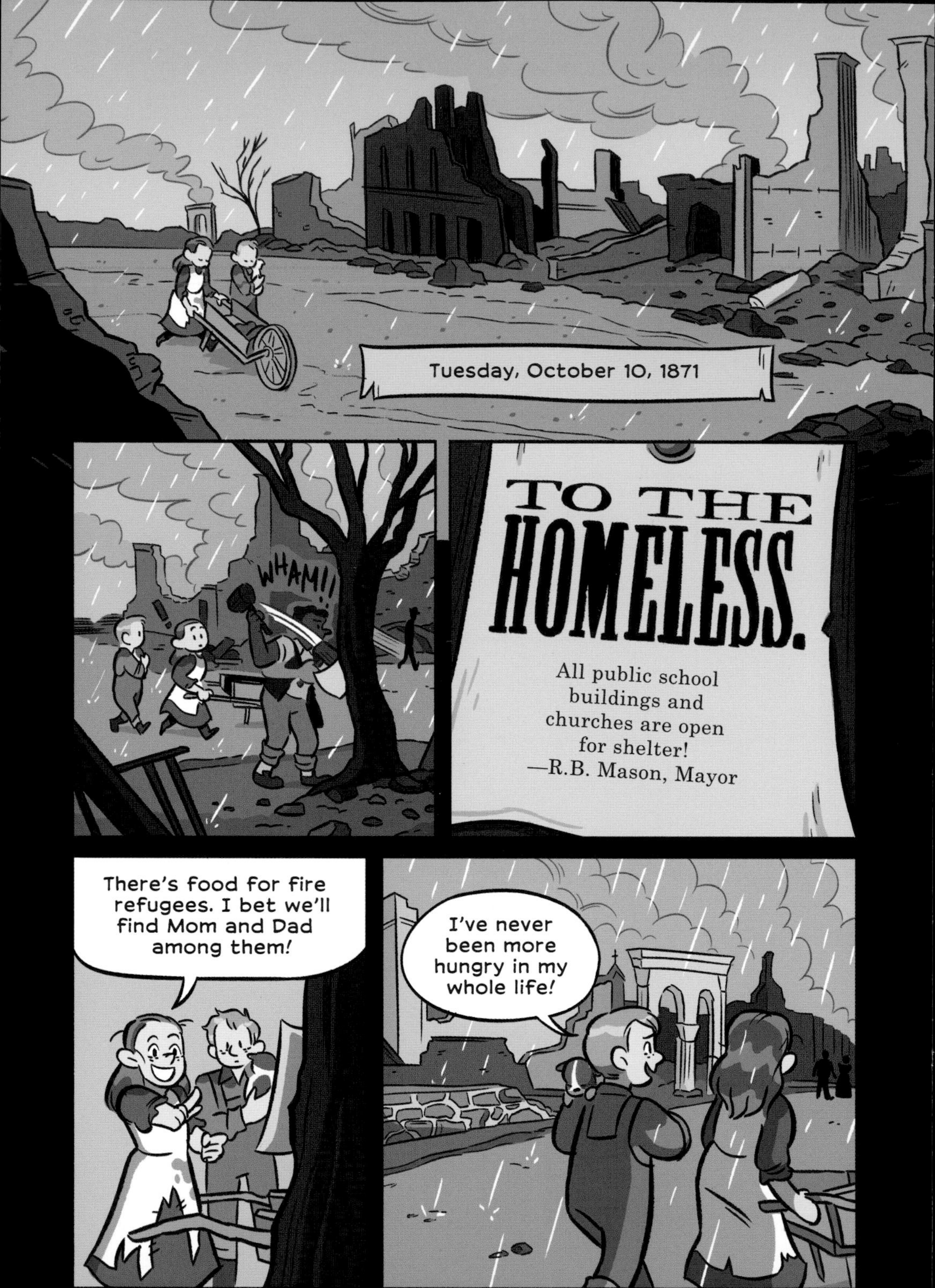
Tuesday, October 10, 1871
WHAM!!
TO THE HOMELESS.
All public school buildings and churches are open for shelter!
—R.B. Mason, Mayor
There's food for fire refugees. I bet we'll find Mom and Dad among them!
I've never been more hungry in my whole life!

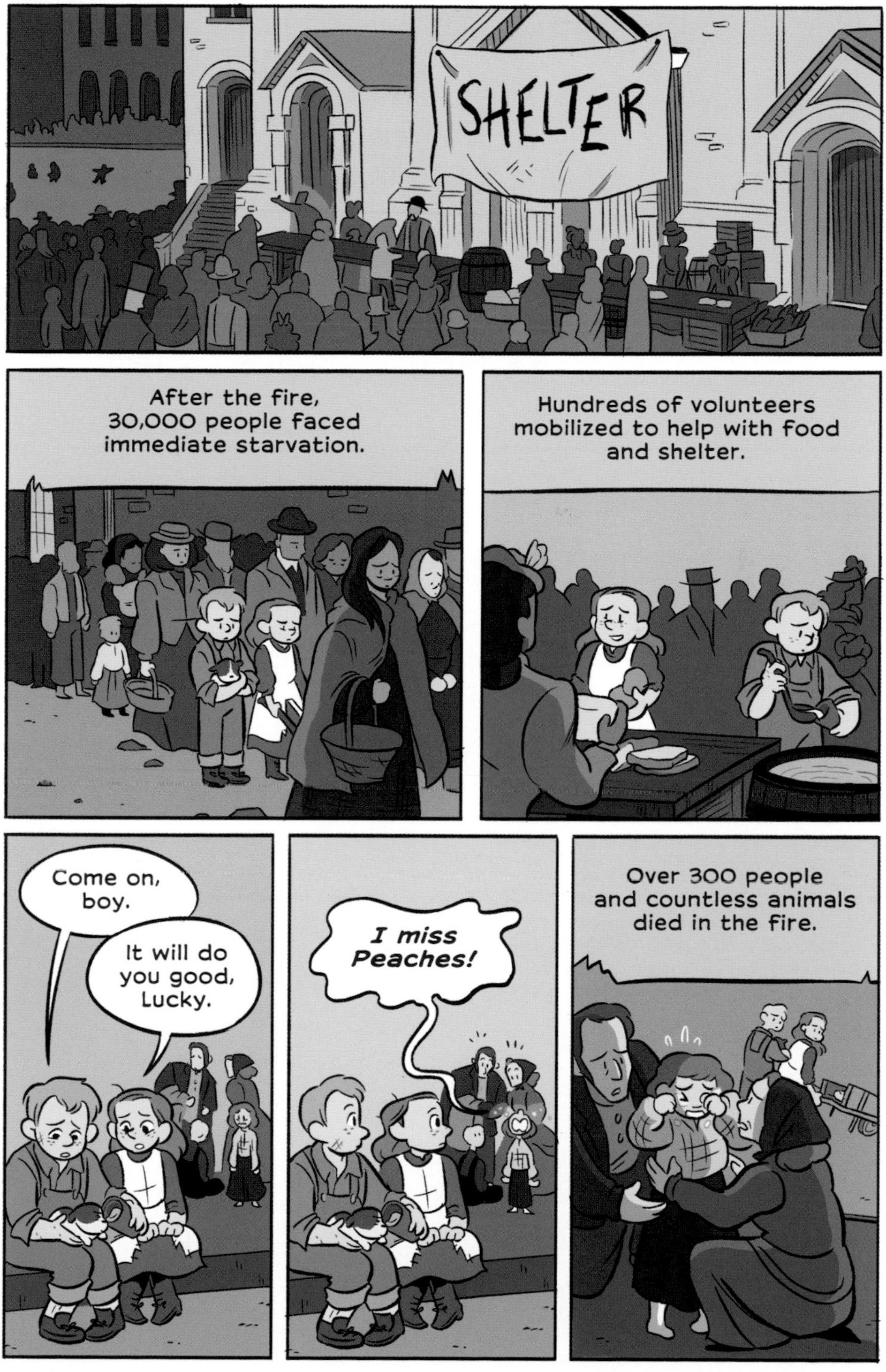
SHELTER
After the fire, 30,000 people faced immediate starvation.
Hundreds of volunteers mobilized to help with food and shelter.
Come on, boy.
It will do you good, Lucky.
I miss Peaches!
Over 300 people and countless animals died in the fire.

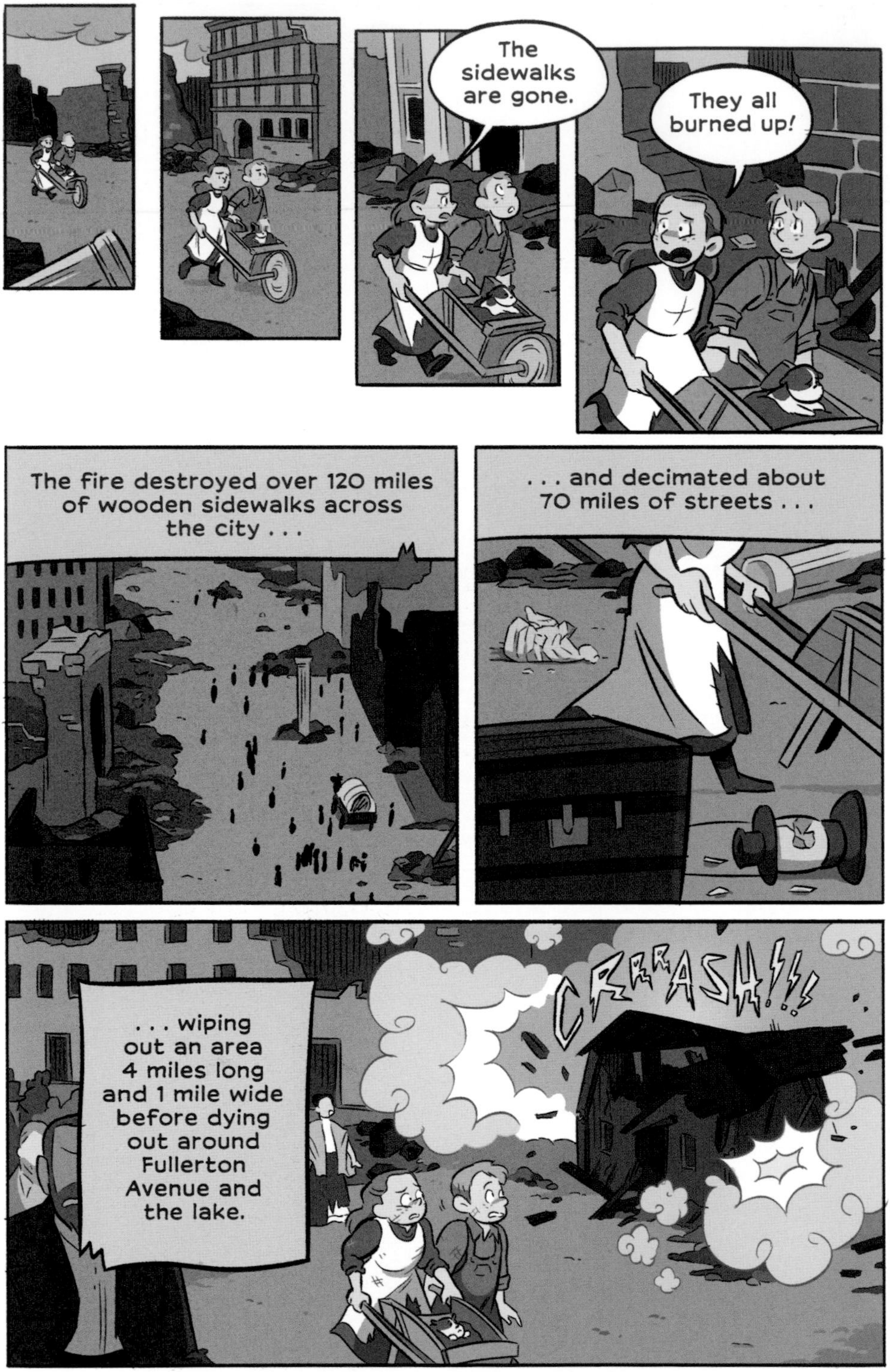
The sidewalks are gone.
They all burned up!
The fire destroyed over 120 miles of wooden sidewalks across the city . . .
. . . and decimated about 70 miles of streets . . .
. . . wiping out an area 4 miles long and 1 mile wide before dying out around Fullerton Avenue and the lake.
CRRRASH!!!

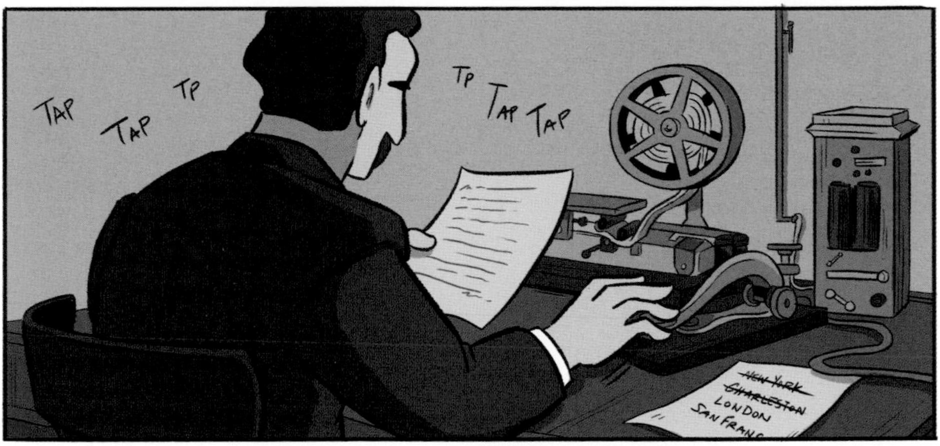
TAP
TAP
TP
TP
TAP
TAP
NEW YORK
CHARLESTON
LONDON

Reporters used telegraph lines to spread
news about the fire around the world.

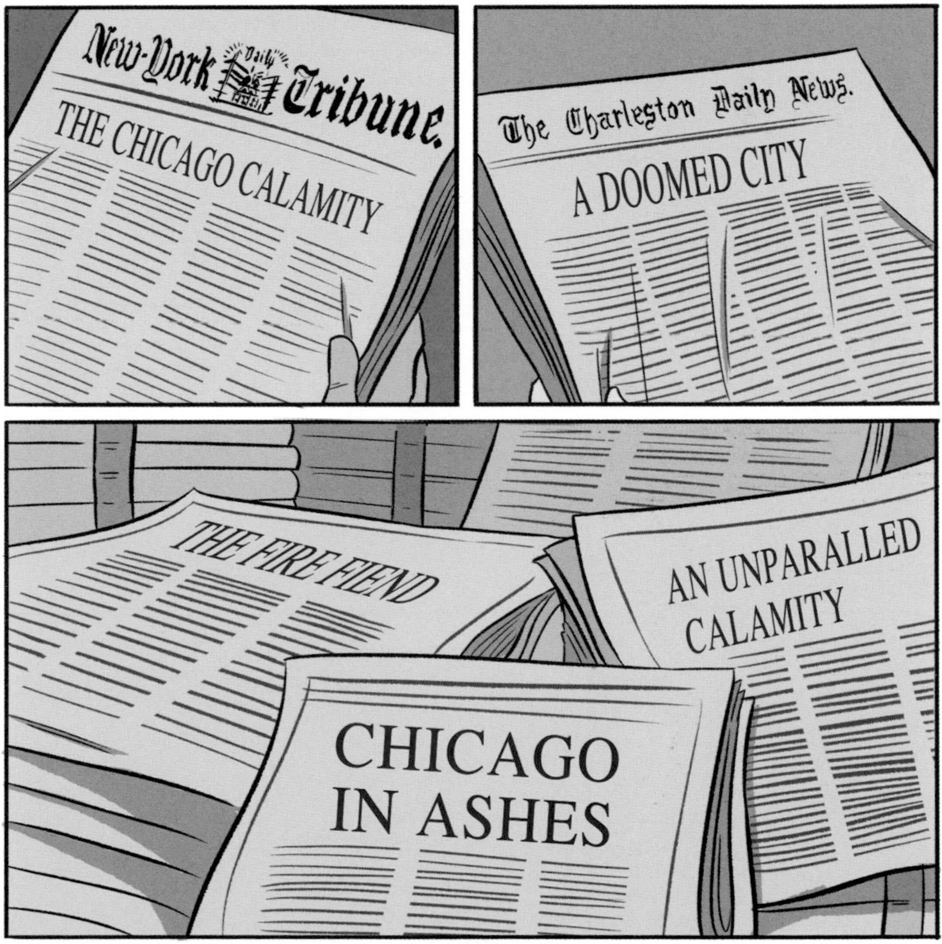
New-York Daily Tribune.
THE CHICAGO CALAMITY
The Charleston Daily News.
A DOOMED CITY
THE FIRE FIEND
AN UNPARALLED
CALAMITY
CHICAGO
IN ASHES

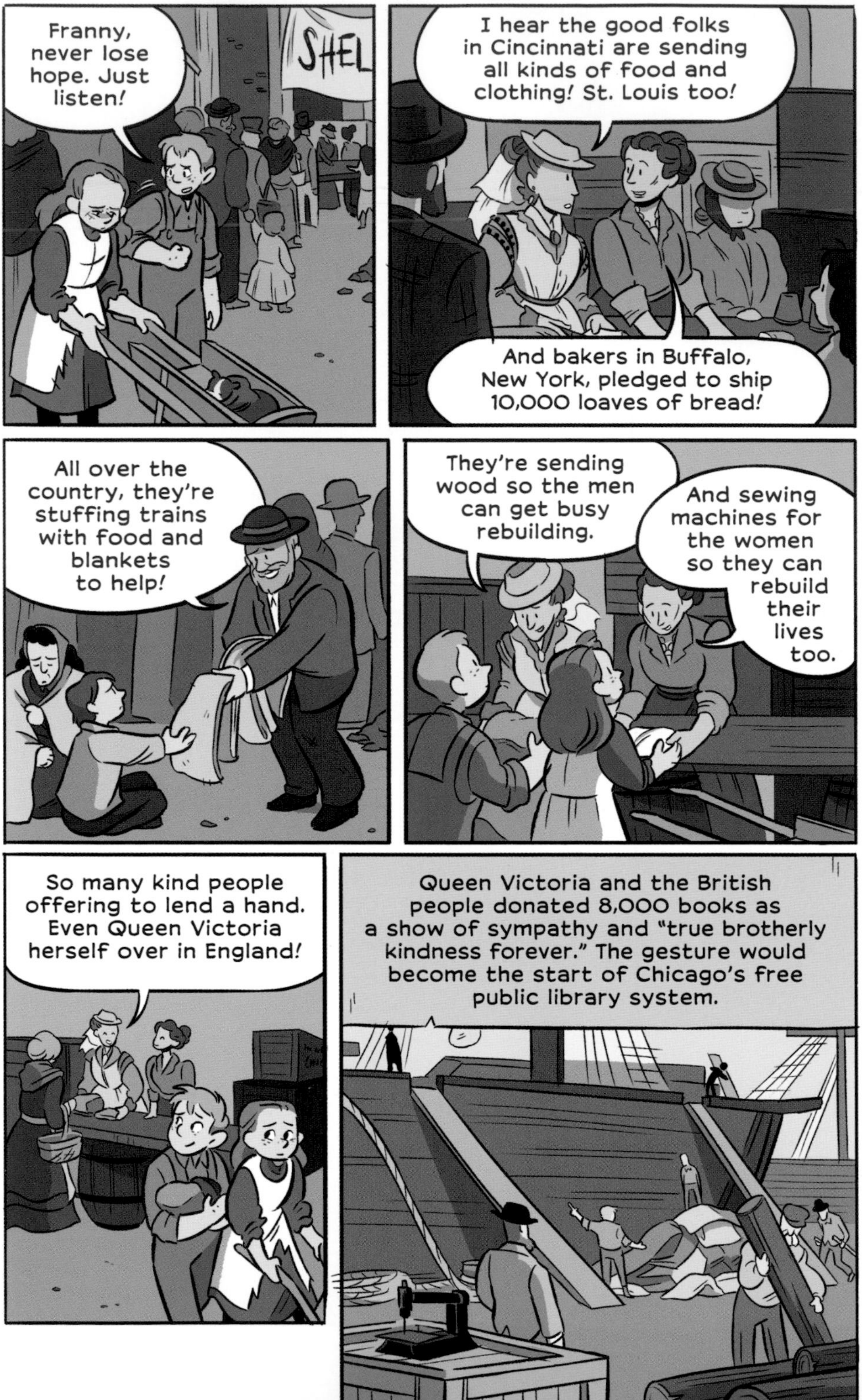
Franny, never lose hope. Just listen!
SHEL
I hear the good folks in Cincinnati are sending all kinds of food and clothing! St. Louis too!
And bakers in Buffalo, New York, pledged to ship 10,000 loaves of bread!
All over the country, they're stuffing trains with food and blankets to help!
They're sending wood so the men can get busy rebuilding.
And sewing machines for the women so they can rebuild their lives too.
So many kind people offering to lend a hand. Even Queen Victoria herself over in England!
Queen Victoria and the British people donated 8,000 books as a show of sympathy and "true brotherly kindness forever." The gesture would become the start of Chicago's free public library system.

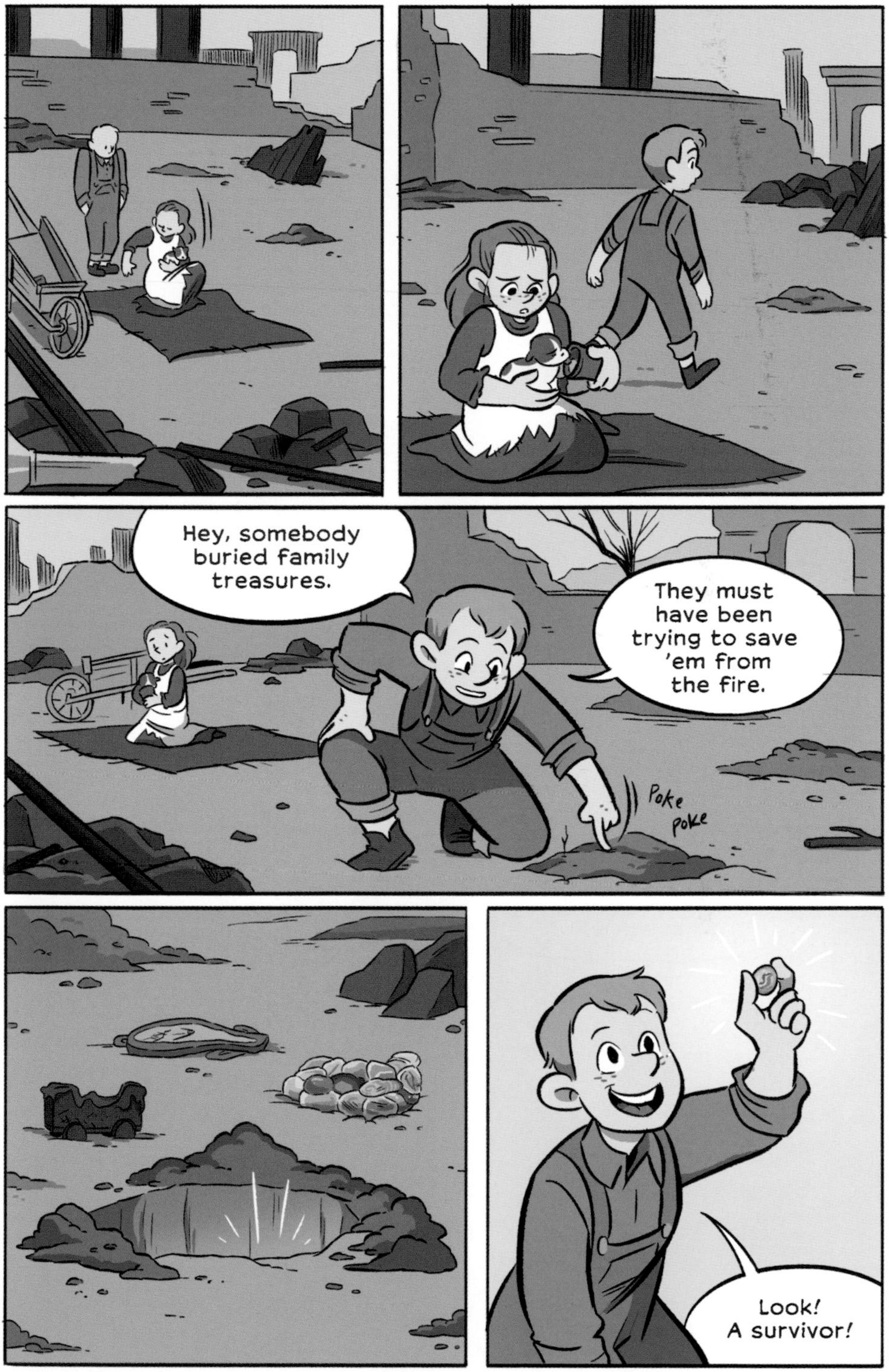
Hey, somebody buried family treasures.
They must have been trying to save 'em from the fire.
Poke poke
Look! A survivor!

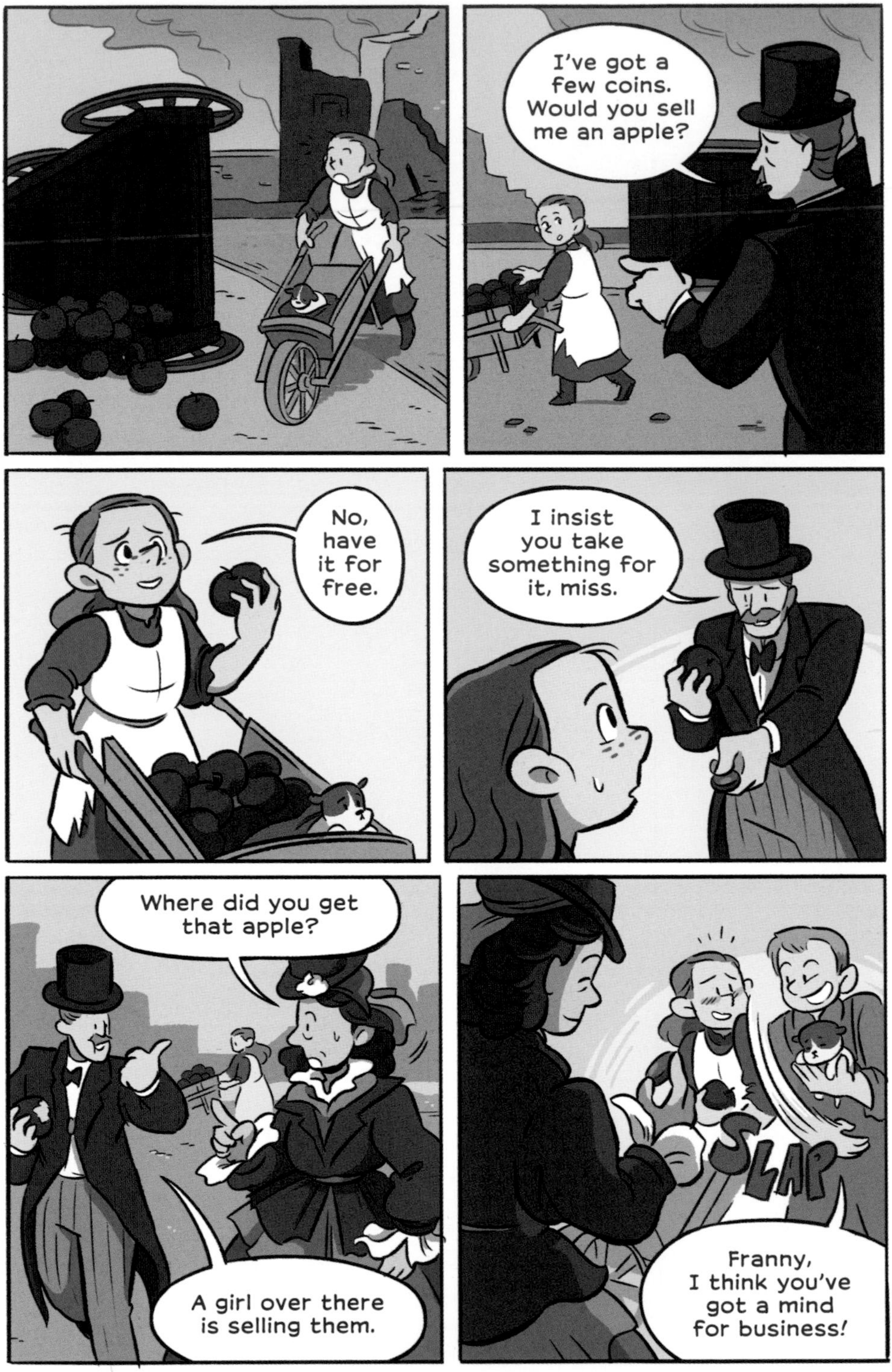
I've got a few coins. Would you sell me an apple?
No, have it for free.
I insist you take something for it, miss.
Where did you get that apple?
A girl over there is selling them.
SLAP
Franny, I think you've got a mind for business!

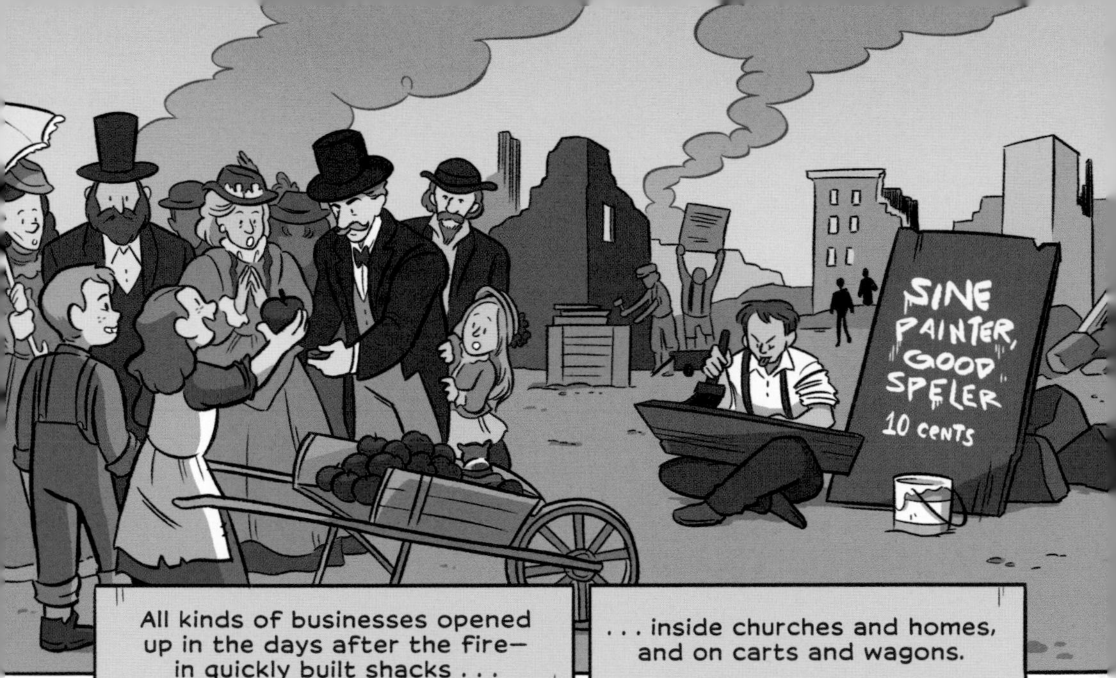
SINE PAINTER, GOOD SPELER
10 CENTS

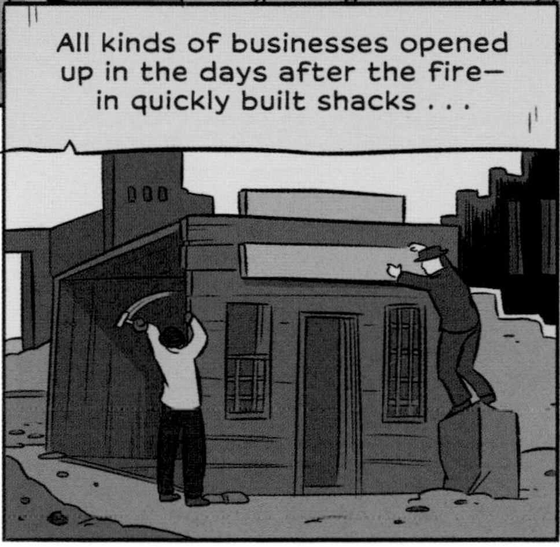
All kinds of businesses opened up in the days after the fire—in quickly built shacks . . .

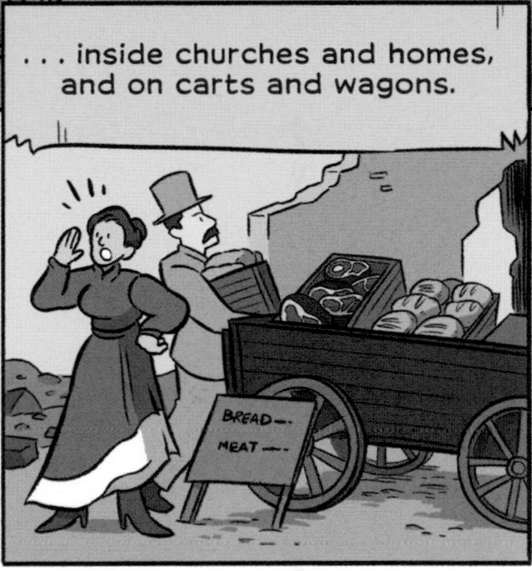
. . . inside churches and homes, and on carts and wagons.
BREAD
MEAT

Kids got into the act too, selling items like melted marbles and burnt-edged books to the curious tourists who soon began pouring into Chicago.

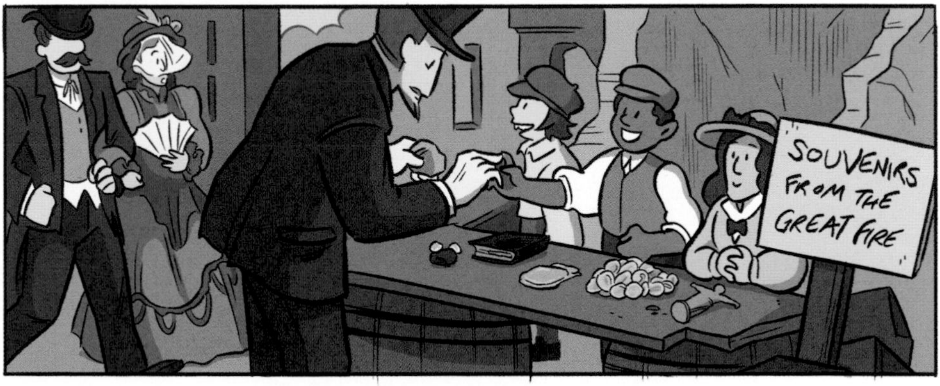
SOUVENIRS FROM THE GREAT FIRE

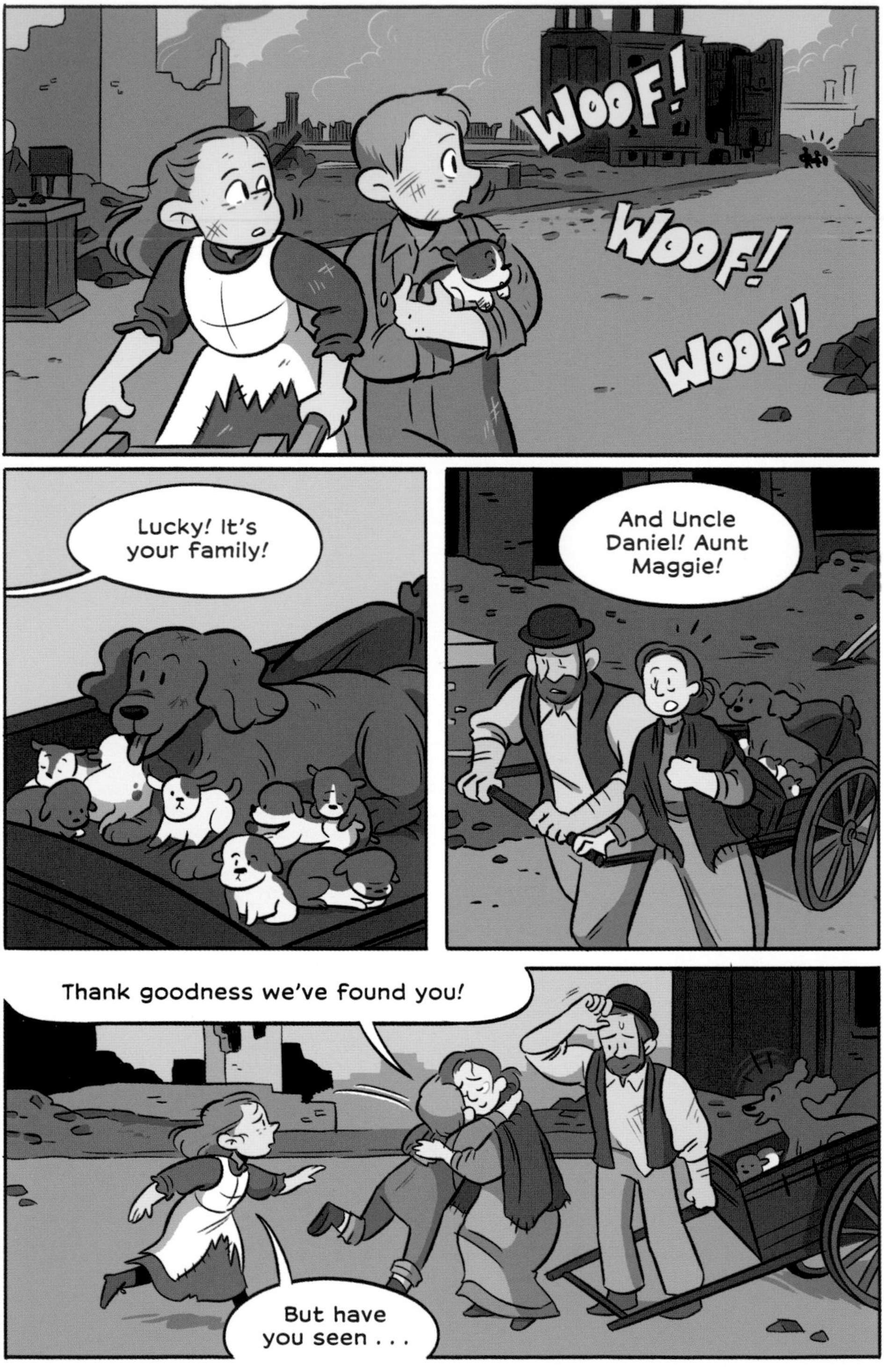
WOOF!
WOOF!
WOOF!
Lucky! It's your family!
And Uncle Daniel! Aunt Maggie!
Thank goodness we've found you!
But have you seen . . .

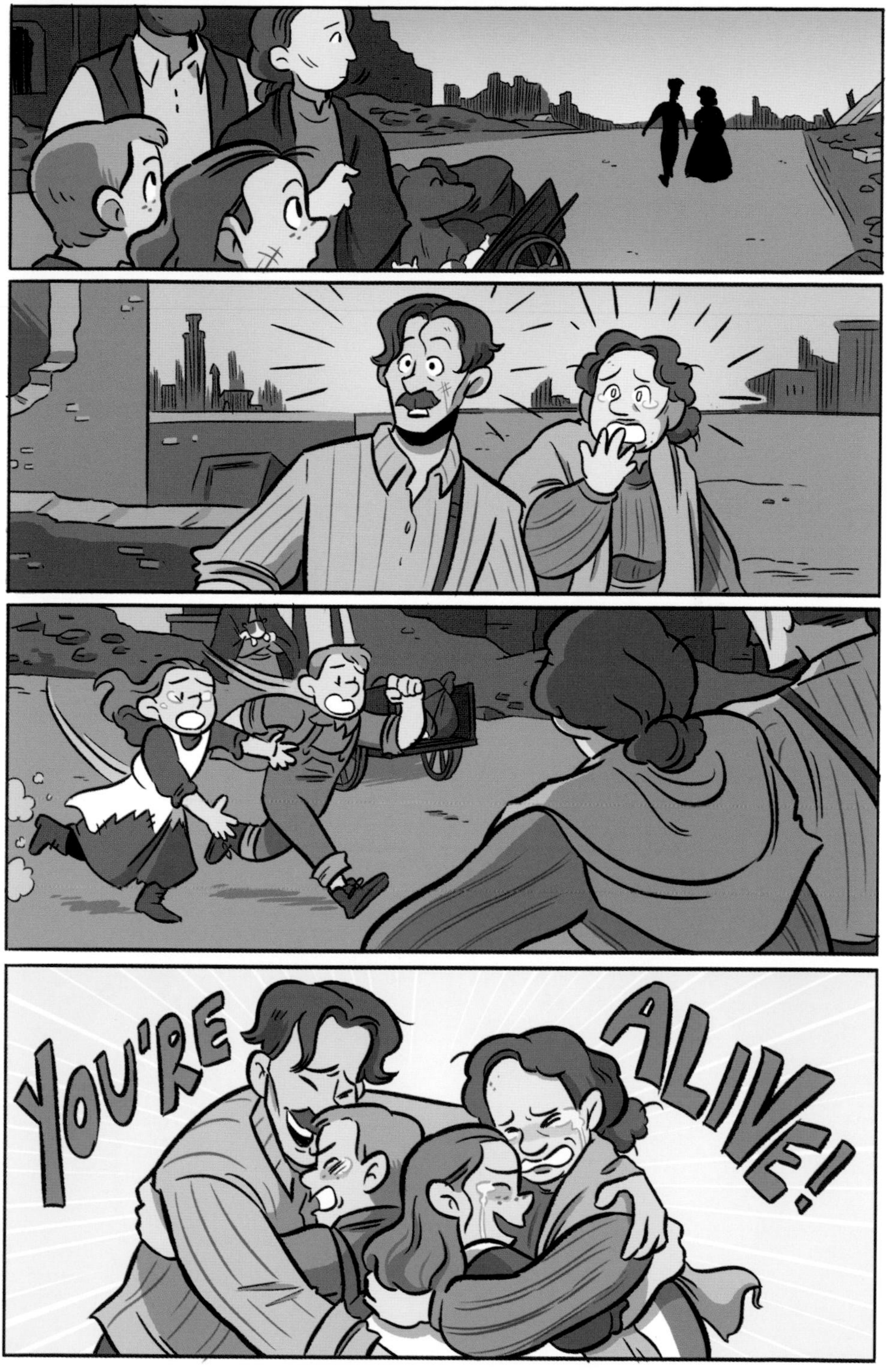
YOU'RE ALIVE!

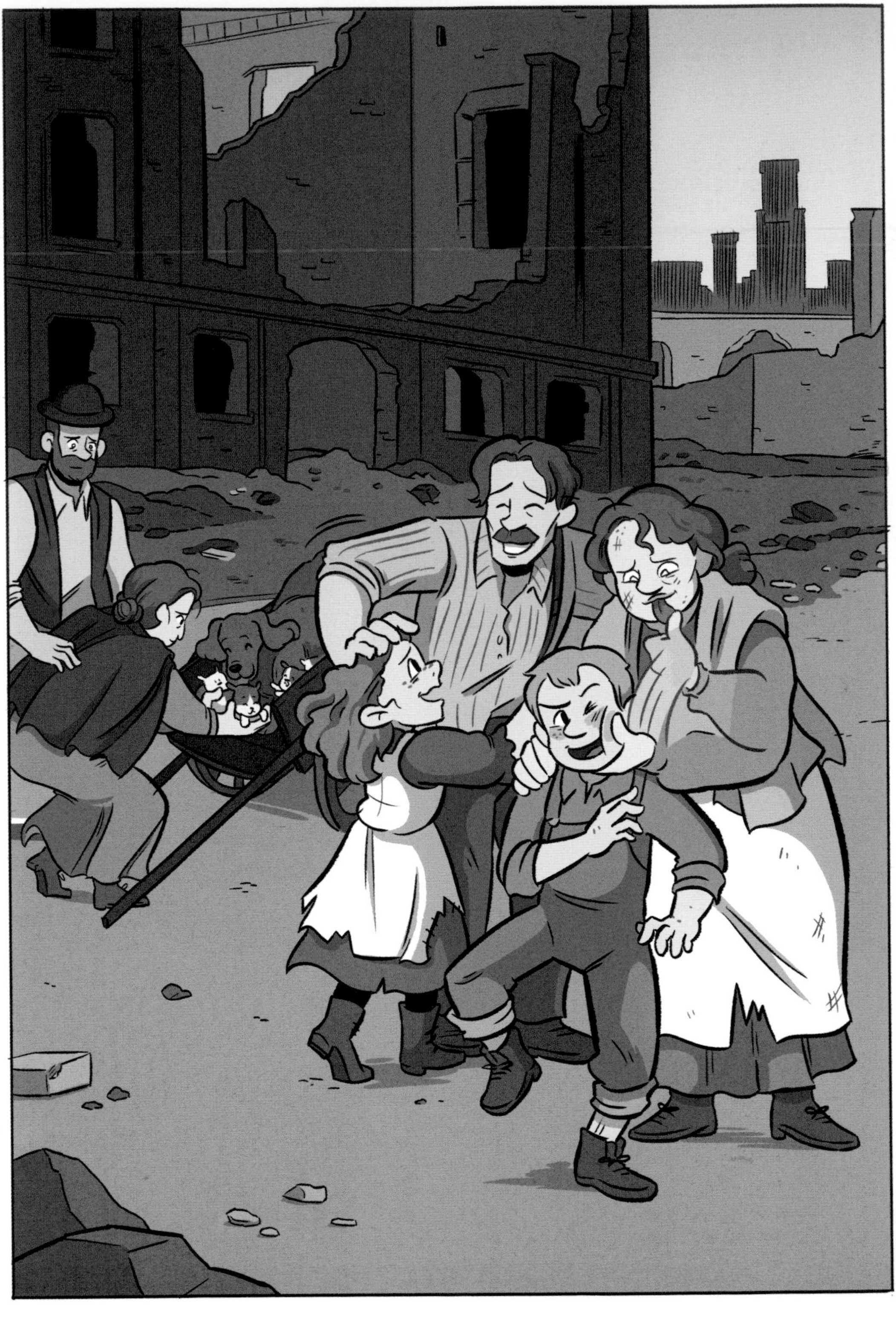

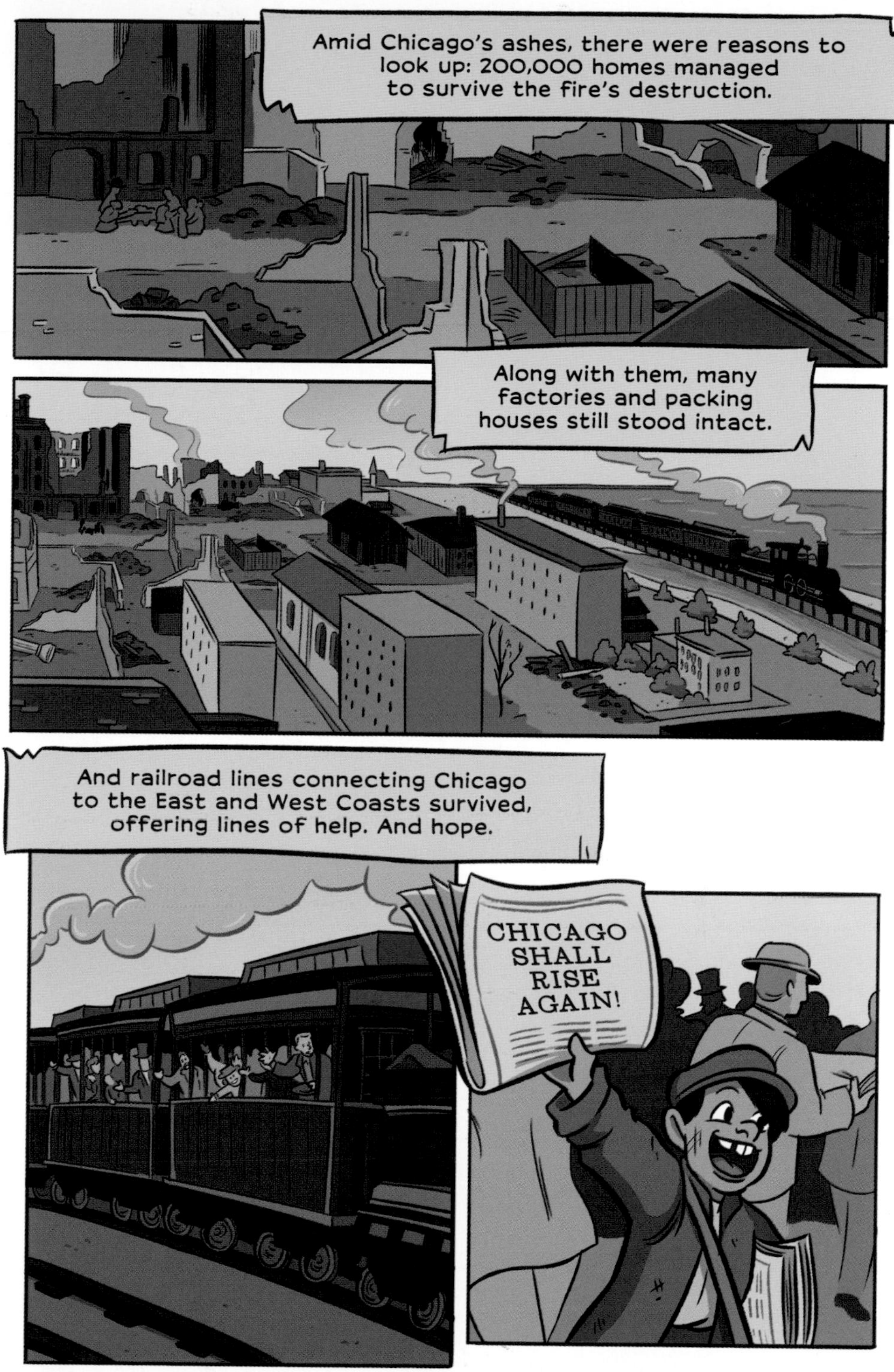
Amid Chicago's ashes, there were reasons to look up: 200,000 homes managed to survive the fire's destruction.
Along with them, many factories and packing houses still stood intact.
And railroad lines connecting Chicago to the East and West Coasts survived, offering lines of help. And hope.
CHICAGO SHALL RISE AGAIN!

22 years later,
June 21, 1893

WORLD'S COLUMBIAN EXPOSITION

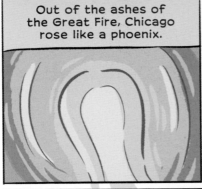

Out of the ashes of the Great Fire, Chicago rose like a phoenix.

The city grew from 300,000 people in 1871 . . .

RIDE THE   FERRIS WHEEL!

50 CENTS FOR 20 MINUTES

. . . to over 1,000,000 people by the time of the 1893 World's Columbian Exposition, known as the Chicago World's Fair.

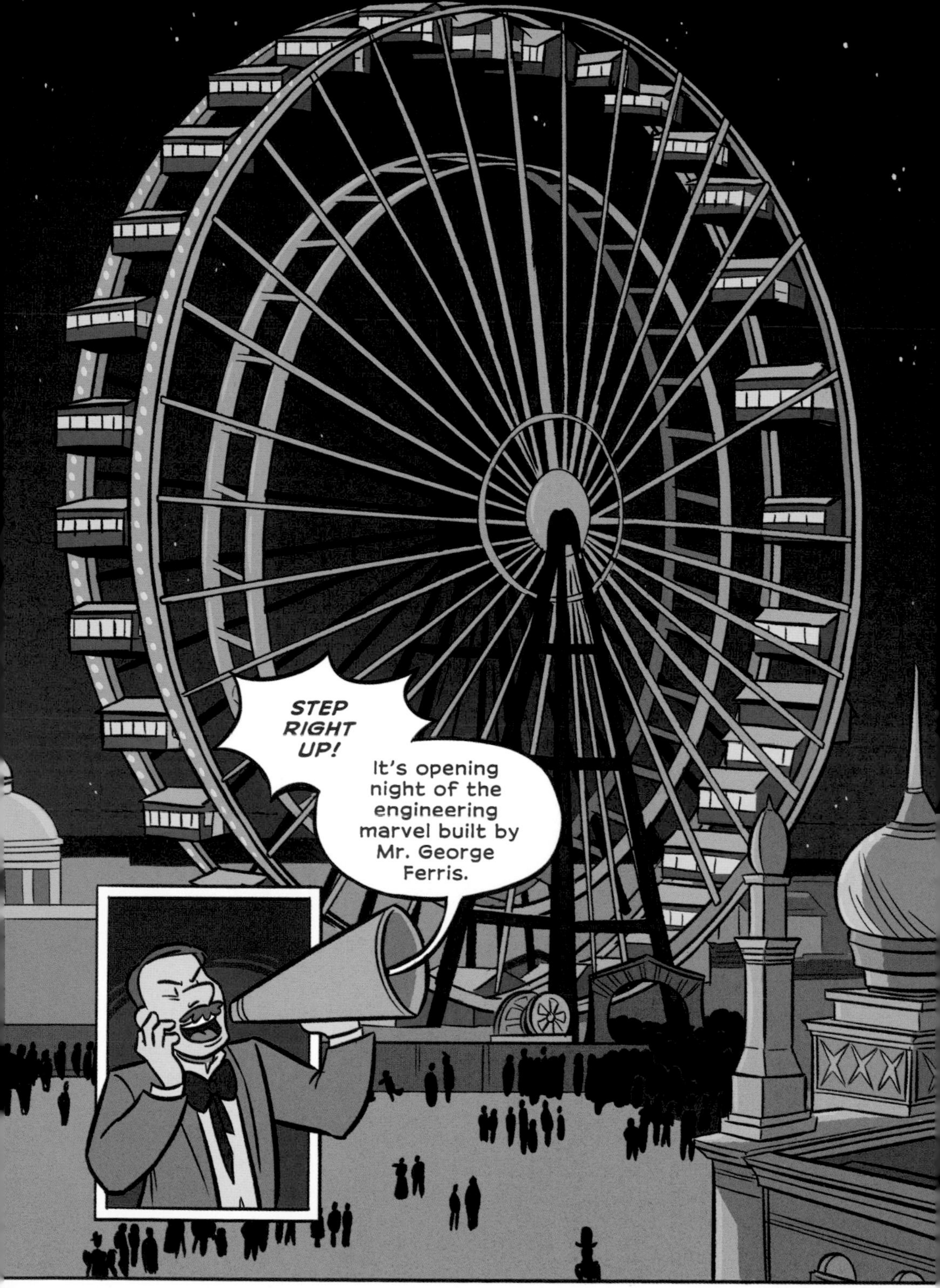
STEP RIGHT UP!
It's opening night of the engineering marvel built by Mr. George Ferris.

So many lights, Mary Frances!

I hear there's 3,000 bulbs on this big wheel alone!

Dad, Grandpa! You've got to see this!

We see it, Patrick. Looks like they've lit up the whole world!

The first Ferris wheel was constructed just for the World's Fair, as Chicago's answer to Paris's Eiffel Tower and New York's Statue of Liberty, both completed a few years before. It stood 264 feet high and had 36 cars, each of which could hold 60 people.

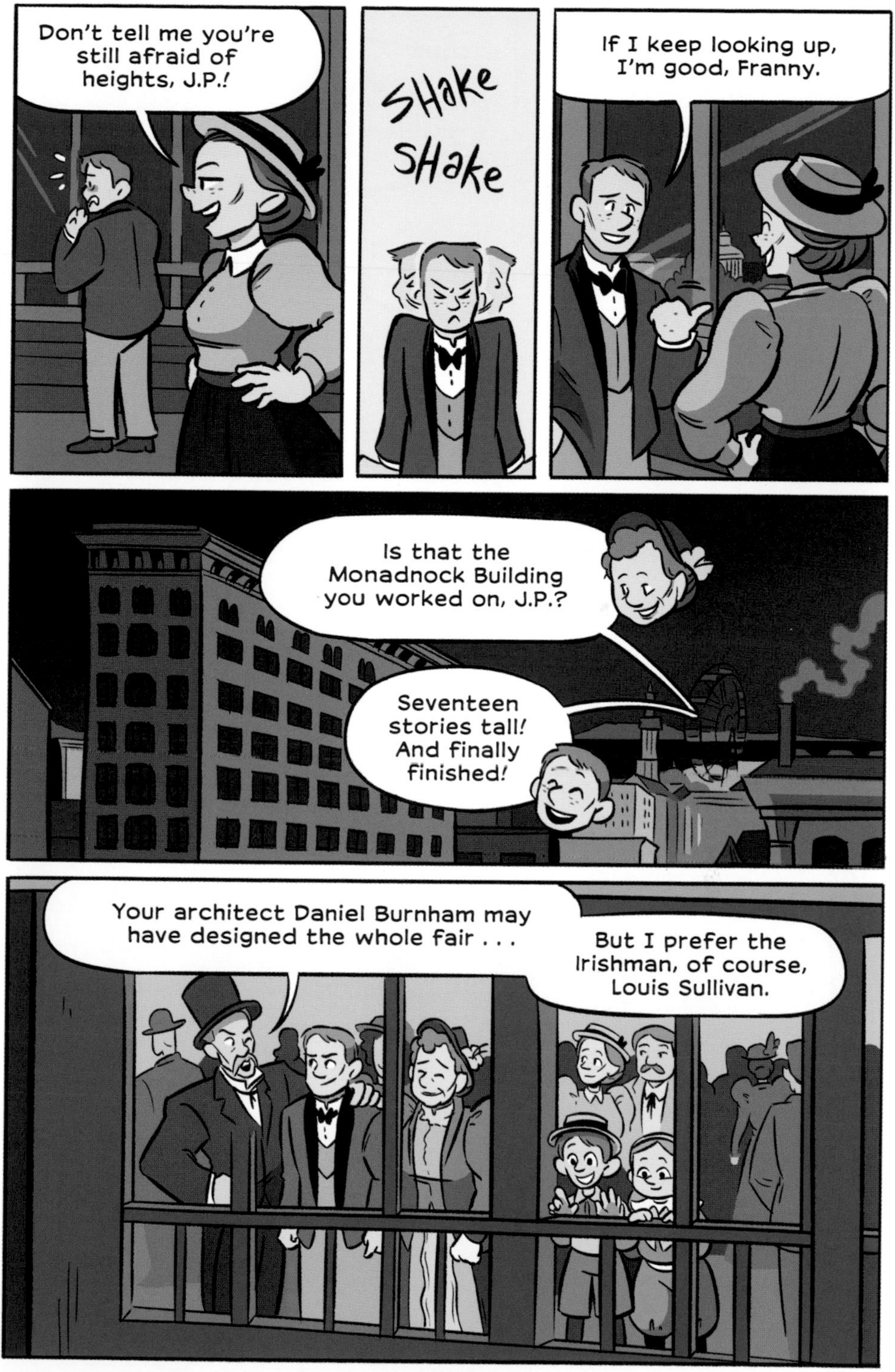
Don't tell me you're still afraid of heights, J.P.!
SHAKE SHAKE
If I keep looking up, I'm good, Franny.
Is that the Monadnock Building you worked on, J.P.?
Seventeen stories tall! And finally finished!
Your architect Daniel Burnham may have designed the whole fair . . .
But I prefer the Irishman, of course, Louis Sullivan.

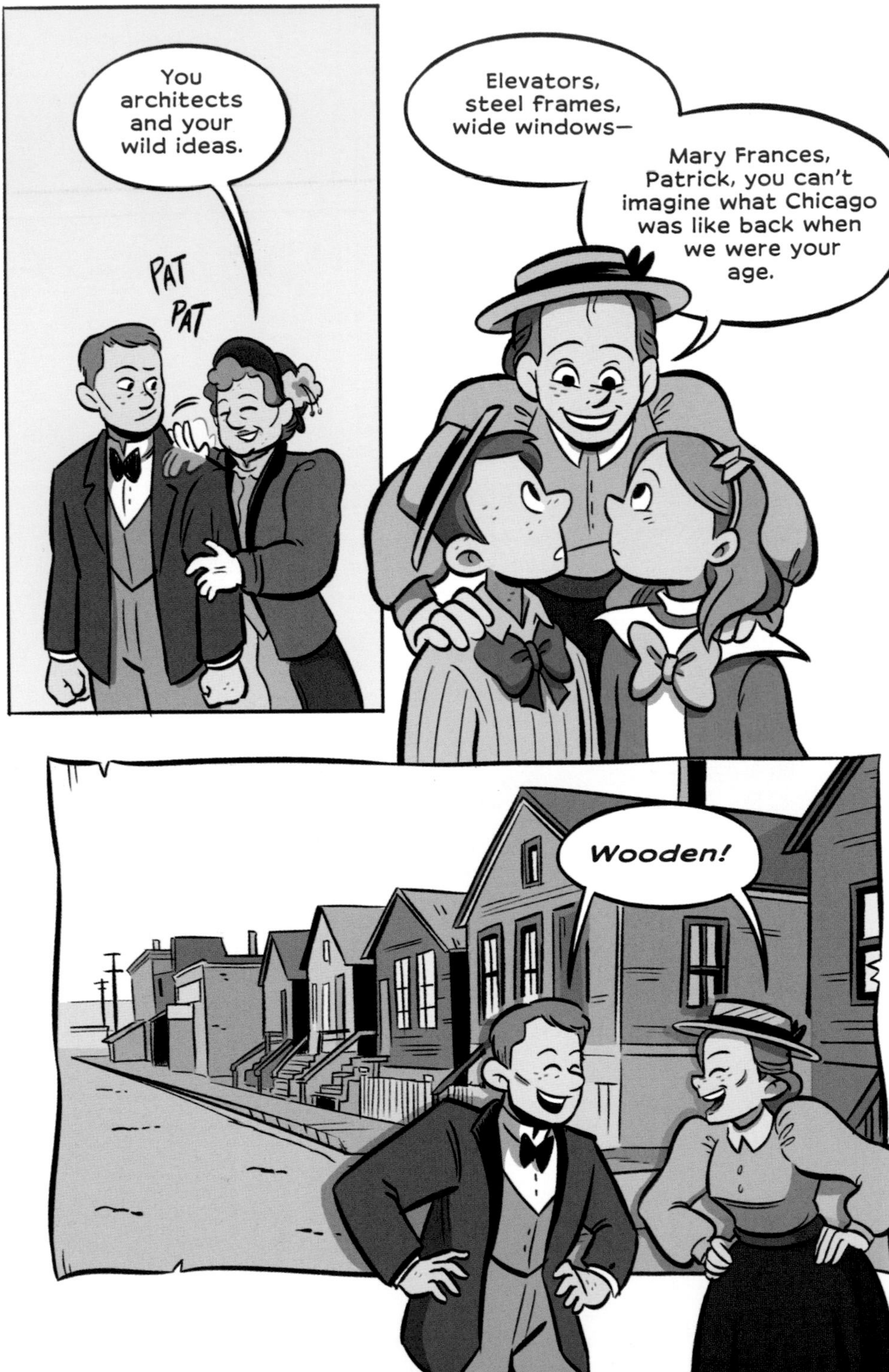
You architects and your wild ideas.
PAT PAT
Elevators, steel frames, wide windows—
Mary Frances, Patrick, you can't imagine what Chicago was like back when we were your age.
Wooden!

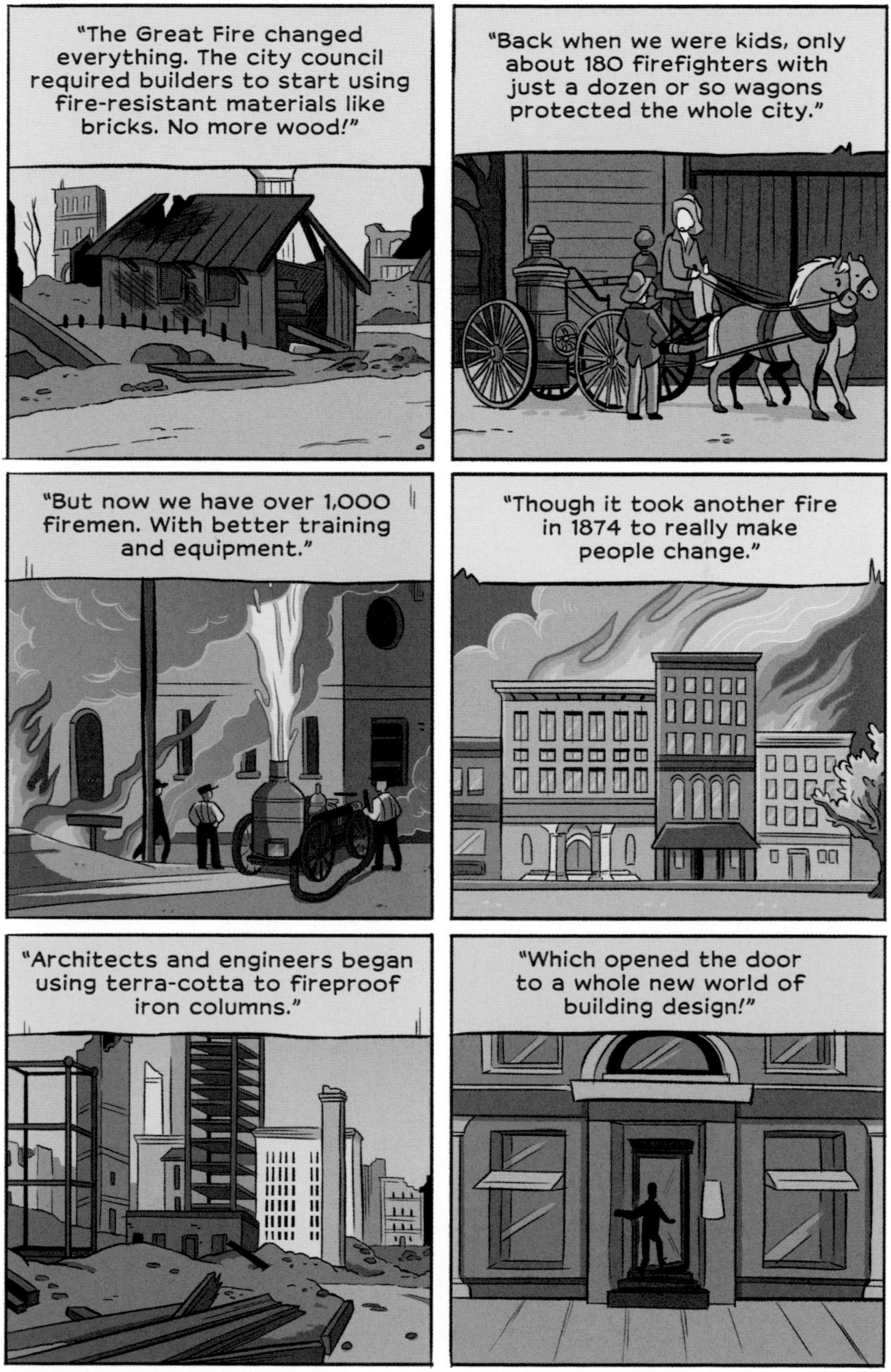
"The Great Fire changed everything. The city council required builders to start using fire-resistant materials like bricks. No more wood!"
"Back when we were kids, only about 180 firefighters with just a dozen or so wagons protected the whole city."
"But now we have over 1,000 firemen. With better training and equipment."
"Though it took another fire in 1874 to really make people change."
"Architects and engineers began using terra-cotta to fireproof iron columns."
"Which opened the door to a whole new world of building design!"

Pioneering architects began building taller buildings, using bold new ideas for fireproofing techniques, lighter materials, elevators, and plumbing.

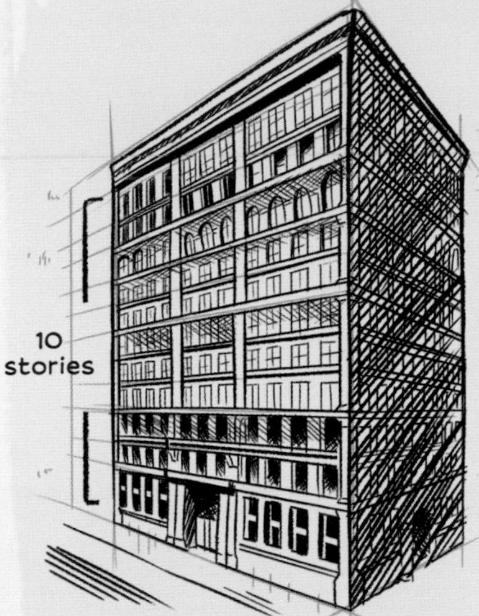
10 stories

HOME INSURANCE BUILDING (1884) BY ARCHITECT WILLIAM LE BARON JENNEY

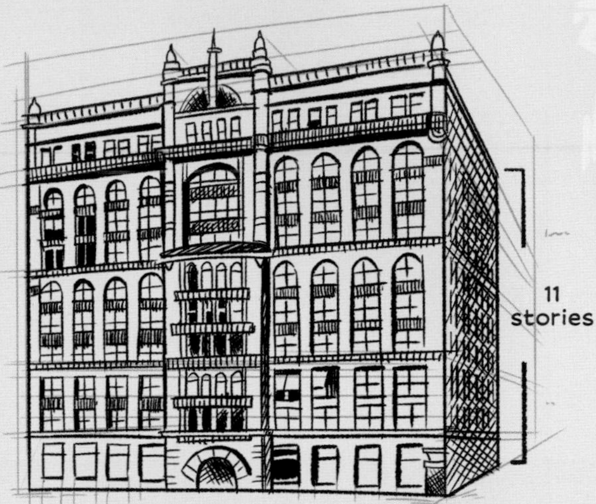
11 stories

ROOKERY (1885) BY ARCHITECTS JOHN ROOT AND DANIEL BURNHAM:
big windows, natural light, load-bearing walls & steel-frame construction

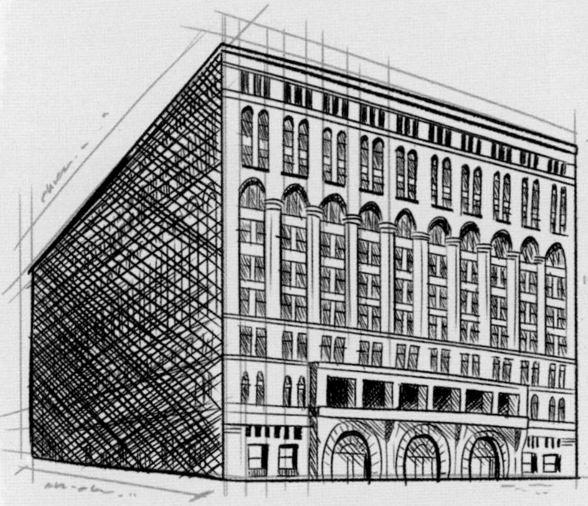

AUDITORIUM THEATER (1889) BY DANKMAR ADLER AND LOUIS SULLIVAN:
10-story hotel, 17-story tower, lavish inside but outside is not ornate

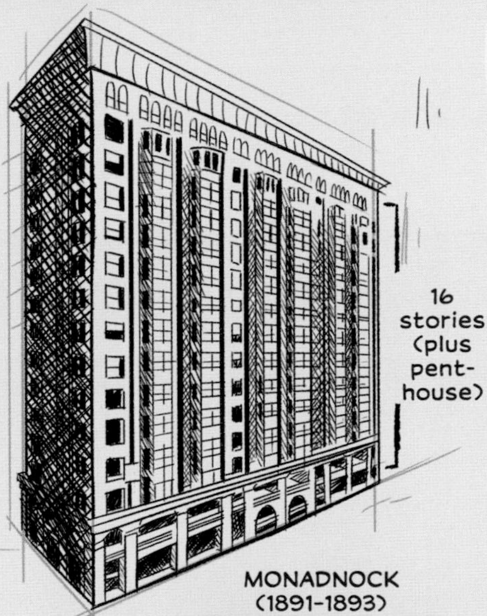
16 stories (plus pent-house)

MONADNOCK (1891–1893) BY DANIEL BURNHAM AND JOHN ROOT:
simple style that serves business interest

Replacing heavy stone with interior steel skeletons, architects were able to create taller buildings that seemed to reach the sky—coining the term "skyscrapers."

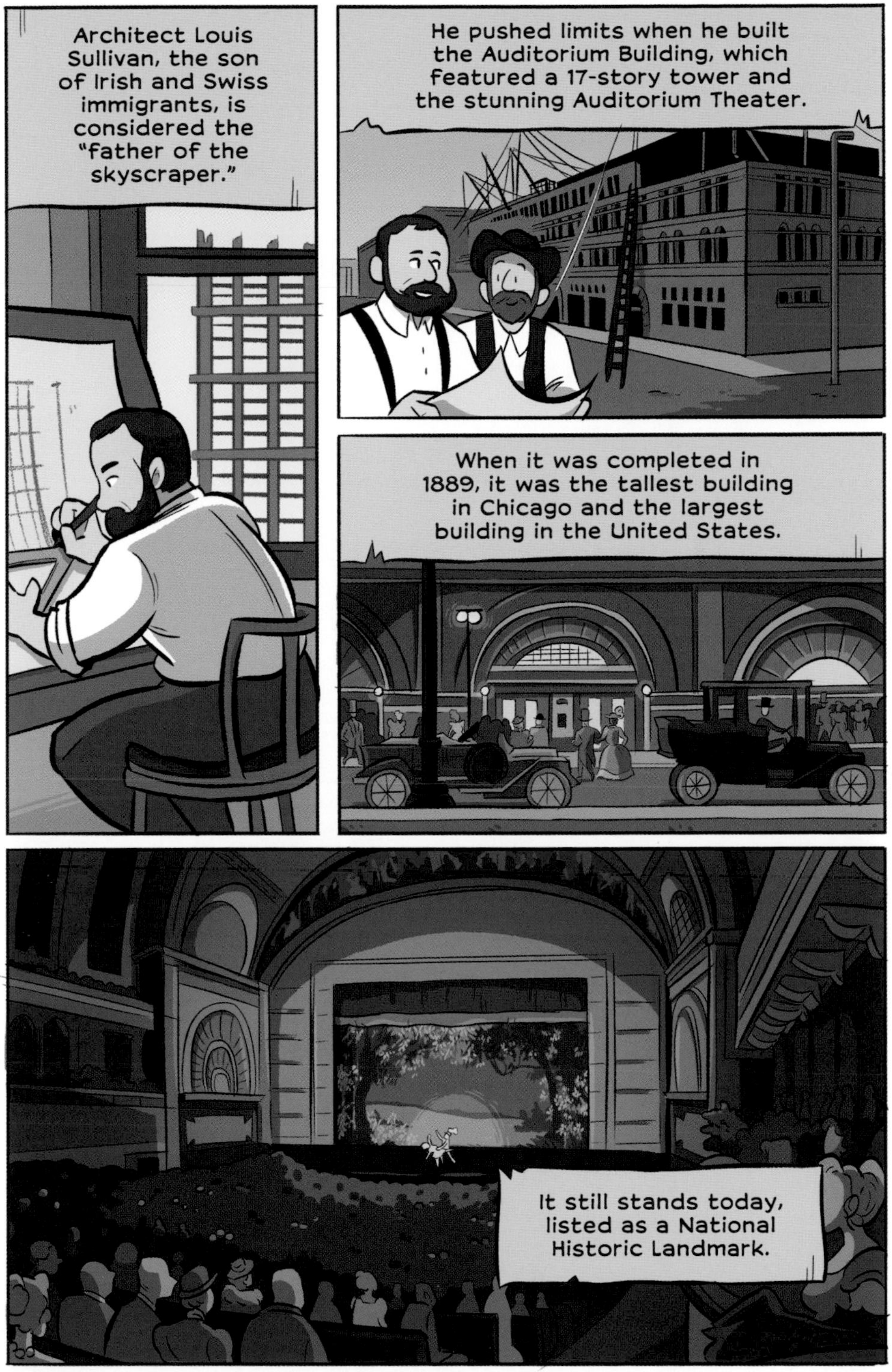
Architect Louis Sullivan, the son of Irish and Swiss immigrants, is considered the "father of the skyscraper."
He pushed limits when he built the Auditorium Building, which featured a 17-story tower and the stunning Auditorium Theater.
When it was completed in 1889, it was the tallest building in Chicago and the largest building in the United States.
It still stands today, listed as a National Historic Landmark.

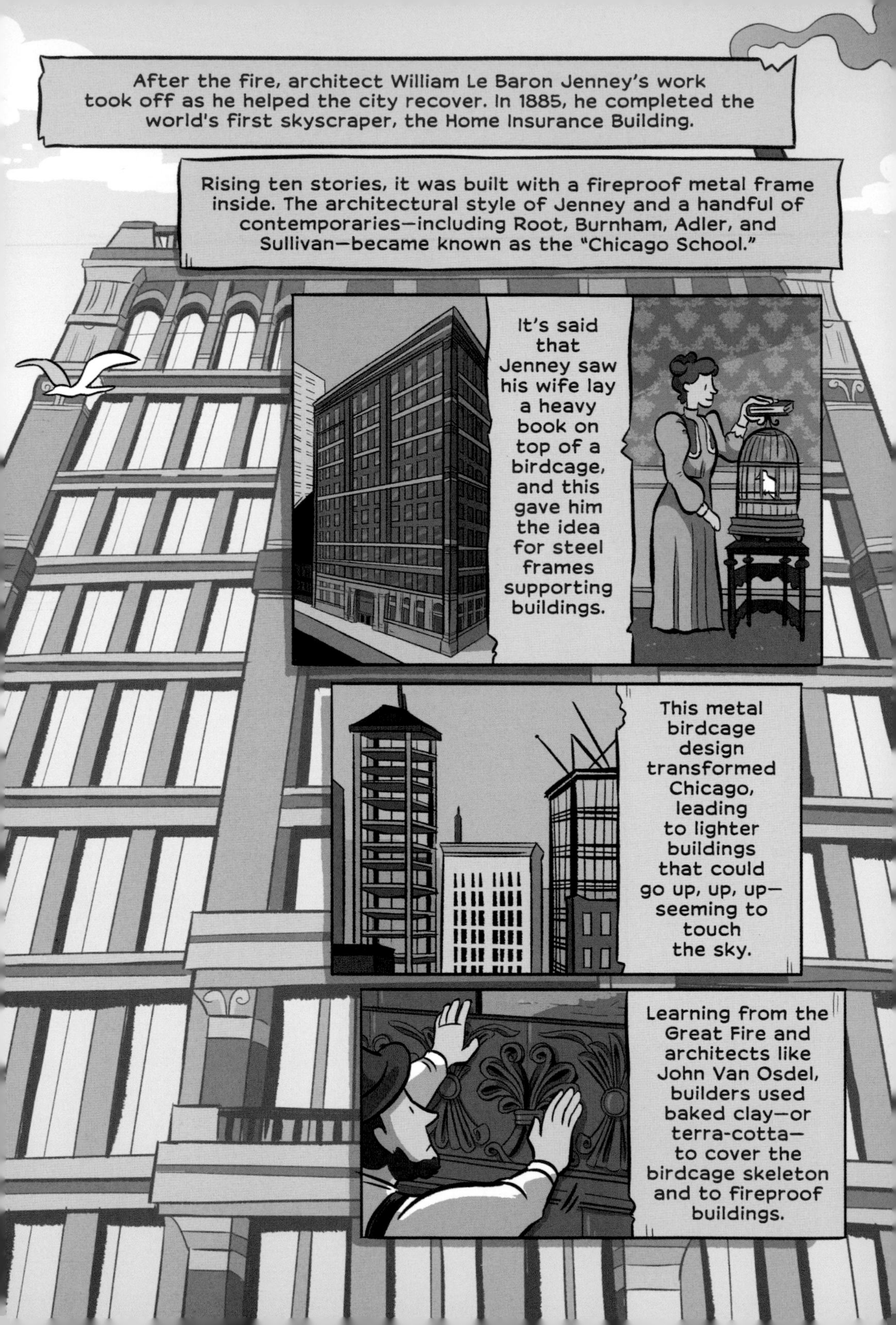
After the fire, architect William Le Baron Jenney's work took off as he helped the city recover. In 1885, he completed the world's first skyscraper, the Home Insurance Building.
Rising ten stories, it was built with a fireproof metal frame inside. The architectural style of Jenney and a handful of contemporaries—including Root, Burnham, Adler, and Sullivan—became known as the "Chicago School."
It's said that Jenney saw his wife lay a heavy book on top of a birdcage, and this gave him the idea for steel frames supporting buildings.
This metal birdcage design transformed Chicago, leading to lighter buildings that could go up, up, up—seeming to touch the sky.
Learning from the Great Fire and architects like John Van Osdel, builders used baked clay—or terra-cotta—to cover the birdcage skeleton and to fireproof buildings.

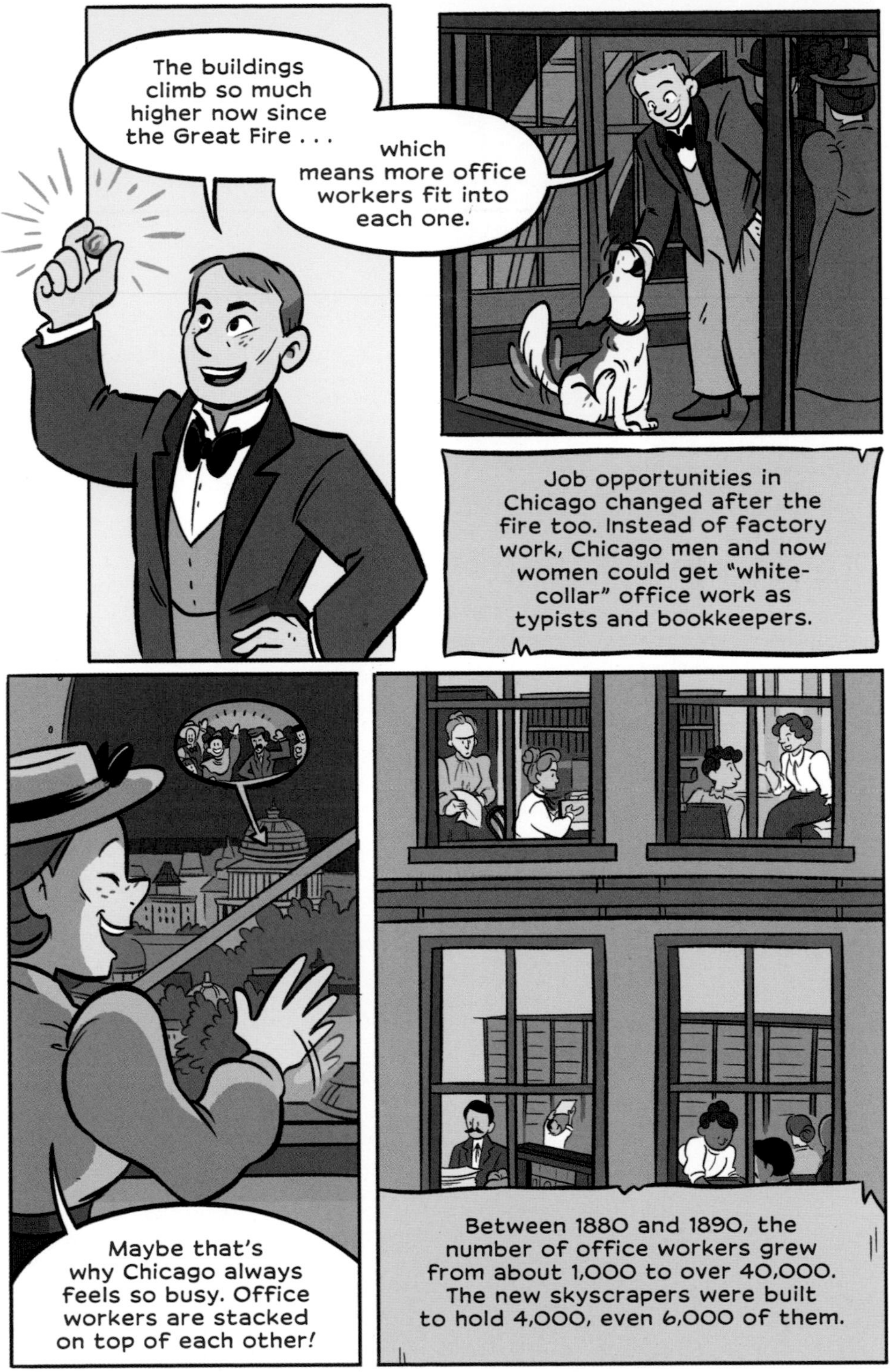
The buildings climb so much higher now since the Great Fire . . .
which means more office workers fit into each one.
Job opportunities in Chicago changed after the fire too. Instead of factory work, Chicago men and now women could get "white-collar" office work as typists and bookkeepers.
Maybe that's why Chicago always feels so busy. Office workers are stacked on top of each other!
Between 1880 and 1890, the number of office workers grew from about 1,000 to over 40,000. The new skyscrapers were built to hold 4,000, even 6,000 of them.

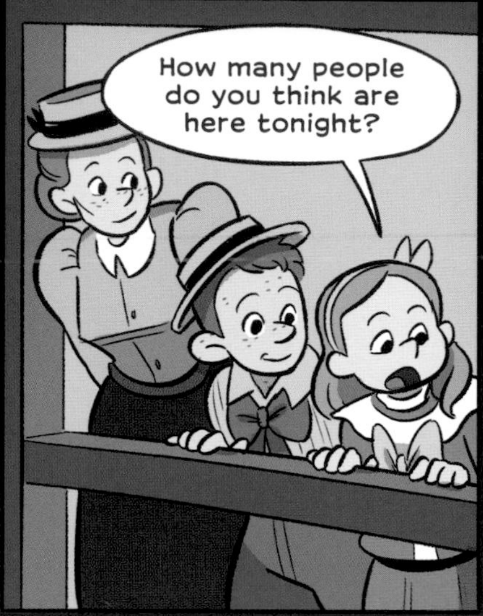
How many people do you think are here tonight?

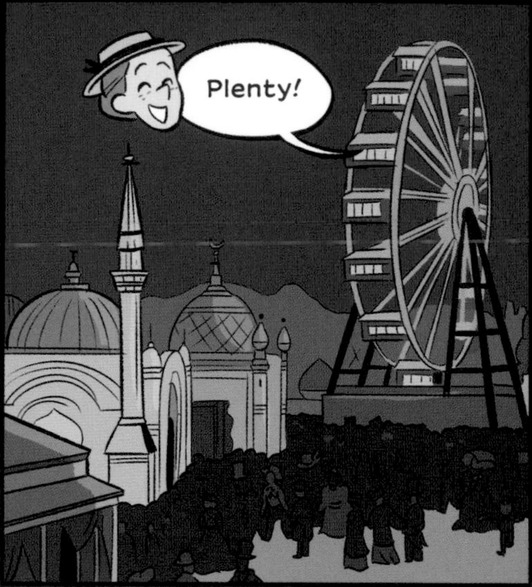
Plenty!

The Columbian Exposition was meant to mark the four hundredth anniversary of Christopher Columbus's 1492 sailing to the New World.

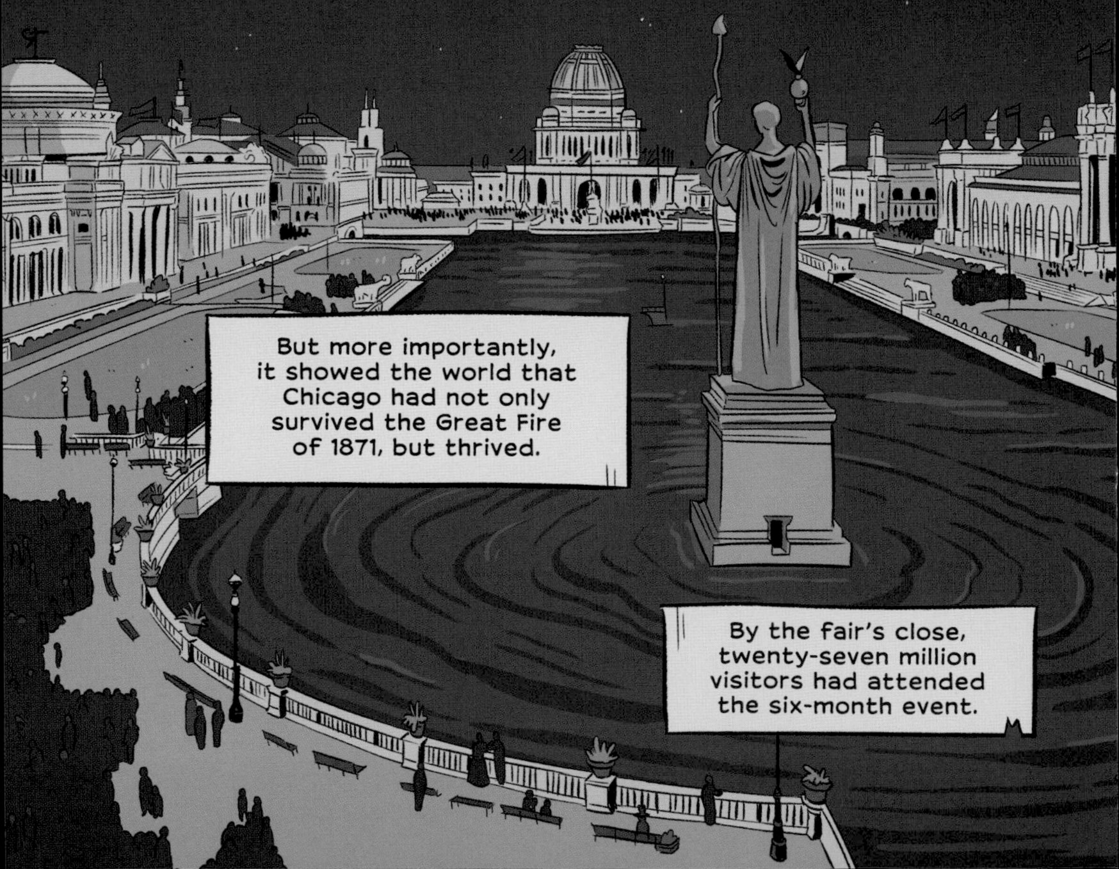
But more importantly, it showed the world that Chicago had not only survived the Great Fire of 1871, but thrived.
By the fair's close, twenty-seven million visitors had attended the six-month event.

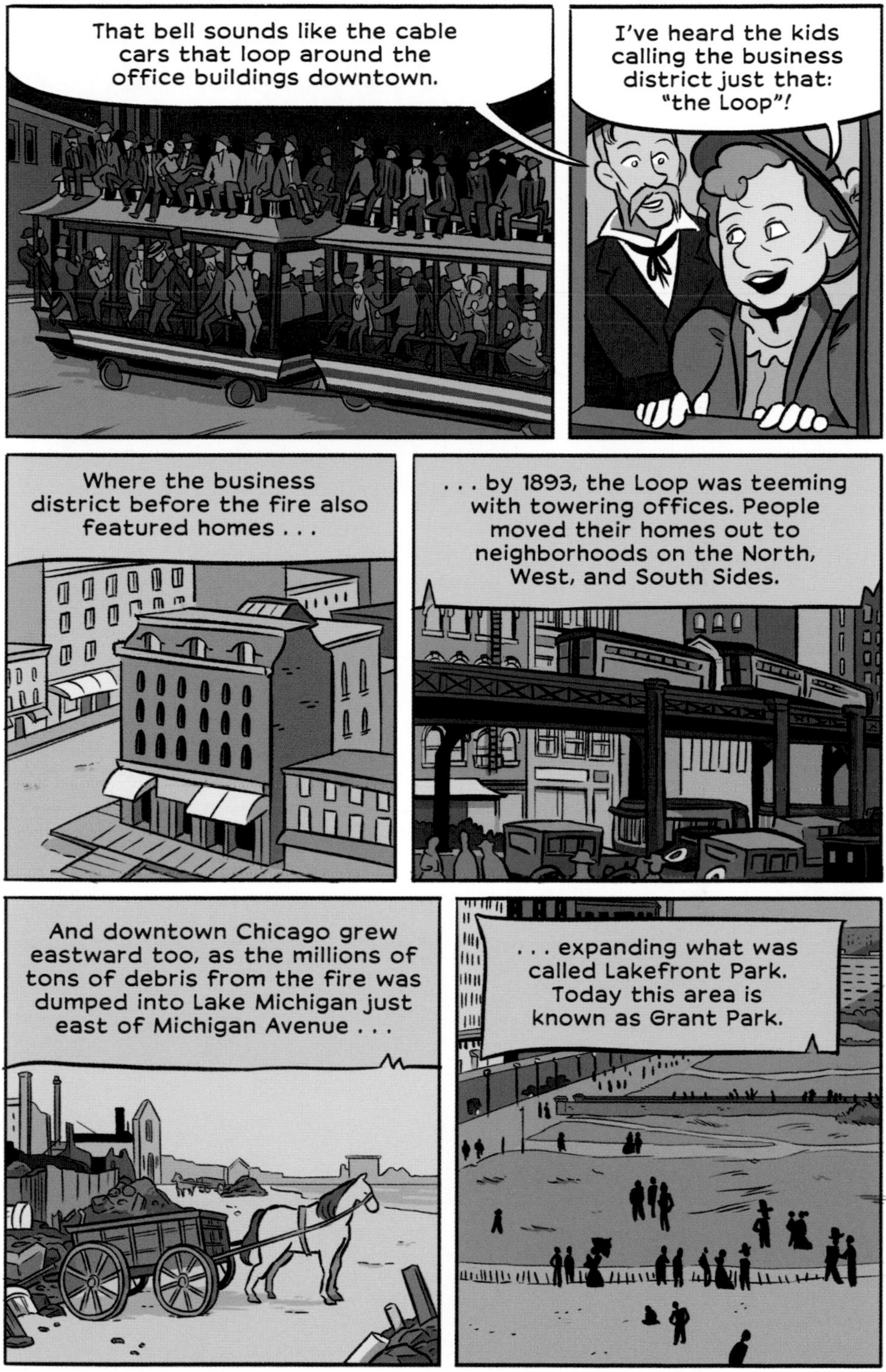
That bell sounds like the cable cars that loop around the office buildings downtown.
I've heard the kids calling the business district just that: "the Loop"!
Where the business district before the fire also featured homes . . .
. . . by 1893, the Loop was teeming with towering offices. People moved their homes out to neighborhoods on the North, West, and South Sides.
And downtown Chicago grew eastward too, as the millions of tons of debris from the fire was dumped into Lake Michigan just east of Michigan Avenue . . .
. . . expanding what was called Lakefront Park. Today this area is known as Grant Park.

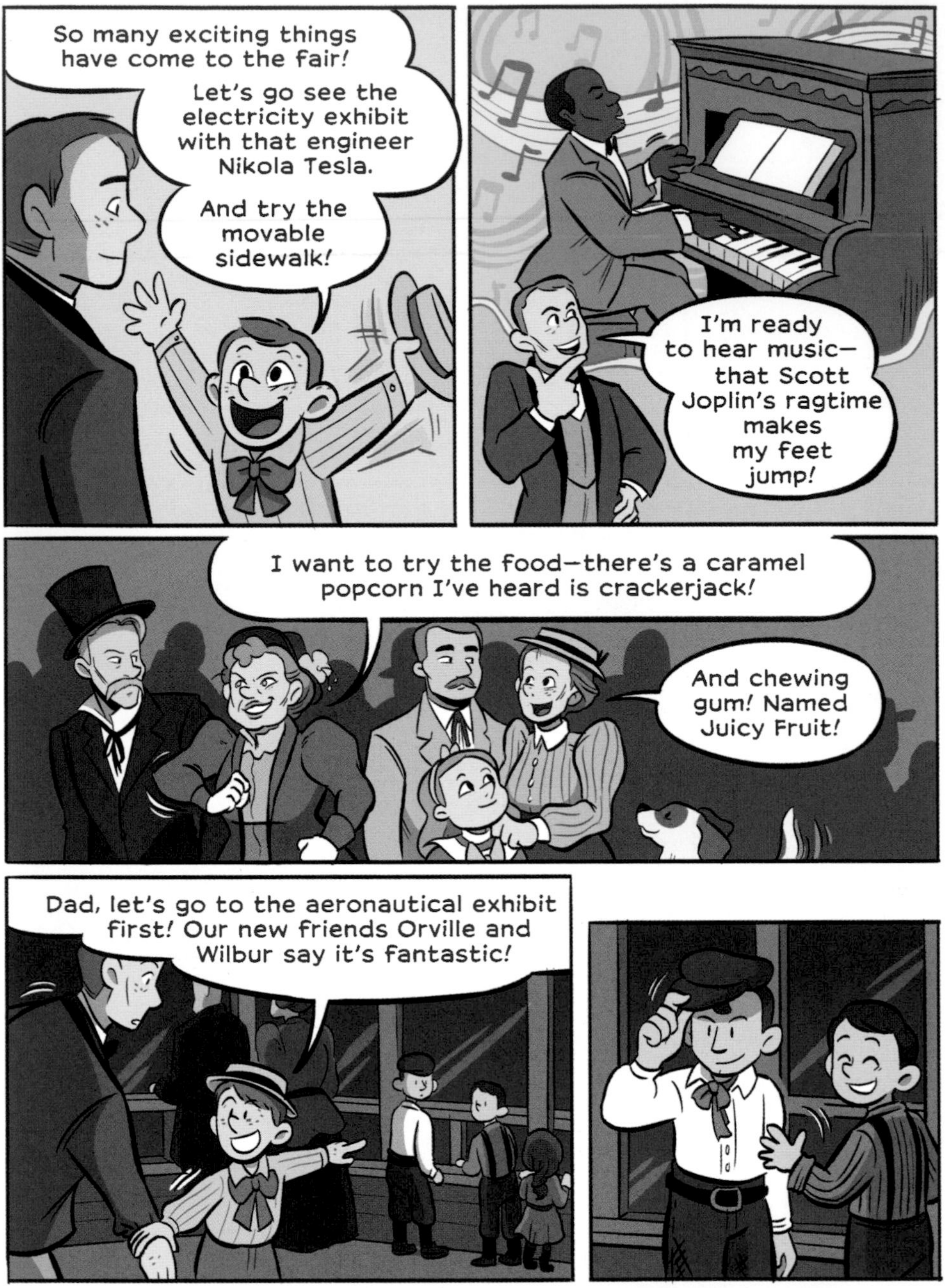
So many exciting things have come to the fair!
Let's go see the electricity exhibit with that engineer Nikola Tesla.
And try the movable sidewalk!
I'm ready to hear music—that Scott Joplin's ragtime makes my feet jump!
I want to try the food—there's a caramel popcorn I've heard is crackerjack!
And chewing gum! Named Juicy Fruit!
Dad, let's go to the aeronautical exhibit first! Our new friends Orville and Wilbur say it's fantastic!

The fair looked back at how far Chicago had come since the Great Fire, but it also inspired the promise of what was to be. Among the visitors were Orville and Wilbur Wright, who were fascinated by the fair's exhibit on flight. Ten years later, they would invent, build, and fly the world's first airplane.

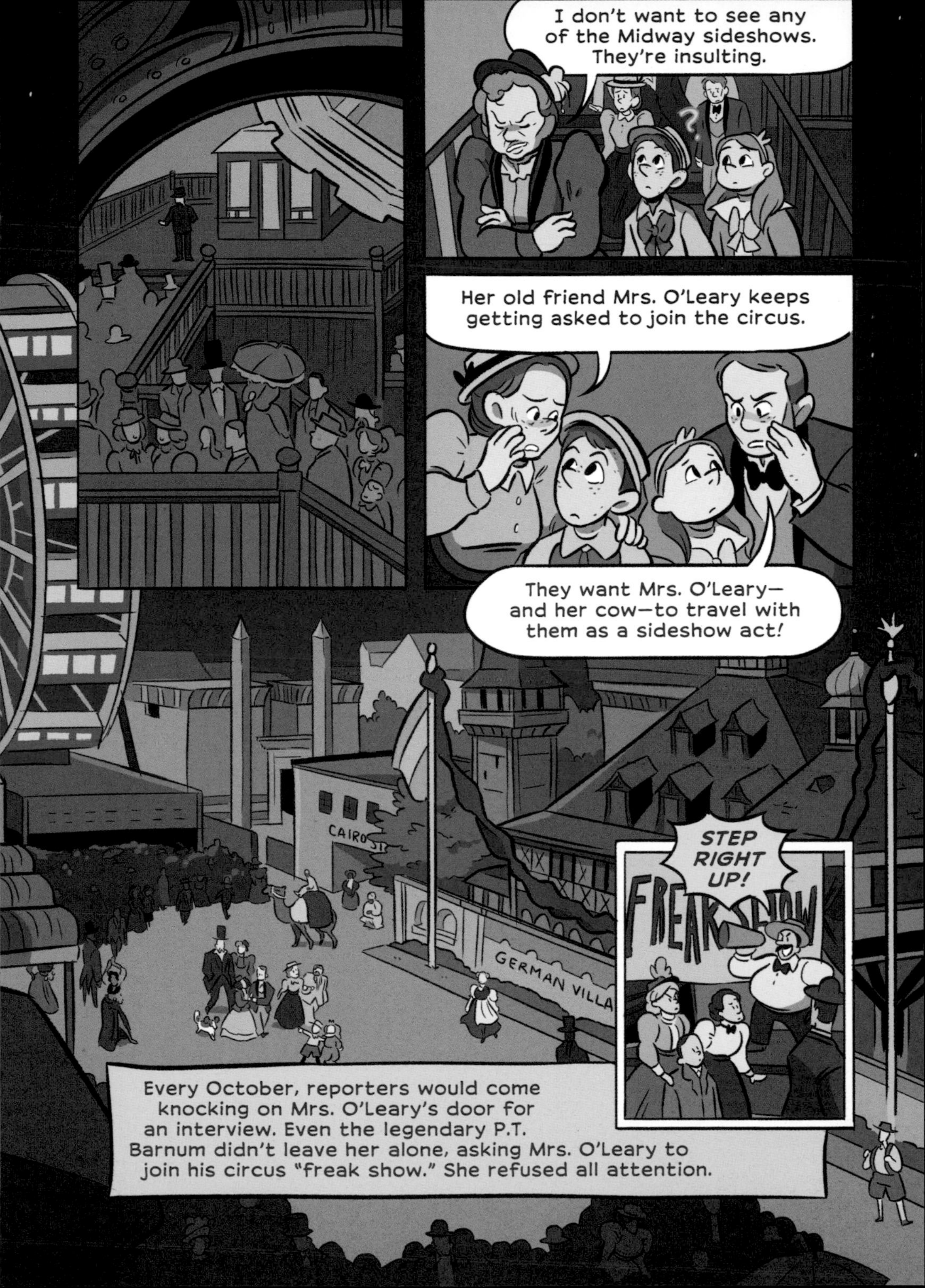
I don't want to see any of the Midway sideshows. They're insulting.
Her old friend Mrs. O'Leary keeps getting asked to join the circus.
They want Mrs. O'Leary—and her cow—to travel with them as a sideshow act!
CAIRO ST
GERMAN VILLA
STEP RIGHT UP!
FREAK SHOW
Every October, reporters would come knocking on Mrs. O'Leary's door for an interview. Even the legendary P.T. Barnum didn't leave her alone, asking Mrs. O'Leary to join his circus "freak show." She refused all attention.

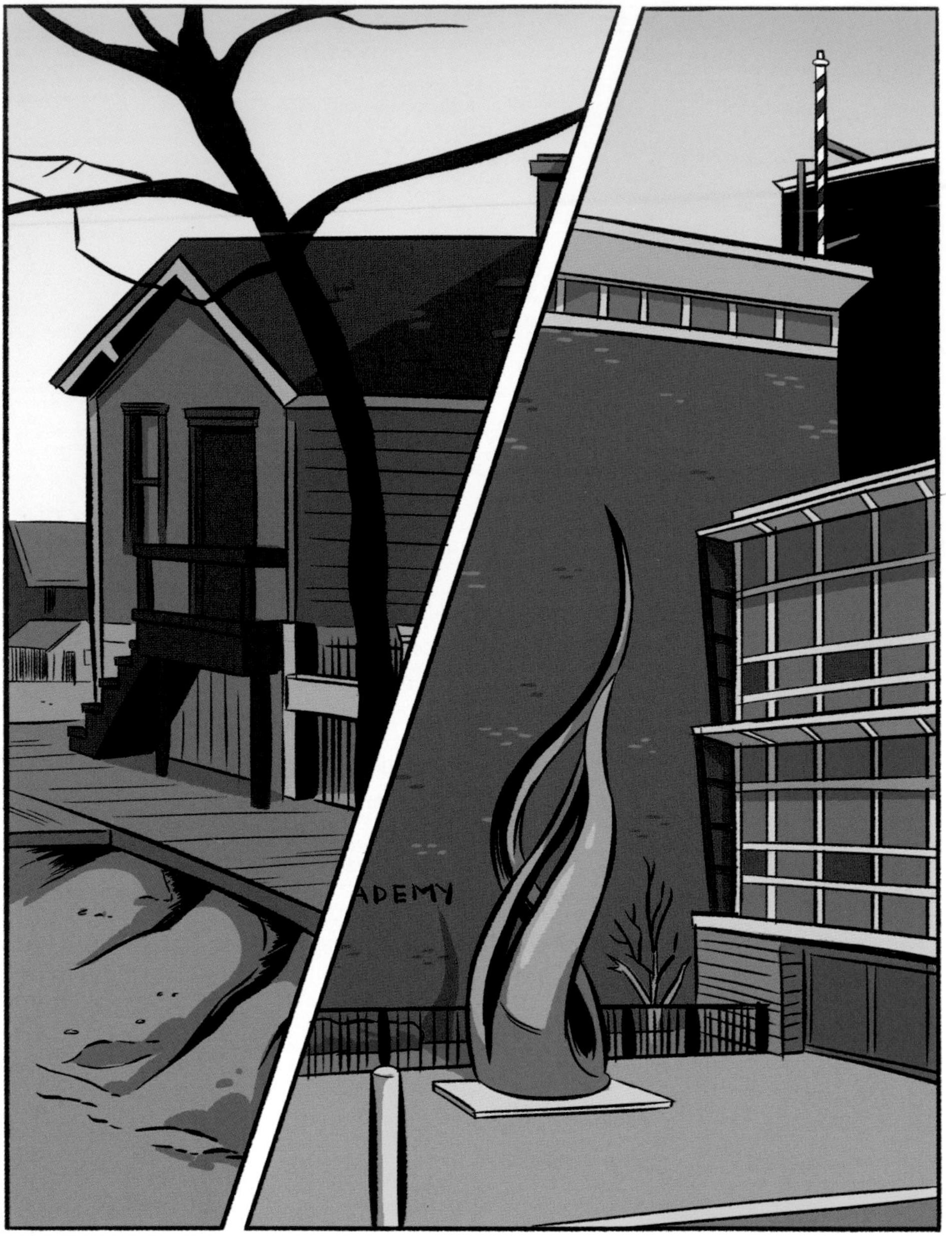
ADEMY

Today, where Mrs. O'Leary's home once stood on DeKoven Street, you can find the Chicago Police and Firefighter Training Academy, one of Chicago's largest centers for training students to become firefighters.

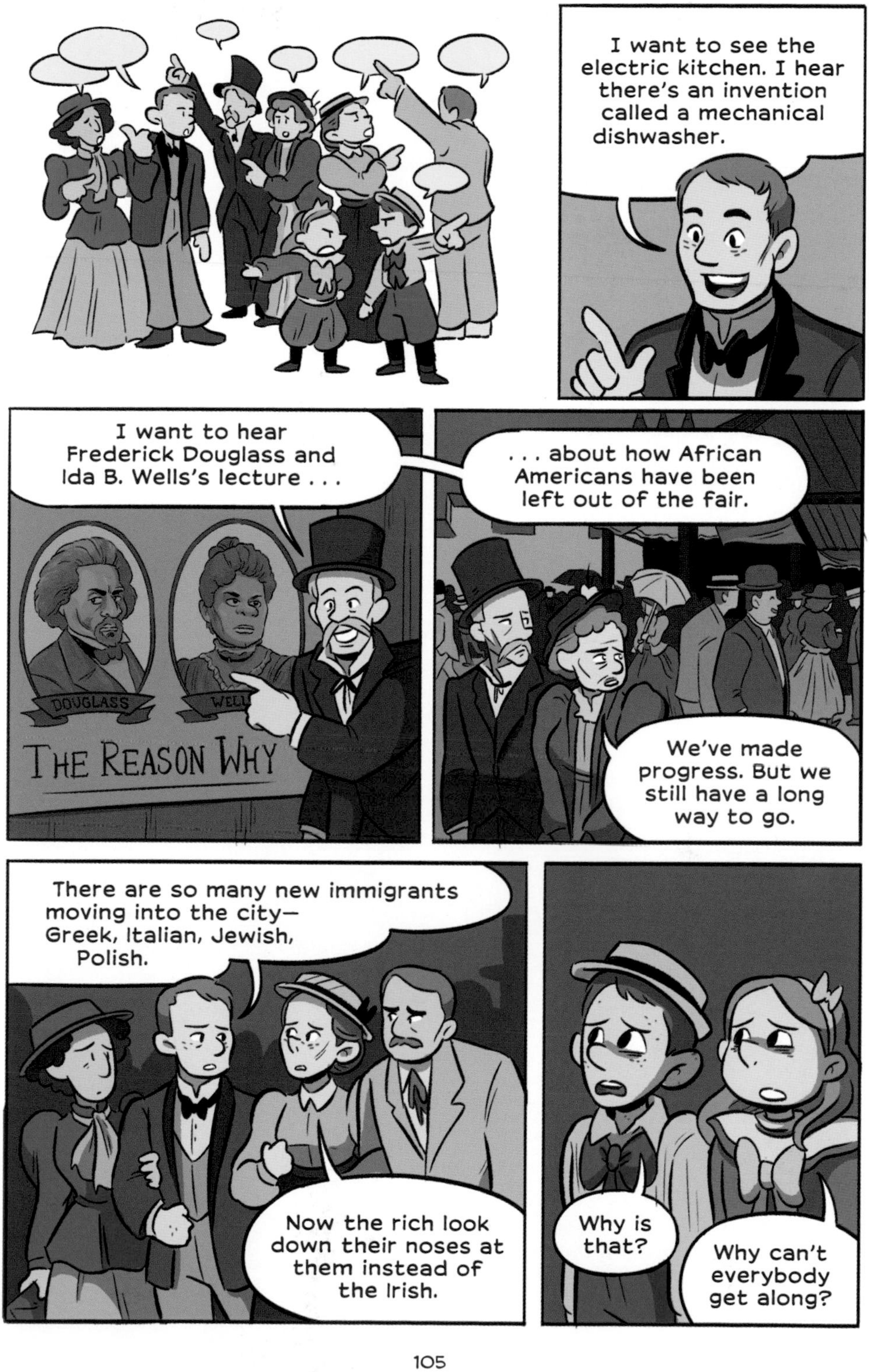
I want to see the electric kitchen. I hear there's an invention called a mechanical dishwasher.
I want to hear Frederick Douglass and Ida B. Wells's lecture . . .
DOUGLASS
THE REASON WHY
. . . about how African Americans have been left out of the fair.
We've made progress. But we still have a long way to go.
There are so many new immigrants moving into the city— Greek, Italian, Jewish, Polish.
Now the rich look down their noses at them instead of the Irish.
Why is that?
Why can't everybody get along?

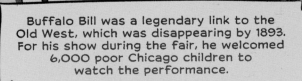

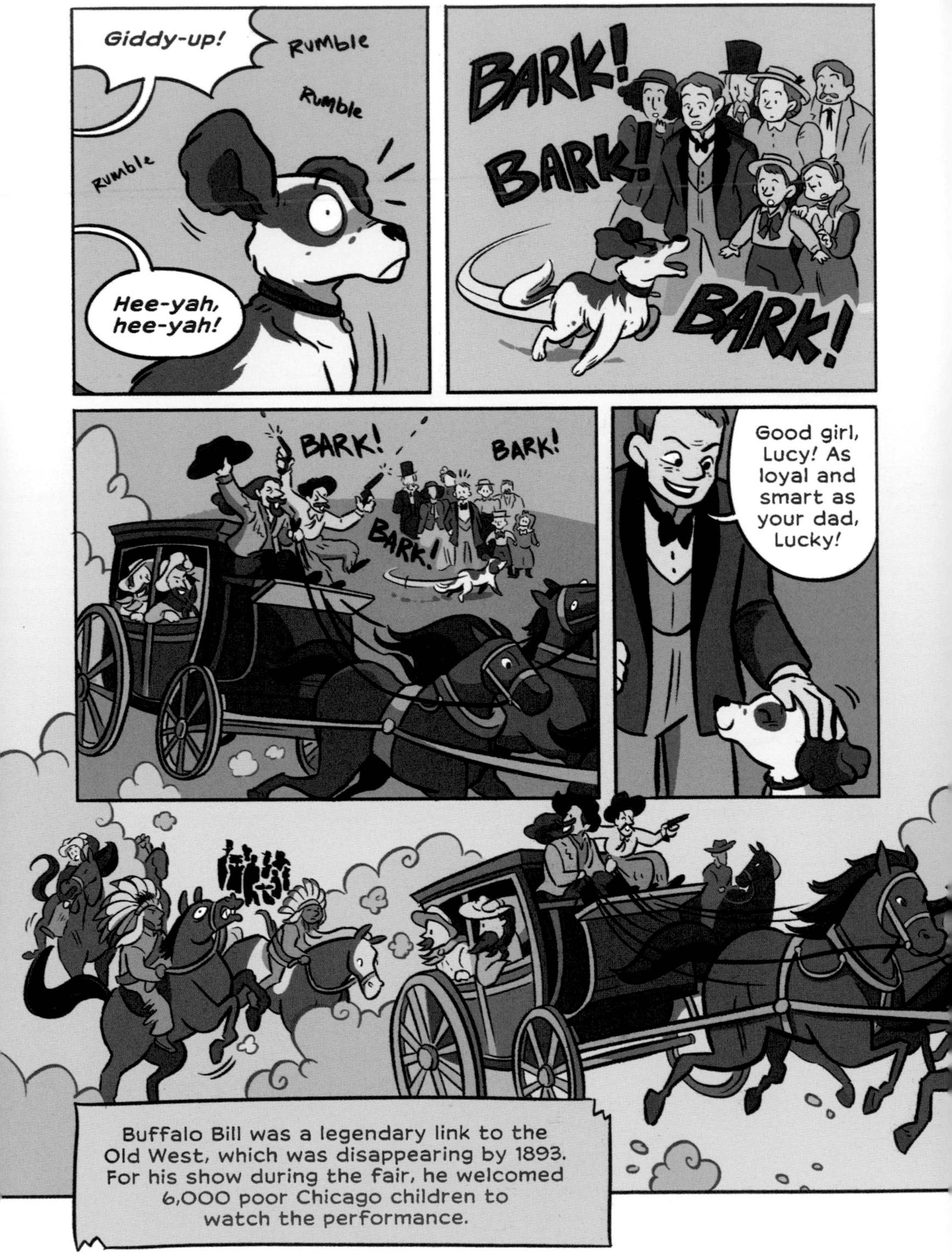
Giddy-up!
RUMBLE
RUMBLE
RUMBLE
Hee-yah, hee-yah!
BARK!
BARK!
BARK!
BARK!
BARK!
BARK!
Good girl, Lucy! As loyal and smart as your dad, Lucky!
Buffalo Bill was a legendary link to the Old West, which was disappearing by 1893. For his show during the fair, he welcomed 6,000 poor Chicago children to watch the performance.

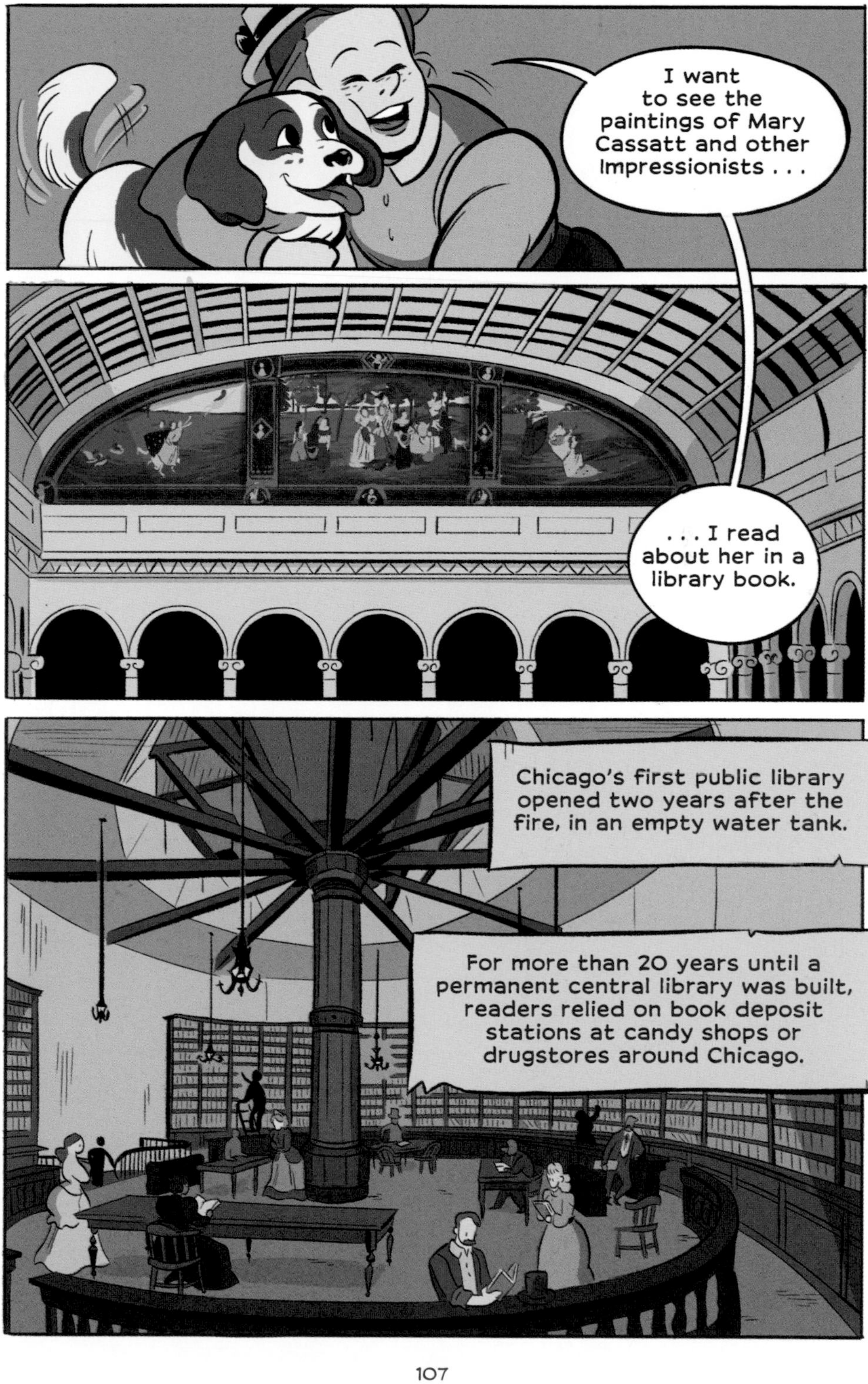
I want to see the paintings of Mary Cassatt and other Impressionists . . .
. . . I read about her in a library book.
Chicago's first public library opened two years after the fire, in an empty water tank.
For more than 20 years until a permanent central library was built, readers relied on book deposit stations at candy shops or drugstores around Chicago.

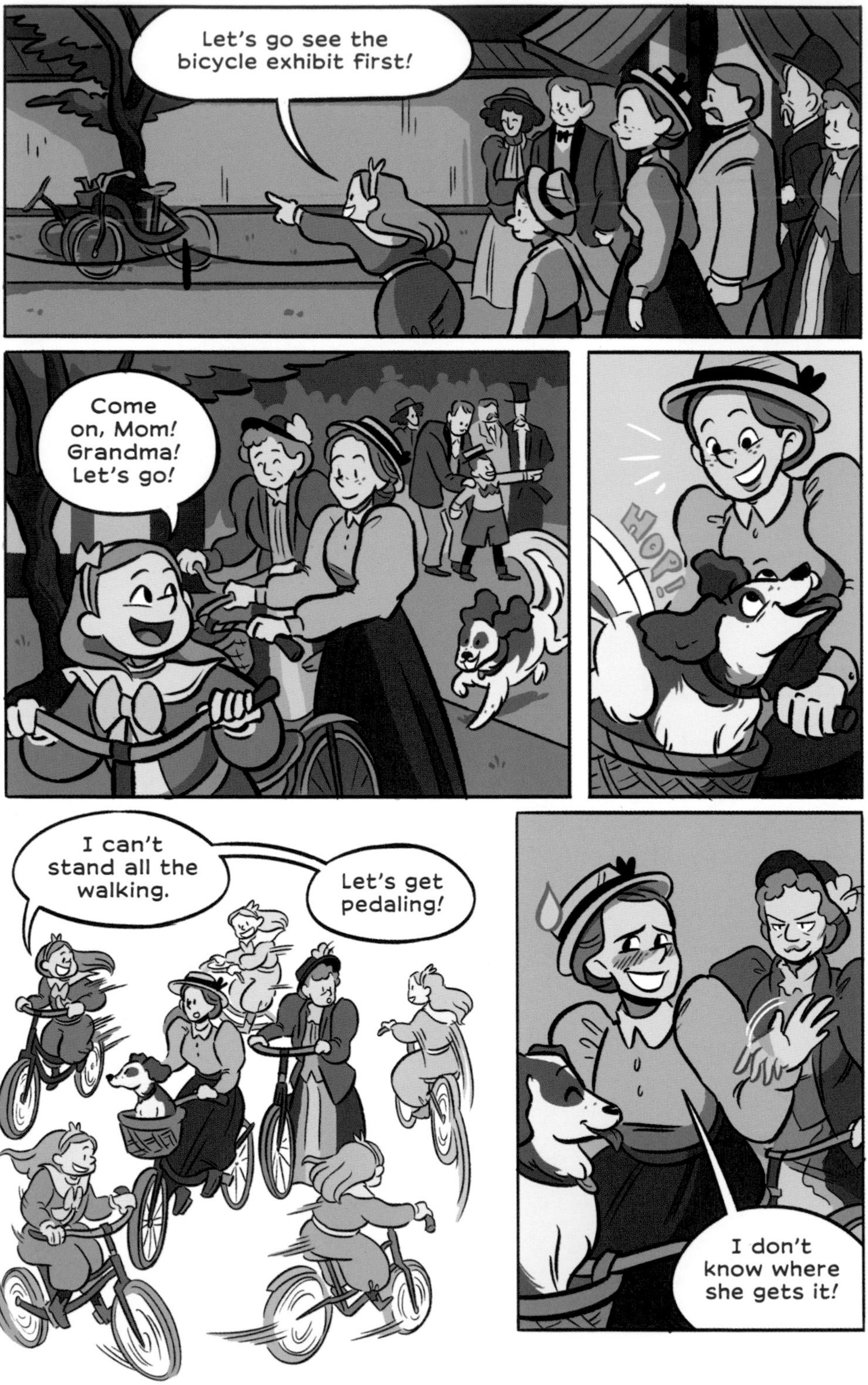
Let's go see the bicycle exhibit first!
Come on, Mom! Grandma! Let's go!
HOP!
I can't stand all the walking.
Let's get pedaling!
I don't know where she gets it!

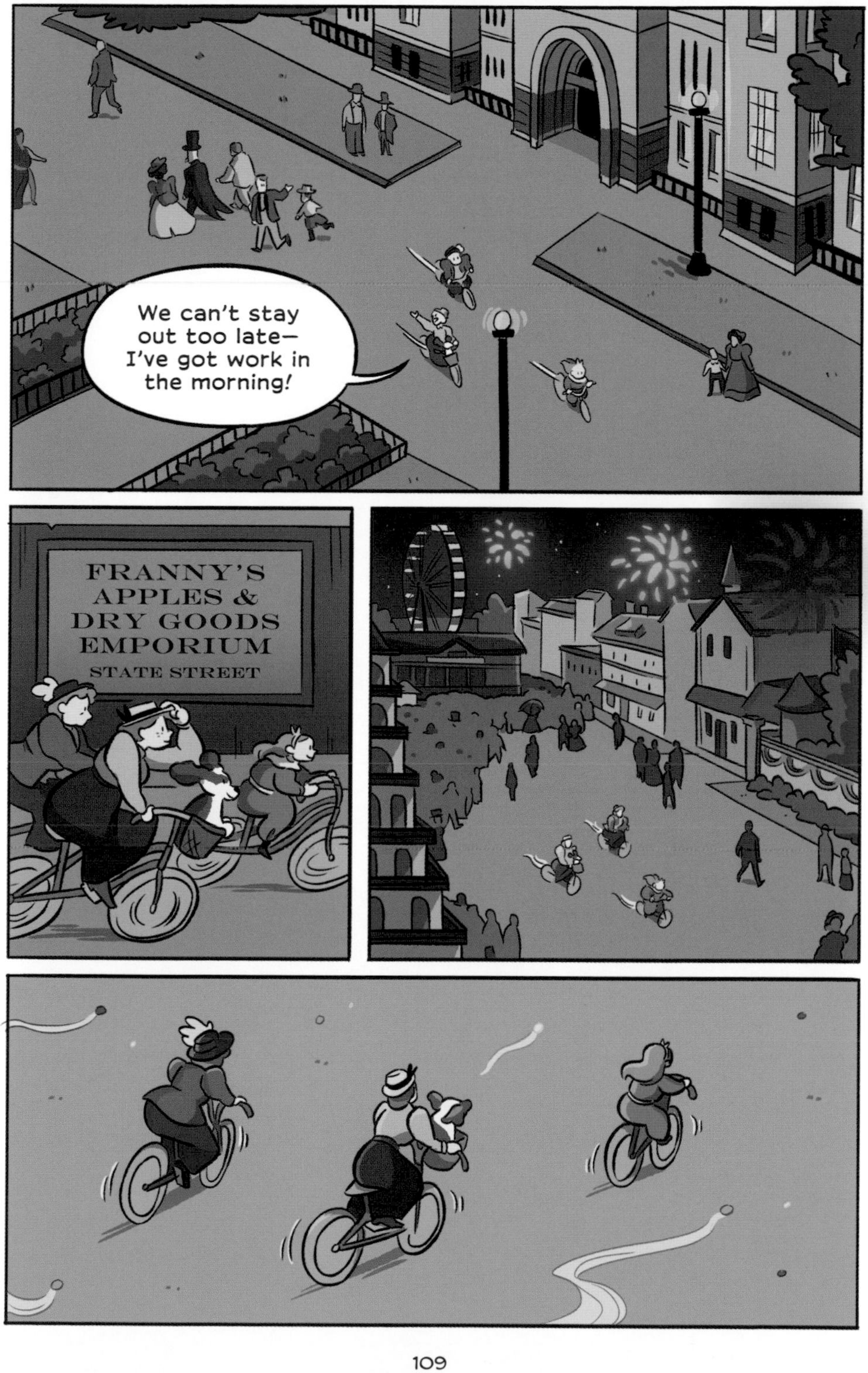
We can't stay out too late— I've got work in the morning!
FRANNY'S APPLES & DRY GOODS EMPORIUM
STATE STREET

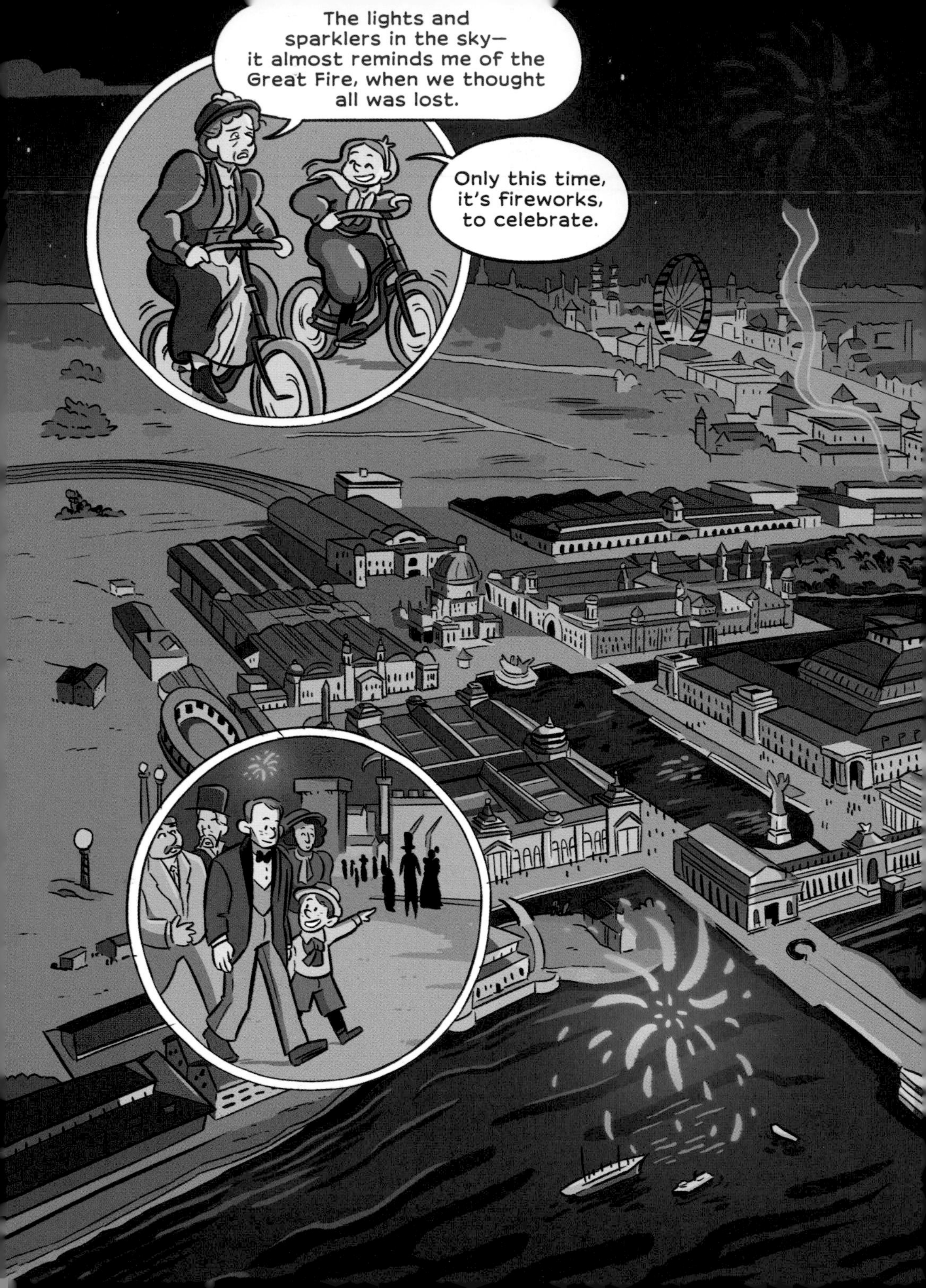

The lights and sparklers in the sky— it almost reminds me of the Great Fire, when we thought all was lost.
Only this time, it's fireworks, to celebrate.

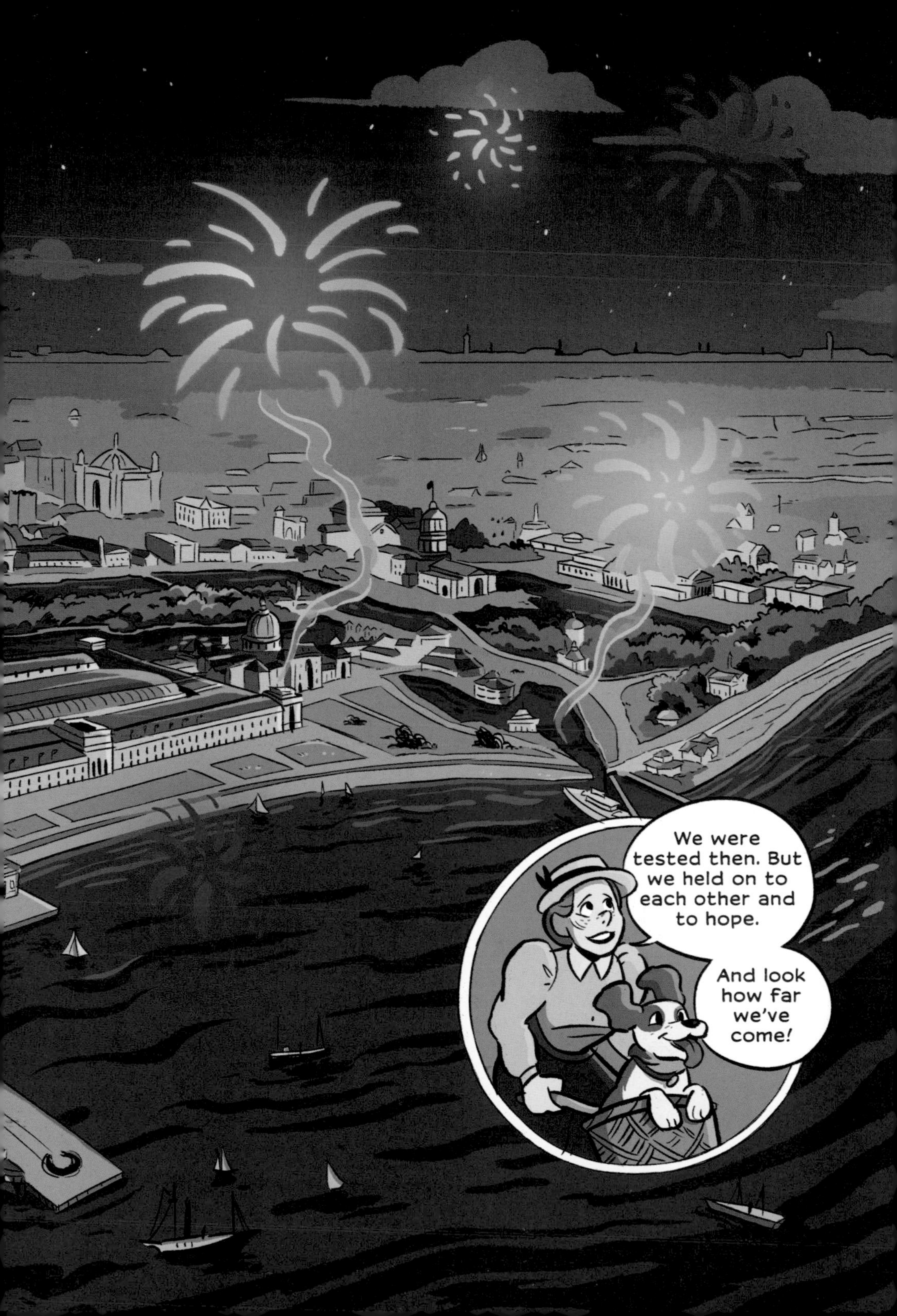

We were tested then. But we held on to each other and to hope.
And look how far we've come!

Author's Note

Thank you to the helpful folks at the Research Center of the Chicago History Museum for patiently allowing me time with files and folders. And to the librarians and staff at the Blackstone Branch of the Chicago Public Library, who never ever give me the stink-eye for returning late books or reserving too many titles. I appreciate your support!

As a Chicago resident and fan of this amazing city, I take great delight in learning new and interesting facts about the Second City (also known as the Windy City, City in a Garden, City of Big Shoulders, Queen of the West, even Hog Butcher of the World). Big thanks go out to my family—Gabriel, Nolan, Olivia, and Norm Issa—for joining me on outings to explore architecturally significant buildings, riding on architectural boat tours, visiting cemeteries and touching gravestones, wandering museum exhibits, and staring off into the distance and imagining what once was.

Since I live just blocks from the site of the 1893 World's Columbian Exposition, I had an especially wonderful time researching the Great Fire and the spectacular fair that celebrated the city's rebirth. Thanks to Dave Roman for recognizing me as a Giant History Nerd (GHN) and encouraging my geekdom for this project.

—**Kate Hannigan**, Chicago, Illinois

Timeline

Saturday, October 7, 1871

10 p.m.: After a week of small fires, a new one known as "the Saturday Night Fire" begins. This blaze starts in the lumber district about ten blocks north of the O'Leary residence on DeKoven Street.

Sunday, October 8

3 p.m.: Firefighters finally extinguish the Saturday Night Fire, leaving them exhausted and their equipment damaged.

Around 9 p.m.: Fire breaks out near or in the backyard barn of the O'Leary residence, 137 DeKoven Street.

9:30 p.m.: The first alarm is registered at the courthouse watchtower downtown, but the strong winds, dry conditions, and slow response combine to allow the fire to get ahead of firefighters' control.

11:30 p.m.: Flaming wooden planks soar eastward across the Chicago River's South Branch, setting the business district ablaze, including the Parmalee Omnibus and Stage Company.

Midnight: The city's gasworks catches fire and explodes.

Monday, October 9

1 a.m.: Flames engulf the Palmer, Potter Palmer's lavish new hotel, open just thirteen days.

1:30 a.m.: The courthouse catches fire, and the mayor orders all prisoners jailed in the basement be set free. Soon after, the 11,000-pound bell crashes to the ground after sounding the alarm for nearly five hours.

2:30 a.m.: The fire jumps the Chicago River's North Branch and begins ravaging the North Side.

3:30 a.m.: The waterworks fails as the wooden roof collapses at the Pumping Station near the Water Tower, and the whole city loses water.

3 p.m.: Mayor Roswell B. Mason issues emergency measures for fire victims.

5 p.m.: Fire reaches city limits at Fullerton Avenue in Lincoln Park.

Tuesday, October 10

3–4 a.m.: Rainfall slowly extinguishes the fire after about thirty hours.

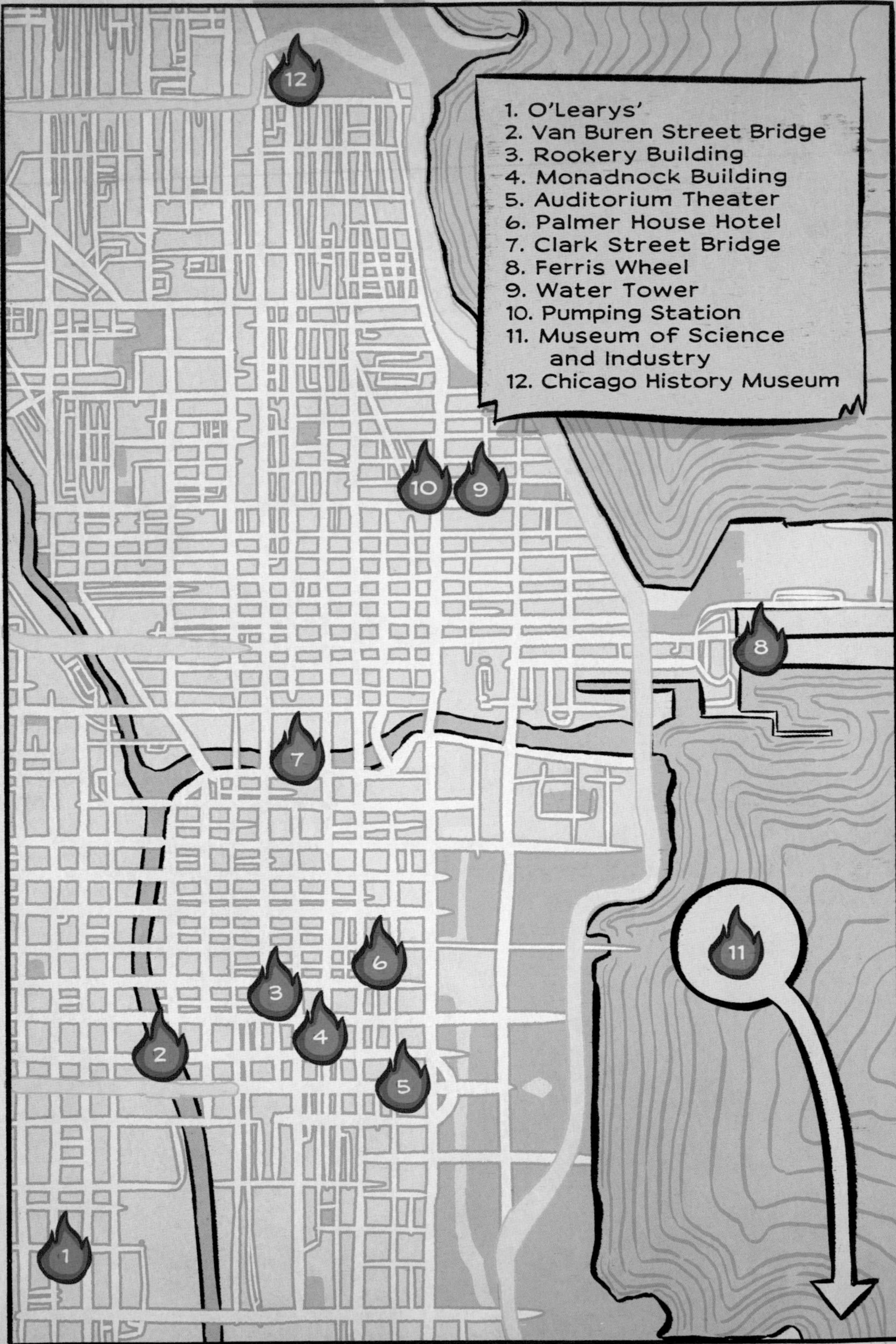

1. O'Learys'
2. Van Buren Street Bridge
3. Rookery Building
4. Monadnock Building
5. Auditorium Theater
6. Palmer House Hotel
7. Clark Street Bridge
8. Ferris Wheel
9. Water Tower
10. Pumping Station
11. Museum of Science and Industry
12. Chicago History Museum
12
10
9
8
7
11
6
3
4
2
5
1

Great Fire Sites to Visit in Chicago Today

Start at **the O'Learys'**, though the 137 DeKoven Street residence no longer exists. In its place stands the Chicago Police and Firefighter Training Academy, 558 West DeKoven Street. Check out the antique firefighting equipment, historical information, and the *Pillar of Fire* sculpture marking the place where it all began.

The Van Buren Street Bridge crosses the Chicago River between Congress Parkway and Jackson Boulevard. Get a sense of what fire refugees would have felt as they fled the flames from the west side, hurrying to safety on the east side of the river. The bridge was destroyed in the fire and has been rebuilt a few times.

Once across the bridge, walk two blocks north to **the Rookery Building** at 209 S. LaSalle Street to see what rose from the ashes of the Burnt City: one of the world's earliest skyscrapers, built in 1885 by architects Daniel Burnham and John Root with a lobby later redesigned by another noted architect, Frank Lloyd Wright.

Just a block or so east stands **the Monadnock Building**, 53 W. Jackson Boulevard, another Burnham & Root building, this time a towering sixteen stories tall. Completed by the time of the World's Fair, it was the largest office building in the world.

Drop a block or two south and east and pay a visit to the beautiful **Auditorium Theater**, 50 East Ida B. Wells Drive. Don't be deceived by its plain exterior. Built by architectural masters Dankmar Adler and Louis Sullivan, this ornate theater is a stunner with twenty-four-karat-gold-leaf ceiling arches, detailed floor and wall mosaics, and gorgeous murals celebrating nature, life, and music. When it was completed in 1889, the Auditorium was the biggest, tallest, and most expensive building of its time, and it became a symbol of Chicago's return to the world stage.

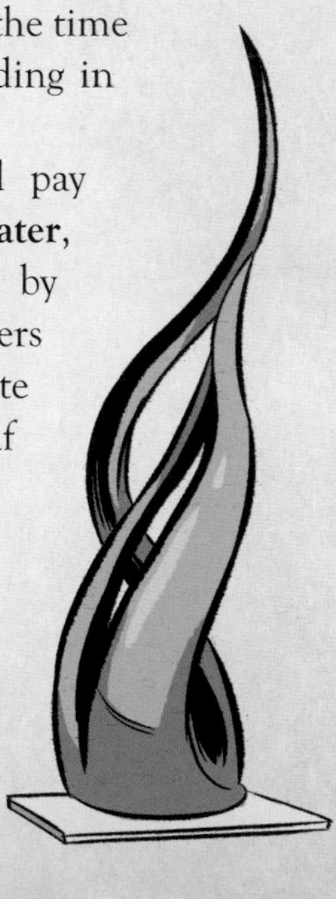

Walk north up State Street to 17 East Monroe Street and check out **the Palmer House Hotel**. Potter Palmer built the hotel as a present to his wife, Bertha, but it burned to the ground after just thirteen days in business. The hotel opened again a year later, then was rebuilt in the 1920s and has undergone significant changes since, but it is considered Chicago's oldest continuously operating hotel. During the Columbian Exposition, Bertha asked the Palmer's chef to create a new dessert, and the brownie was born.

Head north and west to cross the North Branch of the Chicago River at **the Clark Street Bridge** between Dearborn Street and LaSalle Drive, walking to the city's North Side. An architectural boat tour also offers a way to appreciate the bridge, which was destroyed in the fire and has been rebuilt.

From here jump in a cab on Illinois Street and head east to Navy Pier (600 East Grand Avenue) to **ride the Ferris wheel**. It's not the original one built by George Ferris, but it is inspired by the spectacular Columbian Exposition installation and stands as an icon of the city. Towering nearly two hundred feet in the air, it features forty-one cars that hold eight people each.

No trip to Chicago is complete without visiting **the Water Tower** at 806 North Michigan Avenue and **the Chicago Avenue Pumping Station** across the street. Built in 1869 to draw water from the lake so that it would not be contaminated by the filthy Chicago River, the Water Tower and Pumping Station have also become icons of Chicago.

Then race south to visit **the Museum of Science and Industry**, which occupies the former Palace of Fine Arts from the Columbian Exposition.

End your explorations at **the Chicago History Museum**, 1601 North Clark Street, and tour the Great Chicago Fire exhibit, featuring fascinating items, from melted relics to an authentic fire alarm box.

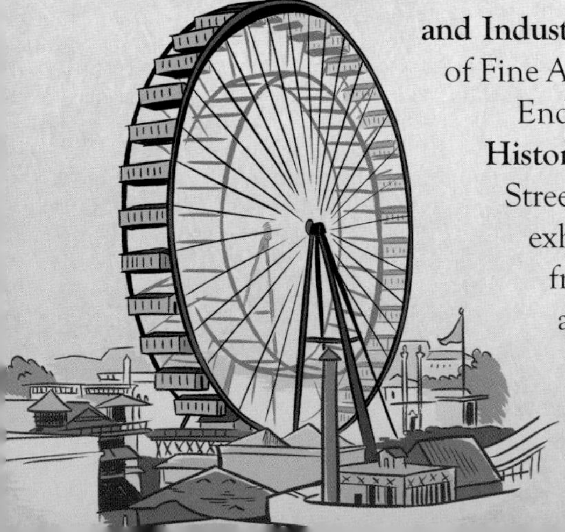

Fast Facts About Chicago & the Great Fire

Did you know . . . ?

. . . that **Chicago has four stars on its flag,** and two of them are featured in this book? According to the *Chicago Tribune*, one star commemorates the 1871 Great Chicago Fire, and another marks the 1893 World's Columbian Exposition. A third star marks the 1933 World's Fair, which was called the Century of Progress International Exposition since it was one hundred years after Chicago's incorporation as a town. The fourth star celebrates Fort Dearborn, the 1803 outpost that marked the beginning of what would become the bustling city of Chicago. (This one was added last but often is considered first.) Curious about the rest of the Chicago flag? The three bands of white stand for the North, West, and South Sides of the city, and the bands of blue represent the two branches of the Chicago River.

. . . that **when the Chicago White Stockings** played a baseball game in late October 1871, just after the fire, they had to wear a mishmash of uniforms borrowed from other teams because their own jerseys and pants had burned in the fire?

. . . that **the Water Tower** is supposedly haunted by the ghost of a worker who was trapped in the building the night of the Great Fire?

. . . that **the city's professional Major League Soccer team,** the Chicago Fire, is named for the 1871 blaze?

. . . that **the railroad companies** offered free passes to those who wanted to flee Chicago just after the fire, but most people chose not to take them—they wanted to stay and help the city rebuild?

. . . that **after the World's Columbian Exposition**—which was in part to celebrate Chicago's recovery and triumph over the 1871 Great Fire—closed to the public in late 1893, almost all the buildings were destroyed by . . . wait for it . . . fire?

Bibliography and Resources

Books:

Atkinson, Eleanor. *The Story of Chicago and National Development, 1534–1940.* Kessinger Publishing, 2010.

Bales, Richard F. *The Great Chicago Fire and the Myth of Mrs. O'Leary's Cow.* McFarland & Company, 2002.

Cromie, Robert. *The Great Chicago Fire.* Rutledge Hill Press, 1993.

The Great Chicago Fire of 1871: Three Illustrated Accounts from Harper's Weekly. Lewis Osborne, 1969.

Lowe, David Garrard. *Lost Chicago.* Watson-Guptill Publications, 2000.

Lowe, David. *The Great Chicago Fire: In Eyewitness Accounts and 70 Contemporary Photographs and Illustrations.* Dover Publications, 1979.

Miller, Ross. *The Great Chicago Fire.* University of Illinois Press, 2000.

Murphy, Jim. *The Great Fire.* Scholastic Press, 1995.

Pacyga, Dominic A. *Chicago: A Biography.* University of Chicago Press, 2009.

Rosenberg, Chaim. *America at the Fair: Chicago's 1893 World's Columbian Exposition.* Arcadia Publishing, 2008.

Sawislak, Karen. *Smoldering City: Chicagoans and the Great Fire, 1871–1874.* University of Chicago Press, 1995.

Museums:

The Chicago History Museum, 1601 N. Clark Street, Chicago, IL 60614. https://www.chicagohistory.org/

Newspapers:

The Chicago Tribune, February 6, 1870. Page 3, Column 1. http://archives.chicagotribune.com/1870/02/06/page/3/article/working-women "Working Women: Some Facts About Domestics and Their Peculiarities. No Irish Need Apply."

The Chicago Tribune, October 11, 1871. Page 2, Column 4. http://archives .chicagotribune.com/1871/10/11/page/2/article/cheer-up

The Chicago Tribune, October 20, 1871. Page 2, Column 4. http://archives .chicagotribune.com/1871/10/20/page/2/article/how-it-originated

The Chicago Tribune, February 9, 1958. Part 2, Page 9, Column 2. "Bird Cage Inspiration for First Skyscraper." http://archives.chicagotribune .com/1958/02/09/page/45/article/builders-are-paid-a-tribute

The Chicago Tribune, November 9, 1996. "Box 342." http://articles .chicagotribune.com/1996-11-09/news/9701150581_1_o-leary -barn-fire-district-alarm

Harper's Weekly, September 2, 1871. Volume 15. "The Usual Irish Way of Doing Things" cartoon.

The Library of Congress, Newspaper & Current Periodical Reading Room. https://www.loc.gov/rr/news/topics/chicagofire.html

The Washington Review and Examiner (Washington, Pennsylvania), November 29, 1871. Page 2. "Mrs. O'Leary's Cow Responsible for the Chicago Fire After All."

Websites:

Curious City, WBEZ public radio, *What If the Great Chicago Fire of 1871 Never Happened?* http://interactive.wbez.org/curiouscity/chicagofire/

Encyclopedia of Chicago http://www.encyclopedia.chicagohistory.org/

Great Chicago Fire and the Web of Memory, created by Chicago Historical Society and Northwestern University. www.greatchicagofire.org

National Geographic, *The Chicago Fire of 1871 and the "Great Rebuilding."* https://www.nationalgeographic.org/news /chicago-fire-1871-and-great-rebuilding/

The Office: Female Office Workers in Chicago, 1870–1930 by Lisa M. Fine, Illinois Periodicals Online. http://www.lib.niu .edu/2003/iht1020324.html

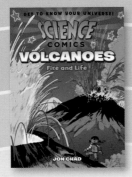